GW01374763

MODEL MAKING
FOR ARCHITECTS

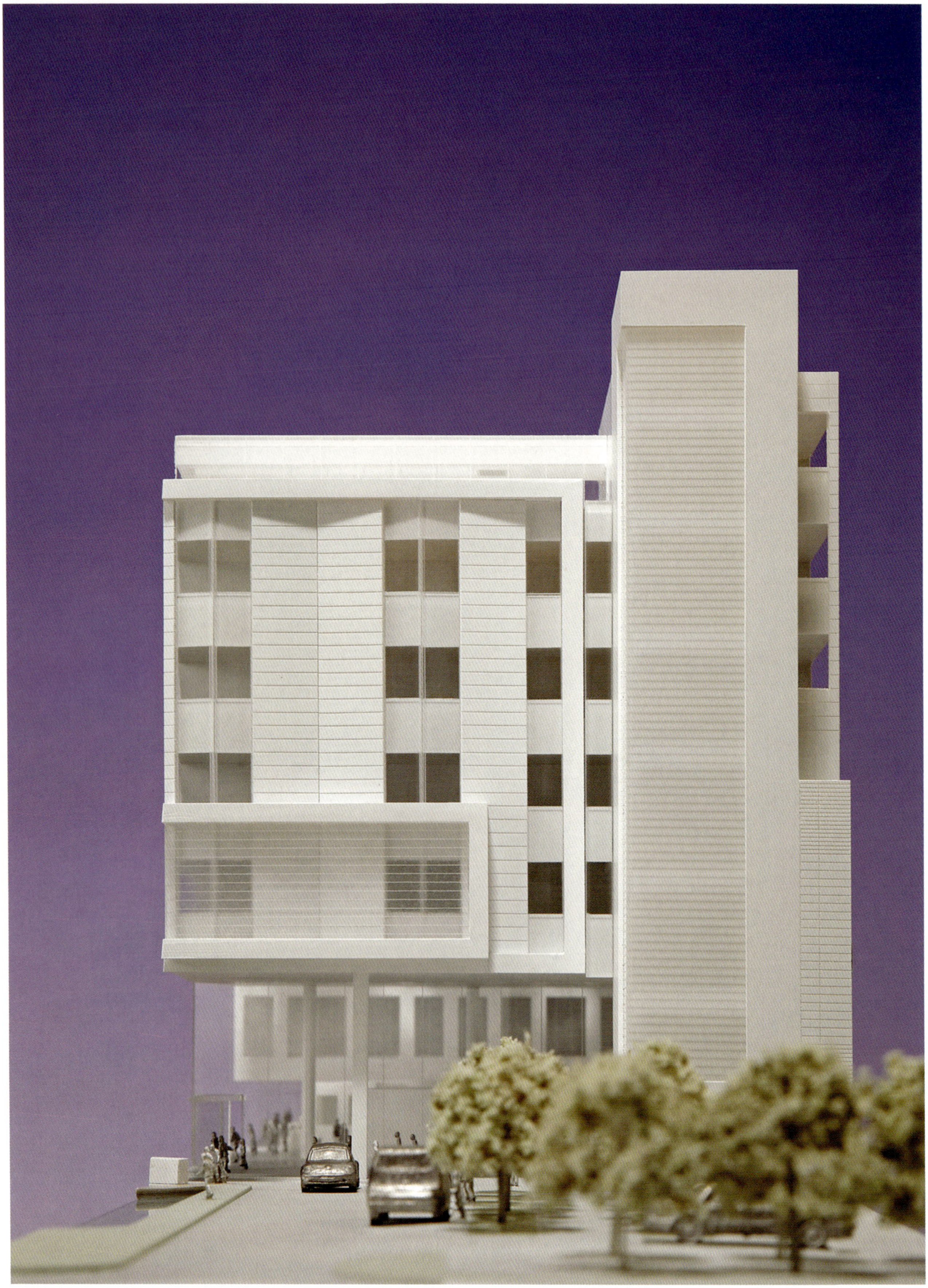

MODEL MAKING
FOR ARCHITECTS

Matthew Driscoll

THE CROWOOD PRESS

First published in 2013 by
The Crowood Press Ltd
Ramsbury, Marlborough
Wiltshire SN8 2HR

www.crowood.com

© Matthew Driscoll 2013

All rights reserved. No part of this publication may be reproduced or transmitted in any form or by any means, electronic or mechanical, including photocopy, recording, or any information storage and retrieval system, without permission in writing from the publishers.

British Library Cataloguing-in-Publication Data
A catalogue record for this book is available from the British Library.

ISBN 978 1 84797 490 7

Frontispiece: Architect's model in sprayed acrylic (Photo: Andrew Putler)

Dedication
To Emily, for making it possible.

Acknowledgements
The author wishes to acknowledge the help and support of all the people who have helped in the making of this book. With particular thanks going to the following people and businesses, without whose time and effort this book would not have been possible: Emily Palmer, who tirelessly interpreted my scrawling into legible English, worked on every facet of the book and finally cajoled me into getting the book finished; Sam Morgan in particular for being the book's hand model, as well as providing insights into his day job as a model maker; Mark Luggie, for his support and insights into model making and the technologies that lead the industry; Phil Wykes for a wealth of information regarding to the in-house model making industry; Sion Driscoll for all of his advice and help with the production of the book cover and book imagery as well as all answering technical questions with regards to computers; and Fosters and Partners for supplying and allowing me to photographs of their models.

Typeset by Sharon Dainton, Isis Design.
Printed and bound in India by Replika Press Pvt. Ltd.

CONTENTS

Introduction 7

1 MATERIALS AND EQUIPMENT 21
2 THE PURPOSE OF A MODEL 35
3 A FIRST EXERCISE IN ARCHITECTURAL MODEL MAKING 49
4 APPROACHES TO MODEL MAKING 67
5 UNDERSTANDING BASES 93
6 MAKING OFFSITE BUILDINGS 111
7 COMMISSIONING A MODEL 123
8 THE FUTURE 131

Glossary 137
Index 143

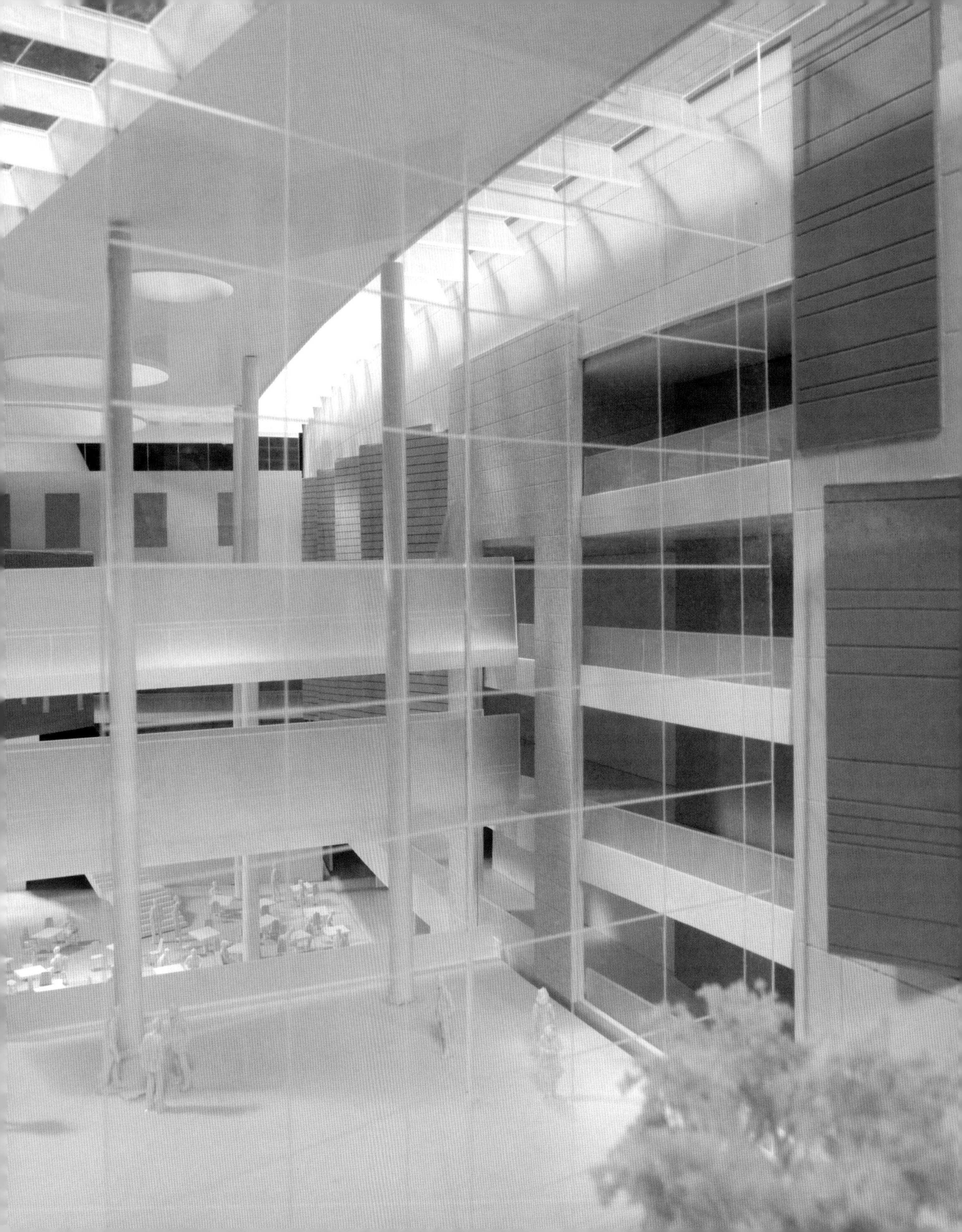

INTRODUCTION

The skills needed to become a model maker are gained over many years and this book brings together an overview of this knowledge across all stages of commissioning and producing an architectural model. This is a guide to building an understanding of the principles, tools, techniques, terms and uses of different types of models and their purposes. It also offers a solid basis from which to decide the purpose of a model and the practical steps which bring a successful outcome, leading to a better understanding of how to approach the designing and commissioning of a model with reference to materiality, colour and finish.

Architectural model making at its most pragmatic is the representation of two-dimensional drawings or plans in three-dimensional form. It is important to understand what an architectural model can do for the design process and most importantly what is to be resolved through the production of a model. Understanding what the model is for is always going to be the key to a positive outcome.

In all aspects of the design world and throughout the history of the twentieth century, from the fathers of modern architecture to some of the most renowned architects working today, the architectural model has played a crucial and relevant role as a visible, integral part of the design process.

Two requirements have to be addressed for a truly successful model: firstly there is a functional need for a scaled representation of a planned building; secondly, there is what we can call the 'obscure need' – this can manifest itself as a visual, cerebral and emotional stimulant. In other words, the aim is to provide a functional model which may also highlight a

'Models should not express the hand of the producer but the spirit of the inventor.'

Leon Battista Alberti,
De Re Aedificatoria, c. 1450.

'Tests on a model ... showed me the way.'

Mies van de Rohe's conclusion with regard to the practicalities of overcoming structural challenges in his design for a 'glass skyscraper'.

'You start by sketching, then you do a drawing, then you make a model, and then you go to reality – you go to site – and then you go back to drawing. You build up a kind of circularity between drawing and making and then back again.'

Renzo Piano, quoted in Edward Robbins,
Why Architects Draw, 1994.

'I love models ... they're perfect worlds, they're perfect imaginings and they are a world where everybody is always happy and there is no weather!'

Kevin McCloud in Channel 4's
Grand Designs, 2011.

LEFT: **A model that makes sense of a complex building layout, with the atrium, walkways and the building's internal elevations modelled. (Photo: Andrew Putler)**

■ INTRODUCTION

Anshen + Allen architects' Karolinska competition model (scale 1:200). (Photo: Chris Edgecombe)

specific area to draw the eye, and/or to create a talking point beyond the immediate functionality of the design. This is especially important when a model is being constructed for a competition where it is required to engage and involve its audience beyond a literal representation of an architect's design; the model gains a value all of its own to express the design in its best light as an almost utopian ideal, which even the finished building may not be able to realize.

When considering the scope for creating a model there are many choices to make, ranging from a simplistic model that explores shape and form, to a detailed model that explains exactly how a building is to be constructed. From the starting point it can be possible, with the use of scale, to understand how the building is likely to look and whether it works in situ. This can be through the production of tens of drawings or just one model. Most commonly, architects themselves are unlikely to produce an architectural model because it would fall under the specialism of an architectural model maker.

This is where the division from study model into the specialism of a professional model maker may be rationalized: basic models of card or foam may be undertaken as study or sketch models by an architect, but for more complicated, developed models the skills and experience needed to produce a model to impress a client, placate a planner or engage the public will involve a team of professional model makers or company to undertake the work. The job title of 'model maker' may be defined as creatively working to a set of plans within a fixed timescale while working to a brief given at the start of a project. Obviously the nuances that are involved in the development of a design during the model build, due to the nature of a model's construction, are far more complicated. It is this level of expertise that has given birth to an industry all of its own, which can be as richly creative as an architect's studio – arguably a creative environment for an architect to 'play' with-

Denys Lasdun (standing) and Philip Wood (centre) with their team in the studio. The architects sit proudly in front of evidence of the design development process.

in. The model, then, offers the architect an opportunity to experiment and engage in a discussion with a physical 'object', so he or she can visualize, then create, the final structure in the real world.

It is often during a visit to the model makers that an architect will see their design in three-dimensional terms for the first time and this is the first step towards getting their scheme constructed. The physical act of getting a model constructed can breathe confidence and life into a design, without which the model might never get past the drawing stage. It is at this model stage that the architect can be parent to their design, physically standing over the model, deciding what's best for its future, discussing potential and considering the beauty of their creation. Flowery language indeed – but in the safe environment of the model there can be a free exchange of ideas and interpretations that aid development of the overall design. The model is often the first time that the design can really be challenged pragmatically. The model then plays its role within the design development, which a building should go through to be built.

A history of the model

The modern understanding of the word 'model' derives from the French modèle and Italian modello – initially from the Latin word modulus, meaning 'a small measure'. The relationship between building design and model making has roots going back almost as far as people building structures. The first model makers were architects themselves, when the ability to see in three-dimensional terms at the design stage helped them to understand materials and their uses to a far greater degree. The more complicated and ambitious the designs became, the greater the need to understand how the materials – timber, stone and eventually metal and glass – could evolve into the envisioned design.

The first architects were masons and carpenters as well as designers. The word 'architecture' comes from the Greek ἀρχιτέκτων (arkhitekton: ἀρχι meaning 'chief', and τέκτων 'builder, carpenter, mason'). So it was these chief builders who created the first models, testing the limits of the material properties to eventually create the columns, porticos, vestibules and great domes of what are today seen as some of the true architectural marvels of the world.

There are examples of models going back to ancient societies such as the Chinese Dynasties. The ways in which an architect approached the design developed and gave birth to the model maker's specialism; this arguably began early in the Renaissance period, when the length of time needed to build some of the breathtaking structures achievable through new building processes began to surpass even the architects' own lifetimes. This is where we see the first recorded writings on the concept of a model, recorded by polymath Leon Battista Alberti in c. 1450–60. Through his wide-ranging knowledge and expertise, Alberti was the first to rationalize the symbiosis of science with art and architecture. In the famous book *De Pictura*, written in 1435, and in a second book, *De Re Aedificatoria*, written c. 1450, he views the architectural model as a field with objective laws.

> You may easily and freely add, retrench, alter, renew, and in short, change everything from one end to the other, till all and every one of the parts are just as you would have them, and without fault.
>
> *Leon Battista Alberti, De Re Aedificatoria*

We can see, therefore, that although early architectural models might well have been in timber or stone, as opposed to today's card and paper, their purpose since the Renaissance has remained the same: to explain and develop the design of architects. Alberti also recommends the duplication of models, so that the original model is preserved; the architect can

INTRODUCTION

then alter and develop while still reflecting on their starting point, original inspiration or design insight. Keeping the original model can allow the original illuminating influence to be articulated even after countless models have been produced. Alberti advises the architect, 'Be sure to have a complete "model of the whole", by which examine every minute part of your future structure eight, nine, ten times over, and again, after different intermissions of times.'

The use of the model beyond design interpretation had some influence in the past in finalizing and getting the construction correct. Alberti confirms this in describing his own undertakings:

> I have often conceived of projects in the mind that seemed quite commendable at the time; but when I translated them into drawings, I found several errors in the very parts that delighted me most, and quite serious ones; again, when I return to drawings, and measure the dimensions, I recognize and lament my carelessness; finally, when I pass from the drawings to the model, I sometimes notice further mistakes in the individual parts, even over the numbers.

This shows how an architect needs to keep working on a design to cut away the imperfections in both the design and construction. Alberti demonstrates that with the use of models, success in creating great architecture lies in continuous endeavour.

It was a requirement to have a representation of the design that manifested all of the details into the scale model, allowing for clarity of vision for the eventual completed building. In cases where perhaps the building was a great cathedral or public building, and therefore took decades to build, having a tool that realized the eventual goal became essential. The construction period for these buildings was so great that technological advancements – and sometimes, more importantly, changing fashions – might allow changes to the design, and this could be reflected in the model. It became vital to have a model as reference, which could reassure those funding the project, allow the public to see the greatness of the architect's vision, and then to update and alter the model as a guide to how the plans were developing.

One of the first extensively documented examples of this relates to the construction of the duomo of Florence's cathedral. There are still in existence today wooden models from the 1350s for the campanile (built by Giotto), and later for the choir chapels and a part of the nave. In a process not unlike today's system, the building authority ordered designs for the completion of the cathedral. In response to this drawing work, a brickwork model was submitted. The model had a dual purpose: firstly it had to represent the drawing; secondly, and perhaps more insightfully, it had to represent how the church was to be built. For technical reasons the project was held up for fifty years. In 1417 Filippo Brunelleschi became the advisor to the project, and soon had many carpenters creating models for the construction of the dome. These were now called for the first time 'modelli'. In the year 1420 one was selected. With the help of further models – also for elevators and cranes – the construction of the dome was propelled forward.

The early models were therefore usually constructed as the building was built. It has only been in relatively modern times that the structure of a planned, 'accepted build', together with the onset of technologies such as CAD (Computer Aided Design) which can measure and provide structural and material answers, has meant that the model has become a tool solely for design, as opposed to a tool for building. The Modernist movement, early in the twentieth century, was a new and progressive way of thinking that challenged the arts and design establishment. The design process advocated by proponents of the Bauhaus movement and its contemporaries was the forerunner of today's rationalized construction planning strategy.

The computer age

Since 1960 the growth of CAD has become interwoven with the design and engineering of buildings, ships and automobiles. Without CAD the widespread use of the electrical circuit or injection moulds that we see as synonymous with modern mass-produced life would not have come to pass. Developed from US military research and predominantly used in the space race, CAD was later made accessible to the public in day-to-day life. In the mid-1960s IBM developed the first CAD programs.

Since the 1980s, architects' use of CAD has radically changed the design process: firstly it has intrinsically changed the perception of models by architects; secondly, it has completely changed the way in which model makers go about constructing models. In the world of computer technology, the coordinates of the drawing on a screen form the essence of a design, but a three-dimensional model is still essential.

> The computer has revolutionised the way architects work, yet the language of drawing and model making still plays a central role in the studio.
>
> *Richard Cork, curator of 'Foster + Partners: the Art of Architecture' exhibition.*

The computer might be the interface that allows architects to view the world from impossibly exciting new perspectives, but it can still (even for some of the most sophisticated architectural practices) have grounding in the concept of a hand-drawn sketch or paper maquette model, just as although we all write on keyboards and send emails, the ability to do so is based on the ability to write with a pencil.

Technological advancements mean that the craft of making a model has moved on, to an almost science-fiction level. Some CAD programs can calculate three-dimensional models from two-dimensional drawings. They can calculate the material requirements and the cost of those materials. While our present is one of laser-cutting components for kits to create models from CAD drawings, the rapidly increasing development of industries that use three-dimensional computer models and print in three dimensions is perhaps the newest technology that has woven itself into the arsenal of the model maker's tool bag.

What does a model bring to the design process?

To understand the purpose of the model is to understand the justification of the design it must convey and a thorough knowledge of what you are trying to achieve. If this is an understanding of massed shape or light on the building, then the model must have a sympathy through materiality, scale or colour that can define this. The model doesn't always need to convey all the detail of the project brief; it can be a general principle of the design that is put across to your audience. This study model is normally an early stage of the design brief but will ultimately guide you through to the important observations of the brief. More detailed commissions can later tell the complete story but a controlled understanding of the core principles will always lead you to the creation of a successful designed model. When trying to perceive a design from the point of view of the layman's eye, architectural models have the advantage over two-dimensional drawings because they make it easier for the observer to form a subjective opinion about the designer's intentions. They serve as the basis of important discussions about design ideas and for negotiating solutions.

An overview of model types

Studies/sketch models

The scale and level of detail of this type of model may vary, but generally these focus on design development. They are usually produced early on in the design process and are tools to express early ideas or sketches in the design process.

Presentation models

This can cover a whole range of models scales and purposes that can be produced to evaluate a range of needs, generally though we can divide them into categories:

PLANNING MODELS
These are typically built at a much smaller scale (starting from 1:500 and less, 1:750, 1:1000, 1:1250), representing large areas, even a whole town or village, large resort, campus, industrial facility, and so on. Planning models are a vital tool for town and city planning and development.

MARKETING MODELS
These usually have a sales-orientated goal and are designed to maximize the aesthetically pleasing aspects of the design – this can range from a large housing development to a block of flats. The ultimate aim is to help create an image of allure that makes people want to live somewhere; developers hope that the selling of a perfect world in which to live helps to sell the properties before they are built.

■ INTRODUCTION

Early sketch model of the Pembury hospital development for Anshen + Allen architects.

Planning submission model of the same complex later in the project's development. Once the initial design development had been decided upon, a 'polished' presentation model was needed to pass the project through the planning stages. (Photo: Andrew Putler)

INTRODUCTION

Marketing model produced at 1:150 scale in conjunction with Millennium Models. The large scale allows for increased gravitas in the marketing suite. The base board size was 1.8m^2, which allowed the impressive nature of the spaces and functionality of the towers and the shopping complex they sit on to be demonstrated. (Photo: Andrew Putler)

13

■ INTRODUCTION

MUSEUM MODELS
Often these have an interactive aspect: members of the public are expected to have something explained to them through the medium of the model. This is often assisted by interactive elements, for example lighting to specific areas on a model to simulate something or moving parts to express things like traffic flows and changing environments.

TEACHING MODELS
These can be used as a tool to explain engineering processes or construction principles and often show isolated structural elements and components and their interaction. There is also a technical application (in the study of 'right of light' issues, for example.)

LANDSCAPING DESIGN MODELS
These models of landscape design and development represent features such as walkways, small bridges, pergolas, vegetation patterns and aesthetic qualities. Landscaping design models usually represent public spaces and may, in some cases, include buildings as well.

Landscape can be expressed using beautiful hand-coloured plans layered into a model. Different inserts are available to represent different options – a clear, cost-effective way of representing large landscaping areas.

Scale

Architectural models are produced at scale. Scale can be defined thus: a representation or copy of an object that is larger or smaller than the actual size of the object, which seeks to maintain the relative proportions of the physical size of the original object. Models representing 1 or 2 buildings and a modest piece of surrounding landscape may be built at a scale such as 1:100 or 1:75. Here is a useful scale guide to obtain more information about standard architectural scales and to help with scale selection.

The scales and their architectural use are broadly as follows:

1:1   Full (or real) size for details
1:10 Details
1:20 Interior spaces/furniture
1:50 Interior spaces/detailed floor plans/different floor levels
1:75 Detailed floor plans/different floor levels

The fully finished model or sections of buildings show the colours, building details, building construction methods, suspended ceilings, window finishes and frame colour, and detailed textured landscaping. The main structure of these models can be similar to the scales listed, with smooth contoured bases to show level changes; within the buildings the detail is embellished with a variety of different materials and finishes. Balconies are often etched out of metal, as are fences, bridge handrails, some complex window surrounds, benches and many other minor details. Plants, trees, bushes and grass effects are created from many different materials. The detail can be as realistic as the client budget can extend to.

1:100 Building plans/layouts
1:200 Building plan/layout
1:250 Layout/site plan
1:500 Site plans

From these scales come detailed models in laser-cut components to create elevation and floor slabs showing windows, elevation details and sometimes the interior spaces, depending on the type and scale of the development. The construction of these models can also show the landscape of the site, the roads, any walls or general site details. The construction used can be of many materials, but modern methods tend to be a combination of wooden veneer and acrylic sheet and a variety of material finishes with the use of metal etchings, spray

A potential fin for a building scale 1:1. The material is bamboo – the same material as the eventual building fin. This was a study in materiality and spacing, investigating the required spacing to adequately shade a glazed building.

INTRODUCTION

Detail of architectural art screening for a building's internal design by Justin Eagles.

Created to explore possible designs for the courtyard of an existing building, this model primarily investigates mass and form but the scale allows the interior layouts to be developed, together with an understanding of its context.

paint and laser-cut surface detail, patterning and texture. Most clients require some compromise to fit with budgets.

1:750   Site plan/location plan
1:1000   Master plan for site or location plans
1:1250   Site plans
1:5000   Site plans/city maps

From these scales we would normally see mainly block work models representing mass and proportions of buildings that are represented in a variety of finishes, perhaps different timbers or spray-finished chemical wood finishes (often referred to as 'chemiwood'). Only the main architectural features could be shown on the smaller scale, so generally speaking no façade detail or specific ground works such as steps, walls and kerb edges are shown; roads, pavements and grasses are often shown on one layer (without kerb edges) and represented by colour or laser scribe. If the site has relatively few contours the model is often produced flat due to the small scale and to fit in with budgetary requirements.

This book will enter into more detail as we progress and will offer you a good knowledge of the reasons for building or commissioning a model; it will also aim to demonstrate how to make all aspects of the models described above. It is a guide for model makers and architects alike, offering tips and advice on the best model to build (or commission) for every situation, ensuring the desired outcome: a beautifully designed and created model.

INTRODUCTION

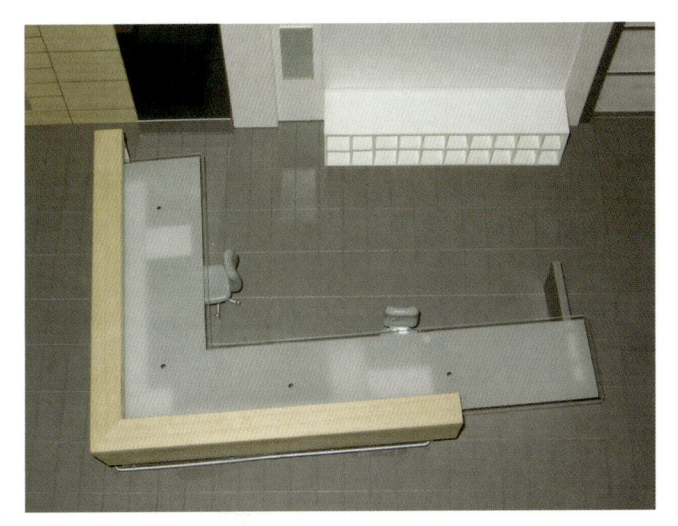

Proposed layout for a reception area, modelled in a realistic palette to investigate the spaces and people flow.

An investigation of a building's façade – colour and panelling in particular – allowing relevant detail to be represented.

Conceptualized timber model. Using a sympathetic palette, the model is freed to present the building's interesting design without the intricacies of the detailing.

■ INTRODUCTION

Timber model that uses frosted acrylic to investigate the key gestures of the new additions to an existing building, while also investigating the design within the building's context.

Timber master plan: while all the buildings are new the overall mass and integration of green spaces is key to the model's success.

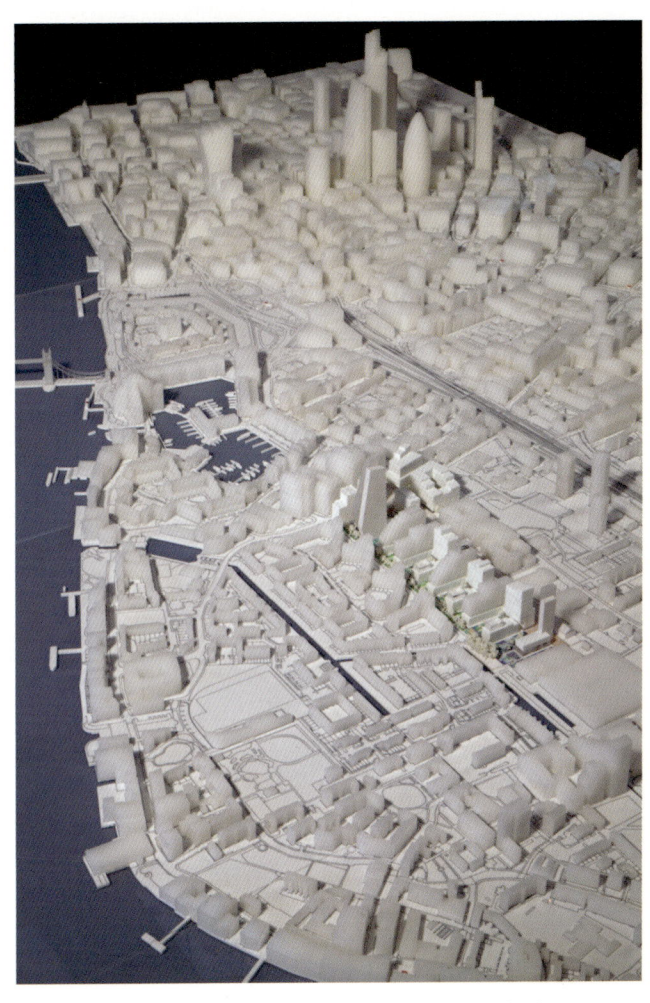

INTRODUCTION

Master plan for a new hospital and retail park. The scale allows the sheer size of the site to be modelled within its context.

A large area is covered to show the proposed scheme's situation in the context of London's City and the Thames. This type of model can instil a 'wow' factor because of its size, and act as a clever design tool when investigating possible heights and views from feature buildings across London. (Photo: Andrew Putler)

BELOW: Model for the design of a bridge. The scale allows the bridge to be put within its context, while also addressing the landscaping of the park below, transport links and key buildings. (Photo: Andrew Putler)

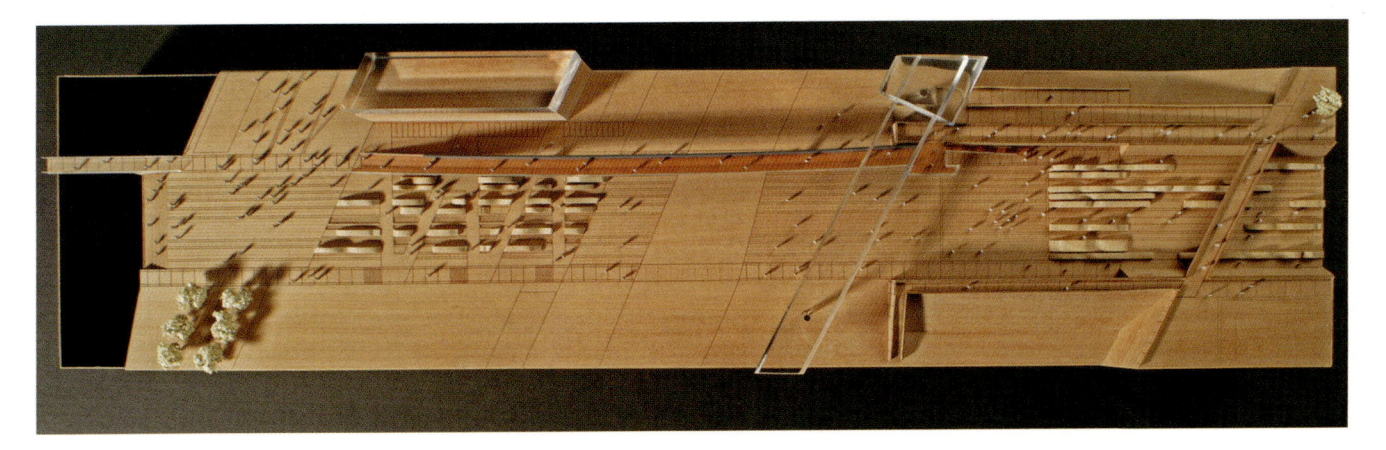

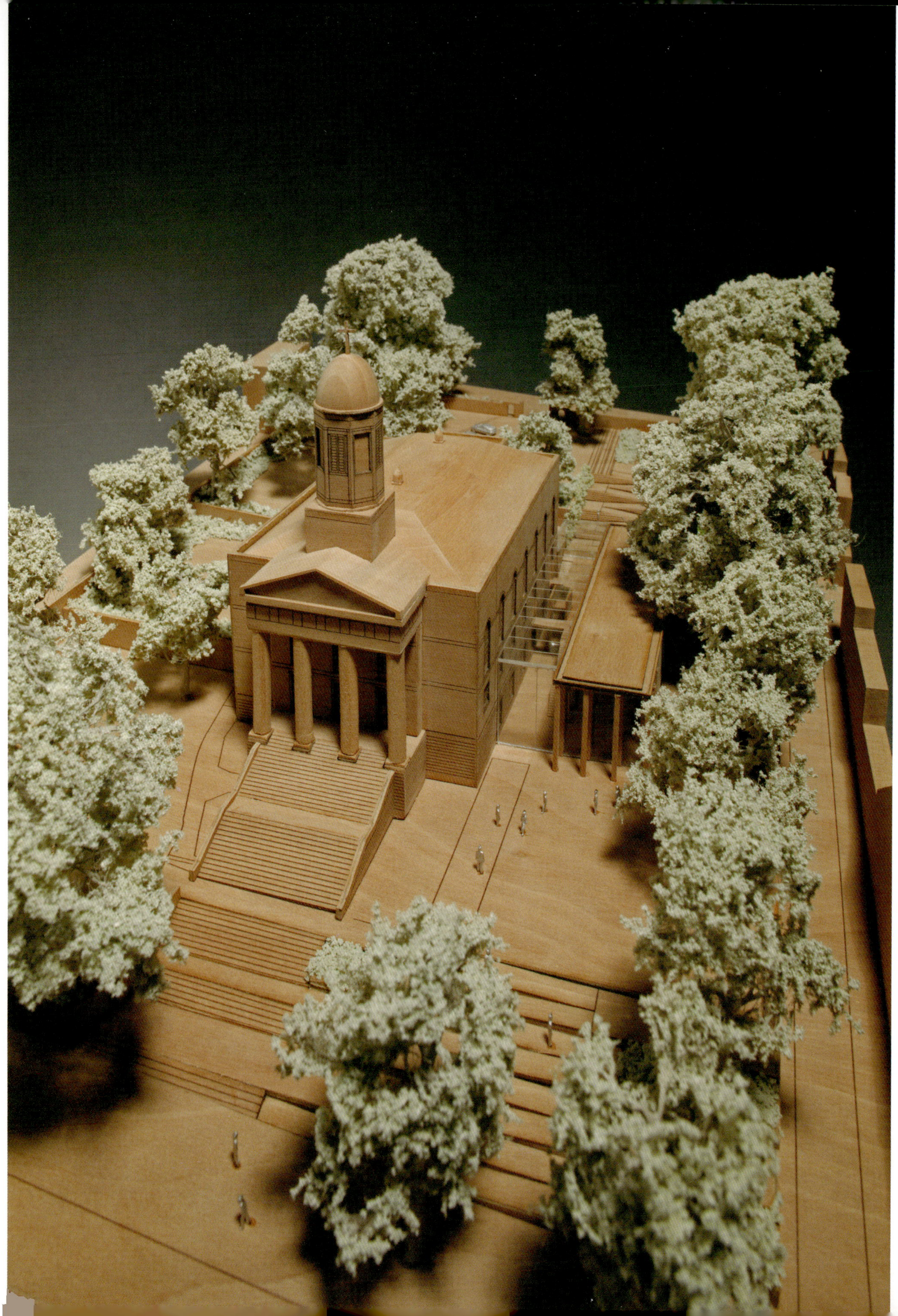

CHAPTER 1

MATERIALS AND EQUIPMENT

A model maker's specialism is to create and produce three-dimensional scaled models from two-dimensional drawings. Beyond the required skills of project management, albeit on a small scale, organizational ability and of course being able to see things in 3D, the work requires imaginative flair, good CAD skills, and practical hand skills. They must also be able to communicate effectively. Most model makers working in the architectural industry are self-employed, and work on a project-by-project basis.

What is a model maker's role?

Model makers are responsible for replicating structures in miniature: for example, they may be required to construct a 100mm-high version of the Empire State building or to make miniature representations in timber of large areas of cities. Models are made in a range of materials including wood, plastic, or metal, using a variety of different techniques. For models with moving parts, model makers may employ basic engineering techniques and, in some cases, for lighting the model buildings, electronics. Using a range of hand, power or machine tools, including computer-assisted equipment, model makers create models that accurately portray the requirements and ideas of architects.

In consultation with an architect, a model maker initially uses freehand drawing skills or computer-aided design (CAD) and sample materials to help visualize the finished product. Once this model is approved, a detailed model will be built and materials and resources will be sought, such as specialist paint, timbers or machinery, three-dimensional printing resources, or large-scale vacuum-formers.

Model makers will also consult with other specific departments or architectural practices such as landscape architects, visualization companies and photographers. Model makers must adhere to strict health and safety guidelines and carry out tasks in a safe work environment, because many of the materials used can be dusty and may produce dangerous fumes.

Skills base

Model makers must have the imaginative flair to help visualize and realize designs in three dimensions and also have good CAD skills with the ability to read and understand plans and technical drawings. Practical skills with hand and power tools are a must for modelling, as is familiarity with a wide range of materials and the techniques required for working with them. To be able to work accurately whilst paying close attention to detail is essential, and being able to discuss ideas and concepts with designers and other colleagues, whilst working to tight deadlines.

LEFT: **Traditional heritage model of development in Bristol. The model palette is sympathetic to the composition; a soft-coloured timber of pear wood is used. (Photo: Andrew Putler)**

■ MATERIALS AND EQUIPMENT

The essentials

1. **Scalpel: Swann-Morton with No. 10A blades**
   This is essential kit and cannot be replaced with any other sort of craft knife or retractor blade (many of which can be dangerous when using them for the relatively fine work of model making). The scalpel is perfect for fine, detailed work and accurate cutting of paper, card veneers, thin ply, styrene sheet and acrylic. It has a strong handle and used with a 10A blade it can perform an enormous breadth of tasks from simple cutting of lightweight paper, scribing lines and splitting thicker materials through to scoring of lines into acrylic sheet.

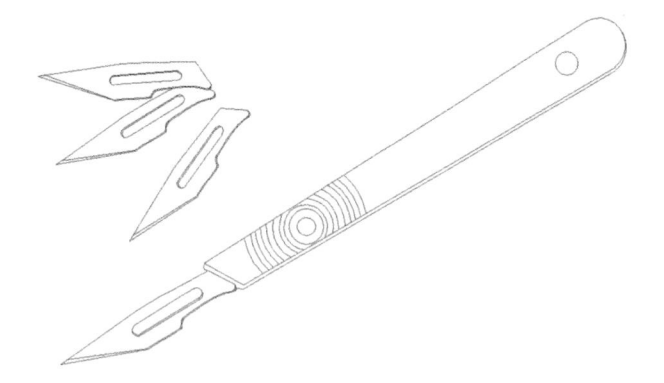

Scalpel and blades.

150mm and 300mm steel rules.

2. **Steel rule**
   This is needed for general measuring and for cutting against. It has to be metal: plastic rules become inaccurate when cutting along them and – more importantly – they can be dangerous as the blade is liable to ride up onto a plastic rule. It is wise to have a selection of sizes; 150mm and 300mm would be considered the essential. A useful tip is to cover one side in masking tape; this prevents damage to the delicate surfaces that you are cutting.

3. **Calculator**
   An incredibly useful tool, even if it doesn't appear so at first; with most aspects of model making a certain level of number literacy is important. Expect to use a calculator for adding and subtracting measurements and more importantly scaling your building to model size.

A calculator.

4. **Engineer's square**
   This is important for a square edge (the constant mantra of all architectural modelling being, 'Does it look square?'). It is one of the first lessons that is needed and is at the centre of what you are trying to achieve. If a series of blocks isn't square then they won't stick together correctly; if an elevation you have cut out isn't square then the building won't stick together correctly. A range of squares from 50mm, 75mm, 100mm and 150mm should cover most eventualities.

MATERIALS AND EQUIPMENT

Range of engineer's squares.

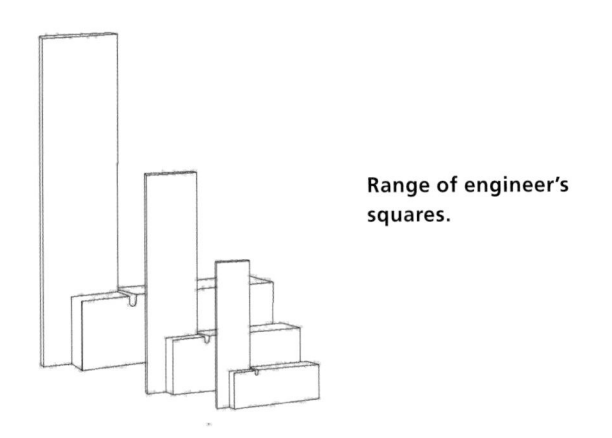

5. **Angle blocks** (123 blocks)
   In the same family as the engineer's squares, these can be incredibly useful for keeping floors in position as they are stacked or elevations square as you glue and assemble them. They are often also very useful as weights to position material as it is gluing.

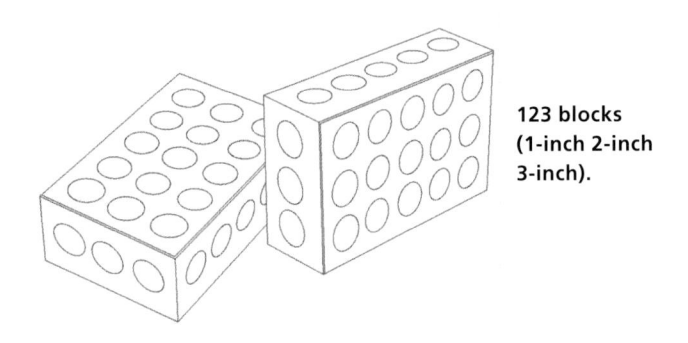

123 blocks (1-inch 2-inch 3-inch).

6. **Tweezers**
   Reasonably self-explanatory, but a must when attempting precision model-making work, tweezers allow for a cleaner, more accurate finish to detailed work, whether it is applying architectural figures to a model or sticking small components together.

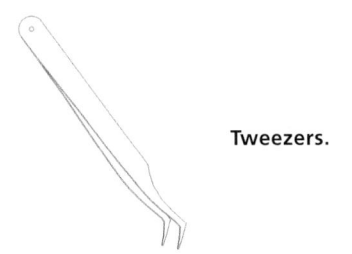

Tweezers.

7. **Veneer gauge**
   The ultimate model-making measurement tool can also be used for scribing materials if the front outside calliper jaw is sharpened. The veneer calliper acts as a three-in-one tool for measuring internal, external and depth values, as can be seen in the diagram. Important for almost all parts of a build, it quickly replaces the steel rule for accurately measuring a three-dimensional object and should be in your hand for the majority of the project.

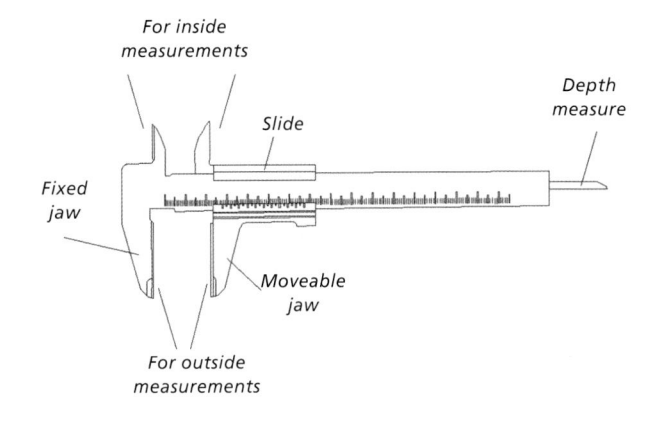

Veneer gauge (callipers).

8. **Superglue: cyanoacrylate**
   Superglue is the generic name for this fast-acting adhesive (commonly sold under trade names like Crazy Glue), perfect for fast, strong joints especially when used in conjunction with superglue activator. It can be used for almost all materials but has to be handled dexterously: it will set fast and if too much is used it can 'bloom' (leave a cloudy residue around the glue point) especially when used on acrylic surfaces. If handled correctly, it can be incredibly useful thanks to its versatility and strength. Superglue comes in different densities – thin, medium and thick – and can be used for filling small gaps; it can also be sanded and can be squeezed into hard-to-access areas. Useful accessories to superglue include nozzles, which can greatly improve accuracy and precision when using the glue. A pipette bottle is useful for storing and applying activator because

MATERIALS AND EQUIPMENT

Bottle of superglue with nozzle, rolls of tape, spray adhesive and lighter fluid.

of the relatively toxic nature of superglue and the activator.

9. **Spray adhesives**
   Two general types of spray adhesive may be used: a low-tack repositionable spray and a high-tack fixed position spray. For usage instructions it is best to follow the specific details on the can. The main use for the repositionable spray (the one more regularly used) is for attaching plans and elevation drawings to material for cutting. This is especially useful in sketch modelling when cutting exact shapes out of sheet material using anything from scalpels through to band saws; it saves time and creates a greater level of accuracy. Any residue after removing the paper master can be wiped away using lighter fluid.

10. **Masking tape**
    Beyond the obvious use, masking tape can be useful to hold model components together while they are being glued or while they are curing. A low tack tape generally will not leave any residue behind on the model.

11. **Double-sided tape**
    This can range from the general double-sided tape to specialist tapes. It is very useful when laminating lots of sheet surfaces together, for positioning things when mocking together a model, and when quickly assembling card and paper studies. (As a general rule try to buy a film tape as opposed to a gel tape; if the tape needs to be removed at a later stage, gel-based tape is almost impossible to remove without leaving a residue.) Stronger adhesive double-sided tapes can be bought for more permanent or stronger bonds such as carpet tapes; there is a wide variety of these on the market.

12. **Lighter fluid**
    This is a good cleaning solvent for removing residue such as spray adhesive or tape residue, and is a good all-round cleaner for machined or worked acrylic, timbers and sprayed surfaces. It is petroleum based and highly flammable, so safety should always be paramount.

13. **Needle-nose pliers**
    Great for holding and fixing when gluing, these can also do the job of tweezers on more robust materials. A long pair of needle-nose pliers may also be particularly useful when scribing and snapping sheet material, such as 1mm acrylic.

14. **Sanding blocks**
    These can be made to an appropriate size, and use paper of various grit sizes, depending on the specific job. The thing to remember is to produce them from robust

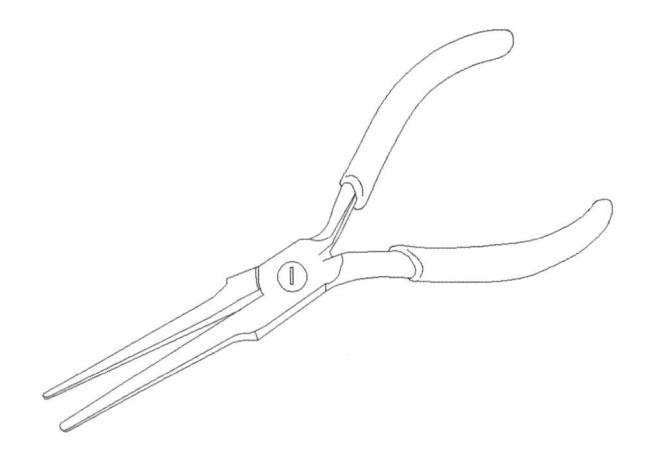

Needle-nose pliers.

MATERIALS AND EQUIPMENT

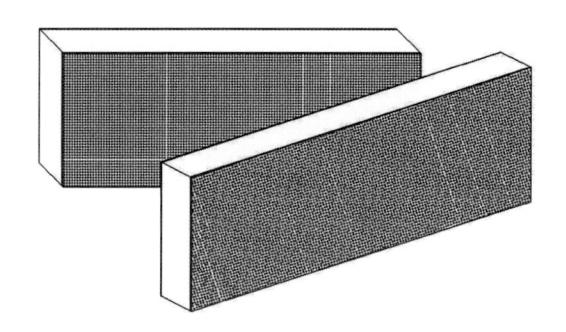

Range of sanding blocks.

materials such as acrylic sheet or MDF in varying thickness. These materials provide a flat, inflexible surface with which to sand from.

15. **Cutting board**
    This doesn't have to be one of the shop-bought cutting mats to protect tables. In fact a piece of MDF cut to size, at least 12mm thick and flat (not warped) is perfect to cut on and to use as a good flat surface on which to build your model. This is a simple requisite, but important. What hope do you have of keeping your model square and even if the surface that you're building on isn't square?

Exploring materials and tools in greater detail

'Wet and dry' sandpaper

To achieve the best and most versatile results, 'wet and dry' (as opposed to ordinary sandpaper) is a better product to use. Wet and dry is available in different grades or grits (grit is a term used for the abrasive measure of the paper) ranging from the very coarse (80 grit) through to the very fine (1200 grit).

Although you may wish to have the whole range of paper grades, and some jobs will demand a specific grit, the desired finish may be achieved using just four grades of paper: the very coarse 80 grit for very rough finishes, 180 grit, 320 grit, and 600 grit, to get a smooth finish.

When sanding acrylic, metals and filler the paper can be wetted. This stops the grit becoming clogged and can reduce friction when sanding delicate objects.

Car body filler

Car body filler – commonly known as 'plod' within the model-making industry – is a two-part paste used in car body repair. It has become widely used by model makers, crafts-people and carpenters to repair and blend plastics, metals and woods. It is composed of a polyester resin, which, when mixed with a hardener (an organic peroxide) or catalyst, turns into a putty which then sets and hardens. You can apply the mixed body filler, and once it has set (less than ten minutes depending on the amount of catalyst used) sand it to shape, and paint it.

Highlighters

These are great for colour-coding areas, especially in the production of context buildings, where defining buildings from one another and their landscape can be confusing. Using highlighters to organize heights, roofscapes and general drawings helps keep processing such large quantities of data manageable.

Lithographic tape

For more intricate masks for spraying, litho tape is far superior to masking tape for achieving a sharper line to a mask job.

Glues

CHLOROFORM
A useful, precise glue that chemically welds acrylic together; it should be applied with a brush. It is worth investing in a chloroform dispensing pot which allows only a small amount of the solvent to be accessible at a time in a well, but it can also be syringed along surfaces quickly before it evaporates. It cures quickly (in a couple of minutes) and generally doesn't

leave marks if applied correctly. Chloroform is the most professional standard of solvent weld and performs most successfully but it can be difficult to obtain, especially in small quantities, because of its more toxic applications.

DICHLOROMETHANE (DCM), OR METHYLENE CHLORIDE

DCM (commonly referred to as 'Di-clo') is part of the same chemical family as chloroform. Often sold under the name 'plastic weld', its main use is for joining acrylic components together before they are painted. Unlike chloroform it does have a tendency to leave cloudy marks and is a little more volatile; it is, however, widely available in model shops. When applying DCM or chloroform, natural hair or sable brushes are best; acrylic brushes will just melt. Choose the size of brush that is most comfortable, but generally a small brush is better for detailed, precise work. A useful tip is to sharpen the end of the brush into a point; this can be useful for moving small components into place or holding them there after gluing.

TENSOL 12

This is glue which hardens due to solvent evaporation and produces a clear bond in acrylic sheets. In appearance it looks like liquid acrylic and is very useful for creating strong, durable joints on unpainted surfaces. It can be thinned down further using chloroform and is best applied from a squeezy bottle with a long nozzle.

CONTACT ADHESIVES

Contact adhesive is a multipurpose thixotropic (non-drip) glue; it should be used with the specific aim of bonding laminated plastics, wood and other materials. It is especially useful for bonding veneers to surfaces when producing timber models, or for sticking buildings to a base. Instructions on the packet should be followed, but the general principle is to apply the adhesive to both sides of the gluing surface, wait for it to tack off, and then place together while applying pressure. Be careful when placing together as it is an incredibly strong bond to separate if positioned incorrectly and will often damage the material being glued if you need to reposition. If you do need to remove the adhesive due to a design change or mistake, lighter fluid acts as a good solvent to weaken the bond, and left over residue can be cleaned away. It can be bought by the can for larger areas such as base boards and large buildings, or in tubes fitted with a nozzle for more intricate work. Certain limitations mean it will melt polystyrene, vinyl, and cellulose paint. It also has a very strong odour while curing and can be harmful to inhale especially in spaces with inadequate ventilation, such as an office environment.

UHU

Although a brand name, the positive properties especially for sketch modelling are that this glue dries strong and clear, is ideal for paper, cardboard, foam board and wood, and is solvent-free and non-toxic: great for an office environment. Because this glue doesn't involve an exothermic reaction it doesn't melt the edge of foam board.

PVA

PVA (polyvinyl acetate) glue is one of the most common forms of adhesive. This (normally) white glue is found in most model studios and is popular because it has an ability to adhere to many different surfaces while not being toxic or releasing fumes. It sets strong while still being quite forgiving during the gluing process because it takes a long time to cure. A good glue for sketch modelling, it works with a range of materials including paper, card, foam board and wood, but it only works on porous material so generally cannot be used with acrylics or metals. It works best when glued under applied pressure.

Model maker's plane

This is the same as any woodworking plane but smaller; it is not essential but useful for trimming down overlaps and flush edging base boards and corners of elevations. Ten minutes of sanding can be reduced to a few moments with the plane.

Micro drill

Essential for planting trees, people and cars, drilling a hole prevents the model animations from falling off the model, creating a far more robust and tidy finish. If you need to cut an aperture out of thin acrylic then drilling a hole in each corner of, say, a rectangle will stop the acrylic splitting and cracking beyond the score line. It is an invaluable tool if you are making alterations.

Rohacell

Rohacell is a type of foam that can be used in the same way as a Styrofoam for massing buildings, but it doesn't melt when in contact with heat-producing glues and can be sprayed with cellulose paint – perfect for representing textured hedges and landscapes.

Styrofoam

A trade name for polystyrene thermal insulation, the word Styrofoam is often used (not always accurately) by the general public in the United States and Canada as a generic term for any type of polystyrene foam. In model making, Styrofoam is the preferred choice material for building topographical models; it is also very often used in conjunction with a hot wire cutter for massing buildings for quick model exercises. It is a cheap, lightweight and sturdy material.

Foam board

Generally used in 3mm, 5mm or 10mm white sheets, although other thicknesses and colours are available, this is singly the most used material for sketch modelling. Its versatile properties include minimal weight, high-impact strength, fine closed cell structure and low flammability. They are easy to cut, saw, drill, and glue. Foam board sheets in many situations are preferable to the very traditional and popular materials in model making, such as styrene and MDF.

Acrylic

This thermoplastic and transparent plastic is known under the trade names Plexiglas and Perspex, but is commonly called acrylic glass or simply acrylic. Acrylics come in almost all thicknesses from 0.2mm through to 50mm and beyond. It is used as an alternative to glass, therefore it is the material of preferred choice for fabrication of protective covers and display cases for architectural models. Cast acrylic is often the preferred material of model makers on account of its stable properties, ease of handling and processing. Acrylic can be machined, sprayed, laminated, vacuum-formed, and polished. Tight-tolerance acrylic is bought in thinner sheet sizes and is more expensive but the accuracy of its thickness for stacking models and producing components is the great advantage of this material. Acrylic's versatility, strength and durability mean that it can be used to build almost all of a model if required and is an incredibly important material to the model-making industry.

PETG

Plastic, glycol-modified polyethylene terephthalate is a clear thermoplastic. PETG sheet has high stiffness, hardness, and toughness as well as good impact strength. It is used to fabricate clear parts and as raw material for vacuum-forming.

Styrene

Styrene is a thermoplastic substance, normally existing in solid state at room temperature; it melts if heated (for moulding or extrusion), and becomes solid again when cooling off, so it is used for both fabrication and vacuum-forming. Styrene is usually white, although it can be transparent or can be obtained in various colours. It is cheap to use and its durability and cost-effectiveness afford it many uses in a model shop, especially because it cuts, scores and can be belt sanded and glued safely and easily. It is often used for sketch modelling as an alternative to card and paper.

Traditional workshop machinery

Disc sander

A disc sander is a stationary electric machine that consists of replaceable circular-shaped sandpaper attached to a disc that is spun at high speed. The disc is placed on a front bench that can be adjusted to various angles. It can be used for rough or fine sanding depending on the sanding grit used. Most materials a model maker would use may be sanded, including woods, plastics, metals and other soft materials.

Bandsaw

The bandsaw, another stationary tool, uses a blade consisting of a continuous band of metal with teeth along one edge. It

MATERIALS AND EQUIPMENT

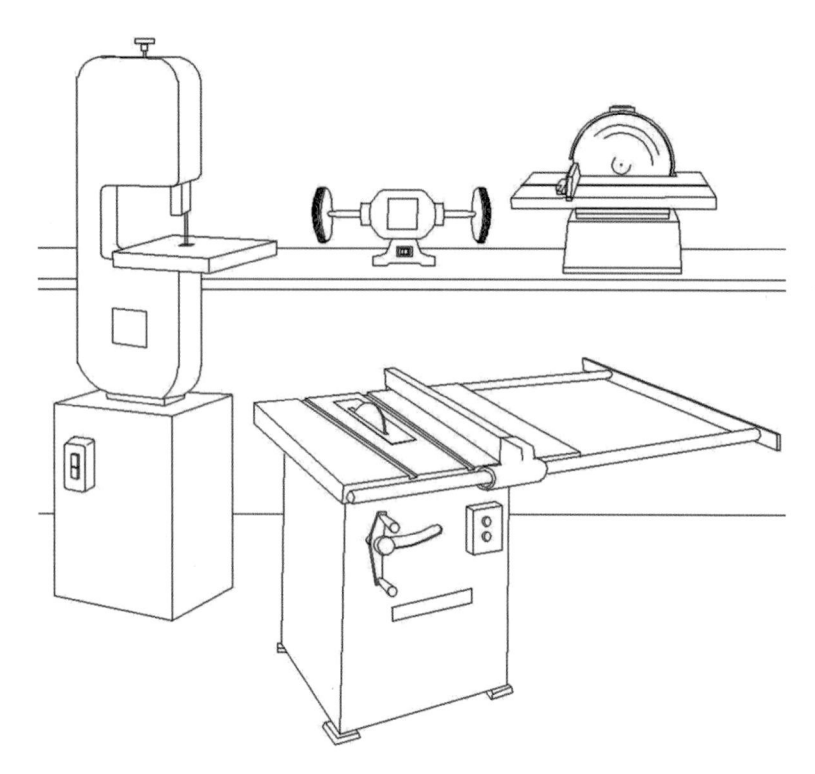

Workshop drawing, including a circular saw, band saw, polisher, and disc sander.

can cut through various materials, including most woods, plastics and metals. The band usually rides on two wheels rotating in the same plane; they are great for cutting curves and irregular shapes, but can also be used for cutting straight lines (although these will usually have to be finished afterwards). Be warned, though: if you attempt to cut within too tight a radius, or if the blade gets twisted or bent in the material, then the blade may snap. Generally this makes a very loud bang and is more frightening than dangerous, but if the guard is not in place, or too much of the blade is exposed, then it could result in serious injury as the blade whips around. It is always worth remembering that these are power tools and should always be treated with respect – they are designed to cut through tougher materials than skin and bone.

Flat bed circular saw / table saw

This wood- and plastic-working tool consists of a circular saw blade, mounted on an arbor and driven by an electric motor. The blade protrudes through the surface of a table, which provides support for the material being cut. The depth of the cut is varied by moving the blade up and down: the higher the blade protrudes above the table, the deeper the cut that is made in the material. The angle of cut is controlled by adjusting the angle of blade. Access to a table saw is essential for making architectural models; whether processing material sizes just to fit onto the laser cutter bed or machining offsite buildings out of chemiwood and timber, the table saw has been at the centre of everything that goes into making an architectural model of virtually any scale. It must be remembered, however, that this is potentially the most dangerous machine in any workshop. Some of the main points to think about before using the saw are listed here; disregard of these could lead to the loss of a finger. It must also be noted that this book cannot be used as instruction for using a table saw. Full training from an experienced workshop user should be sought when using this machinery.

ACCESSORIES

Fence: table saws commonly have a fence (guide) running from the front of the table (the side nearest the operator) to the back, parallel to the cutting plane of the blade. The distance of the fence from the blade can be adjusted, which determines where on the material the cut is made. Most table saws come with a fence as standard.

Push stick: a stick with a shaped end to hook over the material to be cut, allowing you to keep your hands away from the

MATERIALS AND EQUIPMENT

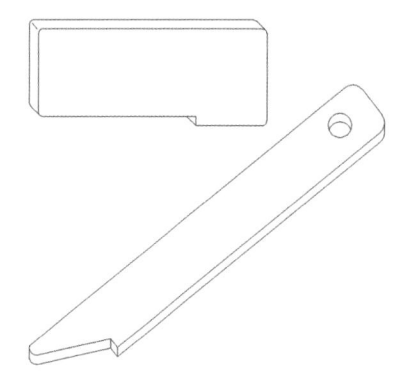

Push sticks for safe use of the circular saw.

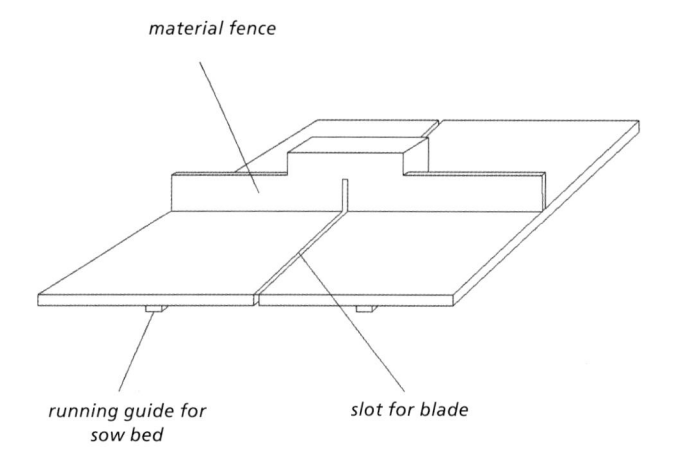

material fence
running guide for sow bed
slot for blade

Cross slide for safe use of the circular saw.

SAFETY USING A TABLE SAW

- Use a push stick when making cuts that would otherwise require fingers to be close to the blade.

- Use the saw such that fingers do not advance into the path of the blade.

- Wear eye protection. Dust thrown into your eyes will be the only distraction you need to push your fingers through the blade or release the material and cause a throwback, taking your eye.

- Do not wear excessively loose-fitting clothing, and tie back long hair.

- Do not use the fence as a guide during crosscuts. If you need to make a series of crosscuts of equal length, use a stop block so the work piece is not in contact with the rip fence during the cut. It is easy for the material to twist out of perpendicular at the end of the cut and get caught by the blade and thrown.

- Check for flaws in the wood or screws and nails. Cutting through a loose knot can be dangerous. Cutting a warped or twisted board along the fence is dangerous because it can get pinched between the fence and blade.

- A dust extractor should be fitted. If sawdust is allowed to build up under the cutting blade, the spinning blade will quickly ignite the accumulated dust through friction. The extractor also reduces the risk of a dust explosion and facilitates a healthier working environment.

- Accidents happen when you fail to be alert and pay constant attention.

blade during close cuts. Metal push sticks shouldn't be used; if they do come into contact with the blade they can act as flying projectiles that can cause extreme injury.

Crosscut slide: generally used to hold the material at a fixed 90º angle to the blade, allowing precise repeatable cuts at the most commonly used angle. The slide is normally guided by a runner fastened under it, which slides in the table mitre slot. This device is normally made in the workshop.

Laser cutter

The laser cutter has become the mainstay tool of architectural model making. This technology cuts parts out of sheet material using a high power laser. The output of the laser is directed by computer software which acts somewhat like a printer driver. Due to this technology the process of cutting multi-layered elevations, floors for architectural models as well as other flat component parts has become faster, more accurate and much more efficient. Laser engraving is the same process as laser cutting, being performed using the same equipment. The difference is that the laser beam does not go through the material, but halfway, engraving ornament or pattern according to the software input.

29

MATERIALS AND EQUIPMENT

Vacuum-former

A plastic sheet is heated to a forming temperature, stretched onto a tool, master or hard mould, and held against the mould by applying a vacuum between the mould surface and the plastic sheet. The vacuum-forming process can be used in model making to make complex hollow parts for models – especially useful if organic, multi-curving shapes need to be produced. The vacuum-former has become widely used to produce curving roofs and buildings, clear domes and canopies. The process is usually restricted to forming plastic parts that are rather shallow in depth, as deeper items become too fragile or brittle to hold their shape. Suitable materials for use in vacuum-forming are conventionally thermoplastics; vacuum-forming is also appropriate for materials such as PETG and acrylic.

Dremel

This is a brand of power tool known for its small drills, although there are many other Dremel products. The Dremel uses its speed (as opposed to torque) to get the job done. By inserting an appropriate bit, the tool can perform drilling, grinding, sharpening, cutting, cleaning, polishing, sanding, routing, carving and engraving. Battery-powered and corded models are available.

Router

A power tool used to hollow out or remove material from relatively hard material, typically wood or plastic. Some makers consider it to be the single most versatile woodworking power tool. It really can do just about anything as long as you have the right attachment or bed. The router has a far more accurate cut than a circular saw especially when used with a bed and fence. It has sufficient durability to be able to produce different shapes and mouldings; indeed, routers are often used in place of traditional moulding planes or spindle moulder machines for edge decoration (moulding) of timber. With the use of jigs and plunge capability then all sorts of irregular shapes to many depths through the material, and cutting straight through, are achievable with ease. Similar to the router is a smaller, lighter version designed specifically for trimming laminates. These are very often used in the model-making industry for smaller-scale general routing work.

Timber

Buying timber

The selection of a wood or sheet material will greatly affect the timescale and budget of your model. As the wood might be the most expensive element of your model it is important to choose carefully the type of timber and the way in which you wish to construct the model.

The selection of good quality timber is essential. First, decide on the type of material most suited for your model, depending on the model or a client's choice – a range of hard and soft woods could be used. Because there is such a range of different woods with different properties, many model makers have a palette of timbers that they use for model making. Listed below is a range of common timbers that are used by model makers. They are popular for numerous reasons, such as colour, density and straightness or size of grain.

Timber types

BALSA (OCHROMA PYRAMIDALE)
Balsa lumber is very soft and light, with a coarse, open texture. As it is low in density but high in strength, balsa is a very popular material to use when making light, stiff structures. Balsa is also a popular wood type in the art of whittling. Most professional model makers don't tend to use this wood; despite all its above benefits it isn't as useful a timber as some as the others listed.

Balsa wood.

30

MATERIALS AND EQUIPMENT

Jelutong.

American white oak.

Lime wood.

Walnut wood.

Swiss mountain pear wood.

Maple wood.

Cherry wood.

Grey tulipwood.

Red cedar wood.

Cork.

MATERIALS AND EQUIPMENT

JELUTONG (DYERA COSTULATA)
Jelutong is technically a hardwood with many similar properties to balsa wood. These properties – such as the low density, straight grain and fine texture – mean it is easy to work with and hence popular with model makers. Jelutong is off-white, sometimes pale yellow in colour, with a fine barely-visible grain. It is exceptionally stable and very easy to shape and smooth to a grain-less finish for paint and lacquer work.

LIME (TILIA)
This is a genus of about thirty species of trees native throughout most of the temperate Northern Hemisphere, generally known as lime in Britain and basswood in North America. The timber is blonde, soft, and easily worked; it has very little grain. Its ease of working meant that in the past (before chemiwood) it was typically used for offsite buildings and could be sprayed and sanded well due to its light grain.

PEAR (PYRUS COMMUNIS)
Sourced from old orchard trees and steamed during kilning to produce an even colour, pear timber is light pinkish-brown with a fine, even grain. Pear turns well and is also popular for model making. Its lustre and light grain make it popular with architects; pear models always seem to go down well in planning meetings, as the notion of a timber architectural model made of pear wood implies luxury and beauty.

CHERRY, AMERICAN (PRUNUS SEROTINA)
Cherry has a warm pink-brown colour with paler greenish bands, a distinctive grain figure and occasional dark pitch streaks. The uniform fine grain works to a smooth finish and ages to a mellow richness. Cherry is a good alternative when pear wood is a little too red; cherry has a rich, light brownness that works beautifully on bases or large-scale buildings, possibly due to its larger grain in comparison with pear wood.

CEDAR (THUJA PLICATA)
Red cedar, from the western seaboard of North America, is well known for its compelling aroma and warm red/brown colour. It is fairly soft and lightweight, with a tight, straight grain and few knots. It is valued for its distinct appearance and there is no mistaking the warm aroma of cedar wood. Arguably there is no better sight than a cedar building on a cork base; although this is considered dated and synonymous with the 1970s, the materials are stunning together and from this writer's point of view, due for a comeback.

OAK, AMERICAN WHITE (QUERCUS ALBA)
American White Oak is generally similar in appearance to European Oak – pale yellow-brown to mid-brown, mellowing with age – but it is rather heavier. It finishes well and is strong, hard-wearing and reasonably stable. The golden creaminess that is synonymous with oak has to be balanced against the fact that for model-making purposes it is very difficult to machine and the strength of its grain limits the scale of models to which it is suited. It does, however, look truly beautiful, particularly when used in conjunction with walnut.

WALNUT, AMERICAN BLACK (JUGLANS NIGRA)
American Black Walnut is a dark, purplish chocolate-brown colour and develops a deep lustrous patina with age. Despite knots, its appearance makes this wood a favourite of architects and stands out as an expensive, lustrous timber. Black walnut is highly prized for its dark colour. It is heavy and strong, yet easily machined and worked. Walnut is less dense than oak, making it easier to use for model making. It seems to work best with very small or very large-scale models.

MAPLE (ACER SACCHARINUM)
Maple is popular for its versatile blonde-white to pale yellow-brown colour, and its close, fine grain which works to an excellent finish. Maple wood is often graded according to its physical and aesthetic characteristics. Some maple wood has a highly decorative wood grain, known as flame maple, Birdseye maple, or burl wood. It is used extensively, from veneers in model making, for the covering of base boards, to cladding large offsite models. It also laser engraves beautifully and takes coloured washes well.

TULIP (LIRIODENDRON TULIPIFERA)
Also known as American Poplar or American Whitewood in the States, tulipwood is a reasonably priced utility hardwood. Its colour is variable, being generally straw-brown to light grey-green sometimes with darker patches. Tulipwood is reasonably stable, having a fine uniform grain. The colour range sets it apart as a timber great for inlays or detailed work within a model.

Sheet material

VENEER LEAVES
There is a variety of veneers available and all of the above woods are readily available as veneer. The best veneers for model making are the paper-backed leaves which have limited shrinkage and do not split or crack as easily. It is also possible to purchase the leaves in 8 × 4 inch or 2440mm × 1220mm sizes. Veneers can be glued or laminated using a contact adhesive.

CORK
This comes in a variety of thickness and is truly stunning when used for a contour stack model; it's easy to cut and glue, although in recent years it has fallen out of favour with architects (perhaps due to its retro quality, harking back to the 1970s). It is fair to say that architectural models, like architecture and all walks of design, are led by fashions, so perhaps cork will enjoy a return to popularity in years to come.

Composite boards

PLYWOOD
A manufactured wood panel made from thin sheets of wood veneer, it is one of the most widely used wood products. It is flexible, inexpensive, workable, reusable, and can usually be locally manufactured. Plywood is used instead of plain wood because of its resistance to cracking, shrinkage, splitting, and twisting/warping, and its general high degree of strength. Plywood layers (veneers) are glued together with the grain at right angles to each other. Cross-graining has several important benefits: it reduces the tendency of wood to split, it reduces expansion and shrinkage (equating to improved dimensional stability), and makes the strength of the panel consistent across both directions. There is usually an odd number of sheets so that the material is balanced – this reduces warping. Because of the way in which plywood is bonded (with grains running against one another and with an odd number of composite parts) it is very hard to bend it perpendicular to the grain direction.

FLEXIBLE PLYWOOD
This is very flexible and is designed for making curved parts.

MARINE PLYWOOD
Marine plywood is manufactured from durable face and core veneers, with few defects, so it performs longer in humid and wet conditions and resists de-laminating.

MDF
Medium-density fibreboard (MDF) is an engineered wood product formed by breaking down hardwood or softwood residuals into wood fibres, combining it with wax and a resin binder. MDF does not contain knots or rings, which makes it uniform (unlike natural woods) during the cutting process. Like natural woods, MDF can split when screwing into it without piloted holes. MDF may be glued and laminated like other woods but benefits from already having a hard flat and smooth surface. As a health and safety note, MDF when cut releases large quantities of dust particles into the air. It is important to wear a respirator, and the material to be cut must be in a controlled and ventilated area.

CHEMIWOOD/TOOLING BOARD
This is a wood-like substance heavily used in modern model making. It comes in different densities, is generally easy to sand and machine, has a good stable strength, and unlike wood it doesn't have a grain and has a uniform content throughout – which makes it great for gluing together seamlessly. It's useful for producing vacuum-form moulds, building offsite models and creating organic shapes.

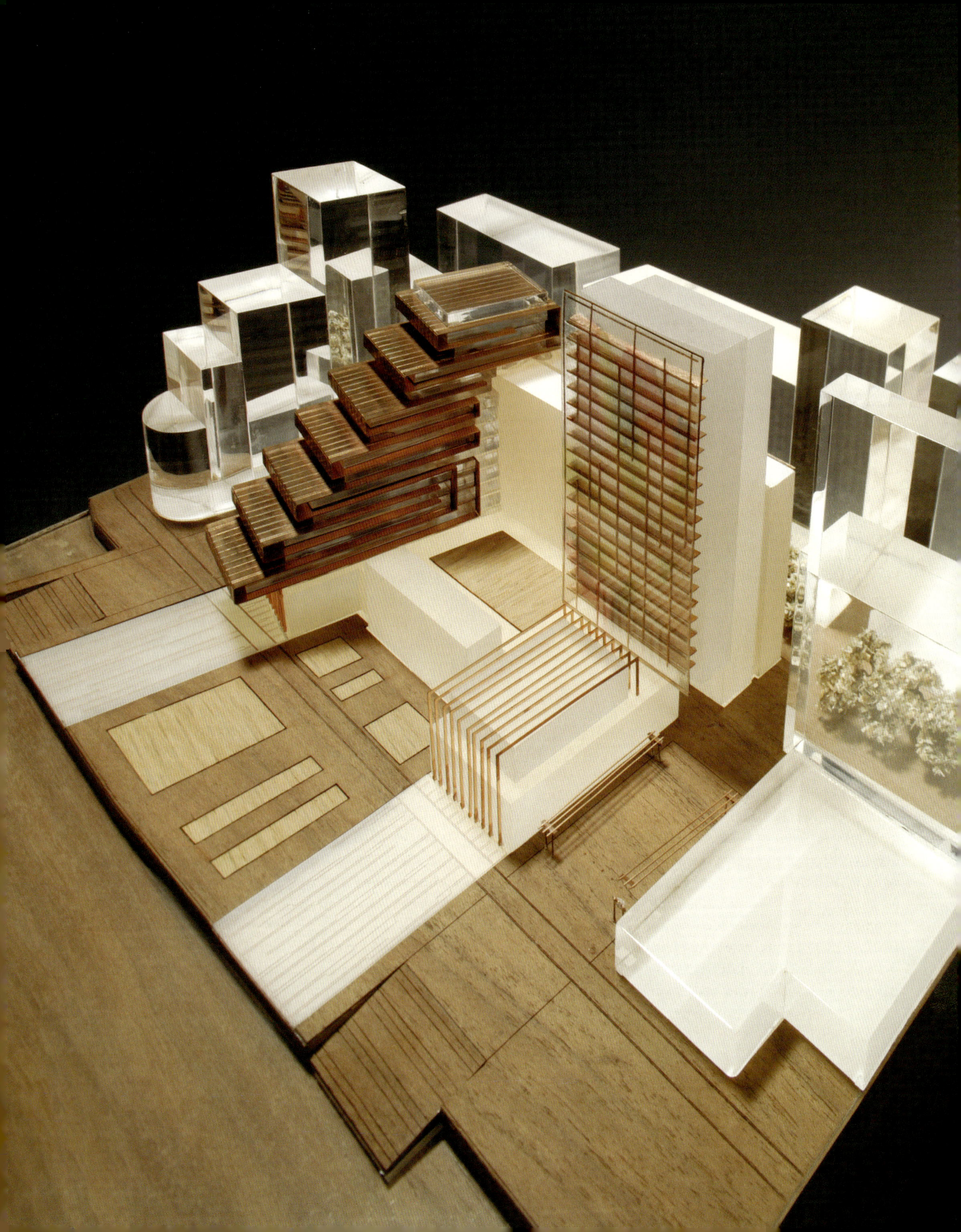

CHAPTER 2

THE PURPOSE OF A MODEL

A main source of our failure to understand is that we do not command a clear view of the use of our words.

Ludwig Wittgenstein,
Philosophical Investigations, 1953

To decide on the best way to approach making a model it is important to consider the purpose of the model. An understanding of the reasons for building will contribute to determining the scale, material and complexity of the design.

All models present a design idea to others. Depending on the element you wish to highlight, some key questions will help you to decide on the type of model required – and will also determine the timescale required for the build.

What is the model for?

This question lies at the root of all subsequent questions that need to be answered in order to create a successful model. Many models are doomed to failure because the reasoning behind building a model becomes lost. The model must be looked at with a calculated view, and it is often the model maker's role to glean what the aim of the model will be or what the underlying hypothesis (reason for the model) is. The series of questions or variables that allow you to investigate the hypothesis are the increments by which a model can be successfully achieved. Without an understanding of these, the model can become compromised, time and energy wasted and the purpose of the model unfulfilled.

A positive outcome arises when a design investigation is brought into clarity by producing the model, and when the model has fulfilled its brief of representing a design and assisted in reaching conclusions concerning design or planning. By exploring different approaches, the model can inform on what can be achieved, and the issues can be analysed at the start, before the building process begins.

The questions key to the project at any 'brief' stage are:

- What is the timescale of the model (when is the deadline)?
- What level of information is there about the model?
- What budget is available for the model?

These questions are not necessarily listed in order of importance, but they are the basis of all builds. Sometimes budget will not be a problem but the model will have an incredibly tight deadline, or there may not be a good level of information to complete the build but there will be plenty of time. (It is unlikely that all three will ever be positives.) The projects to avoid are ones with no budget, poor information and no time – the old adage 'the hours are long but the pay's bad' springs to mind; at least some of these factors should be in place before committing to a model.

If you wish to produce a model for a planning submission, the relevant questions to ask yourself at the start are related to what the final model will need to convey to a viewer. The model will need a good level of detail in order to demonstrate the positive aspects of a design. It will also need to show how

LEFT: **Conceptual model (scale 1:750) for Patel Taylor Architects. (Photo: Andrew Putler)**

35

■ THE PURPOSE OF A MODEL

the building fits into the surroundings, and it will need to be aesthetically pleasing. All of these elements will assist in getting a model passed through a planning stage.

Firstly, find out what level of information is available to build the model; secondly, how much time do you have to gain the information you need in order to complete the model?

Depending on the answers to the first two questions, you need to assess whether there is sufficient budget to staff, buy materials and complete the model. If these three questions can be satisfactorily answered then the model, if managed well, can be successfully concluded. Often you may need to adapt these questions to the specific needs of your client; for

CASE STUDY

A model was originally envisaged as highly complex and detailed 1:200 model. The scheme was for a competition to build a hospital; the client hoped that the model would describe all the building's proposed finishes, from window-frame colour to stone and brick course, etc. For the purpose of agreeing a price, the following was described:

The model will express in a realistic colour palette, sympathetic to the materiality and scale, with Perspex window apertures to reveal the basic layout of the building interior; glazing lines and colour will be present. The feature stairs, main entrance and link bridge will be modelled to detail relevant to scale and interiors will be visible. The existing buildings will be massed showing roofscape and major architectural features with 'blind reveal' detailing of windows and doors, and parapets to the immediate offsite buildings. The context will express site levels with relevant details such as car parking, paving/road layouts, hard and soft landscaping, trees and animation e.g. people, cars, trees, seating, planters etc. Surrounding ground works and buildings will be tonally coloured to reflect the realistic colours of the area, expressing grass paving patterns/colours and road usage coding.

This excerpt allows you to see the detailed nature of the work proposed. The quote was agreed and a timescale decided but this specific version of the model was never built. The architect had been too optimistic regarding the level of information that could be provided to create a detailed model within the required deadline and it quickly became necessary to re-examine the scope of the model. The main question was, 'What is the purpose and how can it still be expressed?'

What became apparent was the need for the model to express the relationship to the surrounding buildings in terms of height and mass, picking out the main feature areas and the use of colour to code them in usage, and finally to represent a dynamic, creative and future-thinking cohesion to their design. The plan became to conceptualize the vision of the building in the model and allow the support information (such as boards and visuals) to do the descriptive work. The model became a very successful vision of what the building could be and architect and client were very happy.

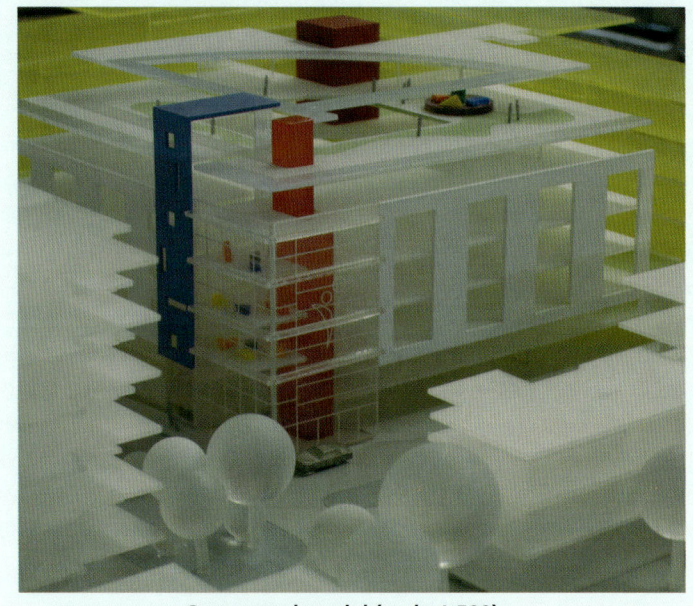

Conceptual model (scale 1:500).

36

THE PURPOSE OF A MODEL

example, your client may be keen to build a 1:50 model of the entire scheme, which would look great, but if you only have a few short weeks and the information is poor then a successful outcome is unlikely. A half-built model is no good to anyone.

Some further questions are listed below to help you decide whether to proceed with a project if the factors of information, time and budget aren't all in place.

- Use: how long should the model last? Is it to be photographed?
- Detail: what is the minimum level of detail the model requires and, once the time and budgetary constraints have been evaluated, can the minimum level of detail then be elaborated upon?
- Budget: what will the model achieve if more time and budget are allotted? Will this make more of the model, and will it increase the perceived 'value' of the model?
- Techniques: which professional construction techniques can do the job economically (as it is often said, 'the quickest way is often the best way')?

These questions are important to help to guide the decision on what type of model to build and what type of construction will assist in bringing the model to its best conclusion.

Model styles

Massing model

This kind of model can be quickly created, and is a non-literal and inexpensive way to show form in simple shapes, primarily to explore volume and how the shape fits within context. (The term 'massing model' is used because you are creating a simple mass to represent shape.) It can be easily changed, which will help to make architectural design changes and decisions regarding an exterior structure. This type of model is preliminary to consideration of the interiors; these will be incorporated at a later date.

Massing model of Tate Britain. This was developed as a puzzle for children and adults alike.

Floor stack model

A floor stack can be used for a larger-scale, more detailed model. One step further than a massing model, this is a way of showing the space that the building will live within, while getting into the detail of the spaces. It is also a good way to give a feeling of lightness to the model, which will help in the developing of the design. These models can be made to represent the floor plates of the buildings or as a floor-to-ceiling slab. From the photos it is possible to see the different effects, colours and styles that this type of model can create.

These models are useful in the early design stages and when working out the volume, usage and flows of a building; they can also be a good intermediate point between a massing model and starting to elevate. The model illustrations show

Simple floor stacking model demonstrating the potential of this style of model in its most basic form.

37

■ THE PURPOSE OF A MODEL

A range of model scenery including furniture, people, cars and trees at a range of scales.

Scale conversions: metres to millimetres

1:1 model	1 metre = 1000mm
1:10 model	1 metre = 100mm
1:20 model	1 metre = 50mm
1:50 model	1 metre = 20mm
1:75 model	1 metre = 13.3mm
1:100 model	1 metre = 10mm
1:200 model	1 metre = 5mm
1:250 model	1 metre = 4mm
1:500 model	1 metre = 2mm
1:750 model	1 metre = 1.3mm
1:1000 model	1 metre = 1mm
1:1250 model	1 metre = 0.8mm

drawings (A4, A3, A2, A1 etc.) will already have sized the drawings to view the model layout at a scale that will best suit their project.

It is important for model makers to operate with scale-related calculations freely; such calculations are sometimes tricky and may lead to mistakes. A simplistic way to scale drawings that are at actual size, or more importantly to quickly understand the sizes of specific parts of the building at model scale, is as follows:

1 metre = 1000mm
1000 divided by model scale (1:100) is 1000 divided by 100 = 10 (i.e. 10mm to every metre)

So if you wish to work out the height at model scale of a 6m building the equation has given us a simple sum to extrapolate the information required (6m × 10mm = 60mm, height of building at model scale).

This equation works for all commonly used model scales: for a 1:500 model, 1000 divided by 500 = 2 (i.e. 2mm for every metre).

This is a quick and reliable way of scaling that can give you heights, lengths and thickness of your model components. It is often a good way to start to shed information that might be irrelevant – the building's details might become too small to represent. (Remember that in many cases what you decide to leave out is as important as what you attempt to force into a model.)

Detailed study of a building, in which particular attention is paid to the articulation.

A 1:50 model would require full drawings with detail of the building's structure and finishes, including plans, elevations and sections to give the model value. Without this the model starts to look 'light'; if the aim of this model is to understand the building's workings, or to impress a client, then the core goal has already failed.

A 1:100 model will need information from plans, elevations, and sections – at this scale there is likely to be treatment of immediate context and definitely ground levels and landscaping; all of this will require the relevant information.

At 1:200 or 1:250 the model will perhaps need less conclusive plans and elevations: there is room to discard some finish-

THE PURPOSE OF A MODEL

Developed study using a variety of material finishes representing the internal spaces within a building. (Photo: Andrew Putler)

A Swiss mountain pear wood model used for a planning application. A good level of detail can be integrated into the model while still allowing the design to be shown within its context.

THE PURPOSE OF A MODEL

A conceptualized frosted and clear acrylic model for planning. The model is built on an insert base to allow it to be placed in a larger model that has its context. This allows for multiple models of the design to be built as it navigates the stringent design and planning process that goes with tall buildings.

ing detail. However, the model is likely to encompass a greater amount of the surrounding area and so the quantity of information for contextual detail and the incumbent landscape and ground levels will increase.

The scale of 1:500 is often favoured by many architects because it succeeds in balancing levels of information against timescale and budget. The model can be produced with less detailed information for the building, whilst showing large areas of context but to a less complete level of detail, often only showing major architectural detail and roofscapes.

Below this scale we start to look at 1:750 and 1:1000 models, which deal with mass and form. The level of detail in drawings may be negligible and it is at this level that a few plans can be created from sketches and through conversations with the architect.

A simplistic way to determine the level of detail to eliminate from your model is to work with the principle of distance. Imagine the level of detail and strength of material colouring that can be seen in a building if you are standing a few hundred metres away and the level of detail and colour that can be seen if viewed from a few miles away; this is often a good way to interpret levels of detail and the strength of the colour palette when considering the scale of the model.

Time versus money

The cost of producing a model can vary from job to job and place to place, but generally speaking, the bigger the model the more detailed the project will become. This inevitably evolves more time and hence greater expense.

If the project is working to a deadline then the need for extra manpower must be taken into consideration. Ultimately the model-making industry is one of deadlines and it is common for model makers to work long hours; sometimes all-night sessions are needed in order to get projects finished on time. It is very often the case that a model is a one-time snapshot of where a project stands within its development. If the model isn't ready for the important meeting then it may not be fit for purpose by the next round of meetings or the competition/planning deadline. By this time the design might well have veered off on a different tangent, making the model – although very expensive to produce – now worthless. It is often, therefore, very important to have a team to guarantee the successful completion of a project on time. As with so many manufacturing industries, especially bespoke industries like model making, the equation 'time versus money' must constantly be juggled.

The costing of materials is the other main factor to take into account. Acrylic and especially veneer can be very expensive (especially some of the more exotic timbers like Swiss pear wood). The costing for the material budget should be taken into account as well as the model finishings, such as trees, people and cars. If a model is expressing a scheme on the edge of a forest then the probable cost of trees for a model could run into the thousands; likewise a client who is particularly enamoured with the sense of people flow on a large-scale model could request thousands of people and cars on the model to best express their design. This can quickly spiral the cost of the model production out of control, making the

THE PURPOSE OF A MODEL

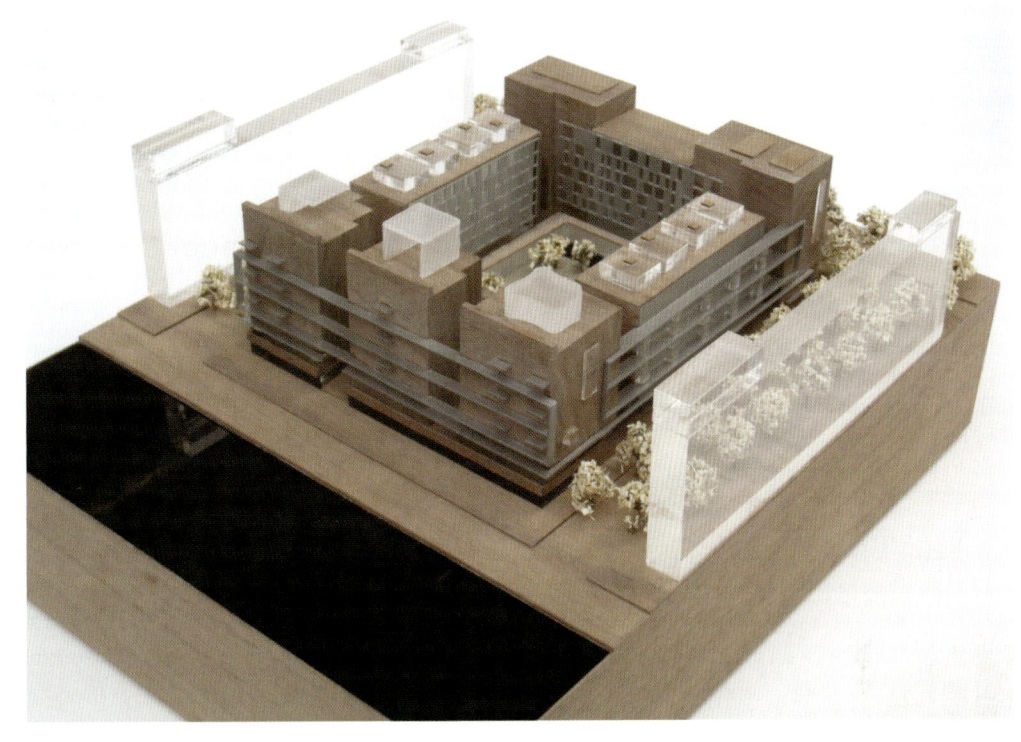

A 1:750 conceptual model from acrylic and walnut. This was an early design for one of the housing blocks for athletes in the Olympic village.

model not cost-productive.

However, the budget is not to be feared but seen as a useful tool in cutting away to the core of what is trying to be achieved. Often the most concise, focused and informative models have, because of constricting allowances, a purity in their design.

Grappling with the variables at the beginning of a model build is the most important confidence-building exercise that can be brought to the process. This then often allows the model maker to focus on the most important elements of a design, such as the feature entrance, a building's relationship with its context, or the feature atria.

Types of model: a closer look

Design development models

These may be produced in several forms: the initial models for design development can be made in block forms with very little detail – these are usually constructed in foam, cardboard

MODEL DEFINITIONS

Listed below are the five most commonly produced models:

Design development models work in a cyclical pattern throughout the stages of a building's design and construction.

Competition models are used by architects involved in a bid to win the right to fully design and construct a building.

Planning models are used to win the approval of the bureaucrats and also to sway public opinion, allowing a building to be built.

Sales models are used just before, during and after the construction period of a build, aiding the sale of the development (whether houses to the public of office space to companies).

Exhibition models retrospectively or currently advertise the quality and achievements of an architect or developer.

43

■ THE PURPOSE OF A MODEL

ARCHITECT'S PROFILE: RAFAEL VIÑOLY

Rafael Viñoly was born in Uruguay in 1944, and by the age of twenty, he was a founding partner of Estudio de Arquitectura, which would become one of the largest design studios in Latin America. His celebrated early work transformed the landscape of Argentina, where this practice was based. In 1978, Viñoly moved to the United States. After briefly serving as a guest lecturer at the Harvard University Graduate School of Design, he settled in New York in 1979. In 1983, Viñoly founded Rafael Viñoly Architects PC, a New York-based firm that has grown to encompass offices in London and Los Angeles.

> The pendulum swing between architects seeing themselves as artists or as technicians exacts a high price on the profession. Architects do architecture, which is a very complex thing in itself.
>
> *Rafael Viñoly*

ments, detailing and landscape of the site. The materials used in modern models tend to be a combination of wood veneers, clear, opalescent and spray-finished acrylic, textured materials (such as flock), and laser-cut surface detail, patterning and texture.

Sales models and exhibition models

These are the fully finished models, showing the colours, building details, landscaping, window finishes, parking spaces, car parks, street lights, and all the street furniture we expect to see in our busy environments. The main structure of these models is similar to competition and planning models, where wood veneers, acrylic, textured materials and laser-cut surface detail are used, but the model is embellished with a variety of different levels of detail. Louvres are often etched out of thin brass or laser-cut from acrylic, as are brise-soleils and 'Juliet' balconies. Further components such as stairs or mezzanine landings, handrails, some complex window surrounds, railings and many other minor details are also modelled. Planting, trees and grass effect are put into place, often with minute detail; this can be important to the design or to sell the illusion of the scheme through a sales suite. The detail can be as realistic or as elaborate as the client's budget allows.

or styrene, all of which have the benefit of being easily workable and cheap, thus allowing for the quick removal or change of the design. These types of maquette are arguably the most adventurous in the design process and may often have the most impressive story to tell, even though initial models may be crude and are tossed aside quickly in the fervour of the design process. Often tens of these maquettes can be made, helping the designer to understand, investigate and develop an idea.

Competition models and planning models

These evolve from the developmental investigations; with greater confidence in the design comes the more detailed model in laser-cut acrylic sheet and timber, showing windows, elevation details and sometimes the interior spaces (depending on the type and scale of development). The construction of these models can also show the roads, pave-

An interview with Phil Wykes

MODEL MAKER'S PROFILE: PHIL WYKES

Can you tell me about the circumstance/perceptions of what the architects wanted from the model shop at Rafael Viñoly Architects (RVA)?

The main brief was, through making their own models, to achieve a highly professional outcome by increasing the work rate and improving the finish of the models. We started the workshop space with just a table in a divided space adjacent to the architects; this was something that, however far we developed the workshop, I tried to keep integral. The model shop needed to be integrated with the architects; there weren't any closed doors; it was all about an infrastructure where the architects could build their own models or have a design input into the models that I, or (as time went on) my team was building. The office environment changed slowly through our influence. Bringing in model-making techniques from my own training was the first major leap in quality but it became about really immersing the office as a whole in this approach. This is what started to really improve the quality of the models and also, hopefully, the quality of the design work, not only assisting to think through ideas but also to communicate an idea to clients.

Much of this integral use of the model was down to Raphael: he saw the use of the model as a highly functional tool, and I think he enjoyed pulling apart a model during a presentation. He was happy to view a sketch model as a presentation model and it was all about communication of design; the model was something that could be changed easily – it was purely a tool. By using coloured paper instead of sprayed material he could use the model and then rip off the coloured paper in favour of a different finish. With a sketch model for Rafael the design of models changed so they could be split apart and easily altered. It was the spirit of the 'sketchbook' allowing for design models. Traditional model makers are used to making things that don't change; models at RVA were built to accommodate the things that were likely to alter and develop. The understanding of the likelihood of change and factoring this in comes through working closely with people in an in-house environment where we were creating models with no fixed, permanent elements.

We integrated laser-cutter technology into the model shop, and this was the last major step towards increasing speed and quality of model production. Having a cut file on computer allowed us to design models that could quickly have new and developed options, replacing superseded designs efficiently and with the accurate knowledge that the new option would

After gaining a BA (Hons) in Model-making at the Kent Institute of Art, Phil Wykes worked as a freelance model maker around London and the British Isles, before joining Rafael Viñoly Architects PC, to create their first in-house model shop in the London office. Phil was with Rafael Viñoly architects from 2005 to 2010 and his résumé includes models of the Battersea Power Station development, 20 Fenchurch Street ('the Walkie Talkie' skyscraper) and major international projects in the Middle East. Regularly liaising with model makers and architects in their New York offices, the communication of the model has become key to the way Phil works. Since leaving Rafael Viñoly architects he has worked for some of the most exclusive architects and established model makers in London. Most recently he has been establishing new and exciting programmes of work and infrastructure for the model-making capabilities of Stanton Williams Architects, recently shortlisted as British Architect of the Year and a company dedicated to the idea of craft within its work. With over ten years of experience Phil has excelled at running teams and overseeing the production of complex models for some of the most prestigious architectural projects happening around the world today.

fit within what was already there, for example the rest of the scheme or base board.

Can you define your role and job title?

My job title at Rafael's was Senior Model Maker Manager and my role specifically was to be responsible for the production of models within the office, advising and overseeing self-led models produced by the architects themselves. I was the main contact for liaising with the New York office and oversaw the production of more traditional models by outside model-making companies.

THE PURPOSE OF A MODEL

What are the most important areas where you see sketch modelling differing from the more traditional forms of model making?
Changeability and value in a design, to be able to take apart and integrate all aspects of the design process within the production of the model. If your model is a success you'll start to see the architects coming to look at the progression of the model and they will develop the design in tandem. When this works well it's an incredibly satisfying process; the model becomes the reference point for the whole design. Producing a beautifully crafted model isn't complementary to the design process; the model should be used as a tool; that's the achievement, rather than the end goal being a beautiful model of a building. The ability to change the model with the speed of the design progression is paramount, so the process of making the model is the aim from the design point of view, as opposed to a finished article.

What is your essential sketch model tool kit and what materials do you use?
Scalpel, steel rule, calculator, square, glues (UHU, emulsion, PVA, dichloromethane), office photocopier/printing facilities, masking tape, double-sided tape, Styrofoam/hot wire cutter, highlighter pens and coloured markers, sprays, mounts for plans, 0.8 acrylic sheet, cardboard/coloured paper, foam board, styrene micro strip, tracing paper.

What level of information do you expect from an architect when approaching a sketch model?
The emphasis is on the development of the design; you can make a sketch model from any level of information. It's the purpose of the sketch model that is important. Those factors don't change throughout the build. The story that the model is attempting to tell is always the key; sometimes drawings are less important but the flavour of the design is what is essential for the model to progress. The base and context for example could demand a reasonable level of detailed information to get a datum and relevant existing building heights correct – although just part of the model it can be a jumping-off point for the design process for a scheme. Initial scheme massing, with something as crude as a ground-floor plan and a few sketches, can form a basic start to some elaborate scheme models. All the time, the development is integrated in the design process. That's the important part.

What information do you tend to receive to produce the model?
What the architect wants from the model dictates the information that you receive. The aim of the model needs to be understood before the information exchange; this focuses the architect on exactly what you require, and saves time sifting through drawings that will have no relevance to the aims of the model. Ultimately though, some typical floor plates, some key ground levels and generic elevation condition can get most things done.

What are the ranges and uses of sketch models?
Sketch models are just that: we put together the design drawings and plans to envisage the three-dimensional view of the building. These models are client-led depending on what the client wishes to see. This can be an investigation into anything that is apt for exploration, whether the model is looking at massing, the building envelope and surface treatments, rights of light with its context, footage allocation for an office, interior layouts and services, circulation or landscaping. This can be at larger scales (1:20/1:50) or the view of a master plan of a city at a small scale (1:1250/1:5000). We can build just about anything depending on the time frame and level of information received. As a general rule, the bigger the scale, the more time and information required.

What are the common issues that you feel the architects come to the process with – what are they looking for from you?
Communication! Lack of communication leads to all sorts of problems, from basic lack of understanding of the design on our part; in many cases the architect may have been working on this project for weeks or even months before we look at it, and there is often a presumption that we know the project instantly as intimately as them. This can cause problems with the perception of the project within the time frame for a model and the desired outcome which obviously will alter the approach. An architect taking for granted that you have the same perception of the job as them, not understanding what's in their mind's eye, can lead to disappointment, abortive work and unsuccessful models. They want the confidence from you that they will have their design treated sympathetically and be represented in the best possible way to tell its story. Understanding this from them in the first place can decide whether you really fulfil the brief.

Did you develop a palette, and if so, why?
A palette is material-led – for me it is all about materiality: this gives you the best ability to understand the properties and finishes that a certain material can give you, how much time is involved in the working of a material, and how easy it is to change. This was particularly relevant when working at RVA, when understanding that you may need to match a particular material. Coloured papers, if coming regularly from a supplier, are easier to match over a period of months as the design progresses. If timber veneers are from different leaves they can start to prove very difficult to match together; when ripping off an elevation because the window layout has changed but the elevation on the next facade isn't changing, or patching in a new pavement layout onto a model that then doesn't match the existing pavements. So I suppose that the palette I use developed on the back of expense: there is no point using expensive timbers if you're likely to rip the same elevation off and replace it three times in a week.

Colour matching, using a range of specific colour cards and papers allows me to envelop changes and therefore not be concerned by having to think about matching. It all comes back to the changeability of the design; it has to be interchangeable so developing a core of colours and materials that you use allows a confidence when making the inevitable alterations.

How do you give an architect direction for the model?
This would only happen if nothing was being achieved – it is largely about investigating the design for them. The idea of sketch modelling is experiencing a functionary role to the model build – the chance to encounter design issues and processes as they build themselves. If you have trouble making a model shape then you may have trouble building the building and this needs to be investigated through the sketch model. It allows architects to experience the design in three-dimensional terms. Sometimes not achieving a positive outcome to a sketch model is the important thing: knowing something doesn't work allows one to focus on other, more viable options, through exploration. Coming to this conclusion is still a successful study. Experienced architects understand the use of someone who chooses to show sketches as opposed to someone who doesn't.

Looking at your career specific to sketch modelling, how has the job changed?
Ultimately the idea of a sketch is still the same; it has become more of an integrated medium through the availability of new technologies. Laser cutters have to some degree merged sketch modelling and presentation models, through improved quality and the ability to use a wider range of materials that wouldn't have been possible to process before without a fully operating workshop with saws and sanders, etc. This though isn't the most important change – laser cutters have brought about the most significant change but not for the above reasons – most importantly they have enabled us to plan models in more modular ways, which allows you to reproduce components and make changes to a model as plans change.

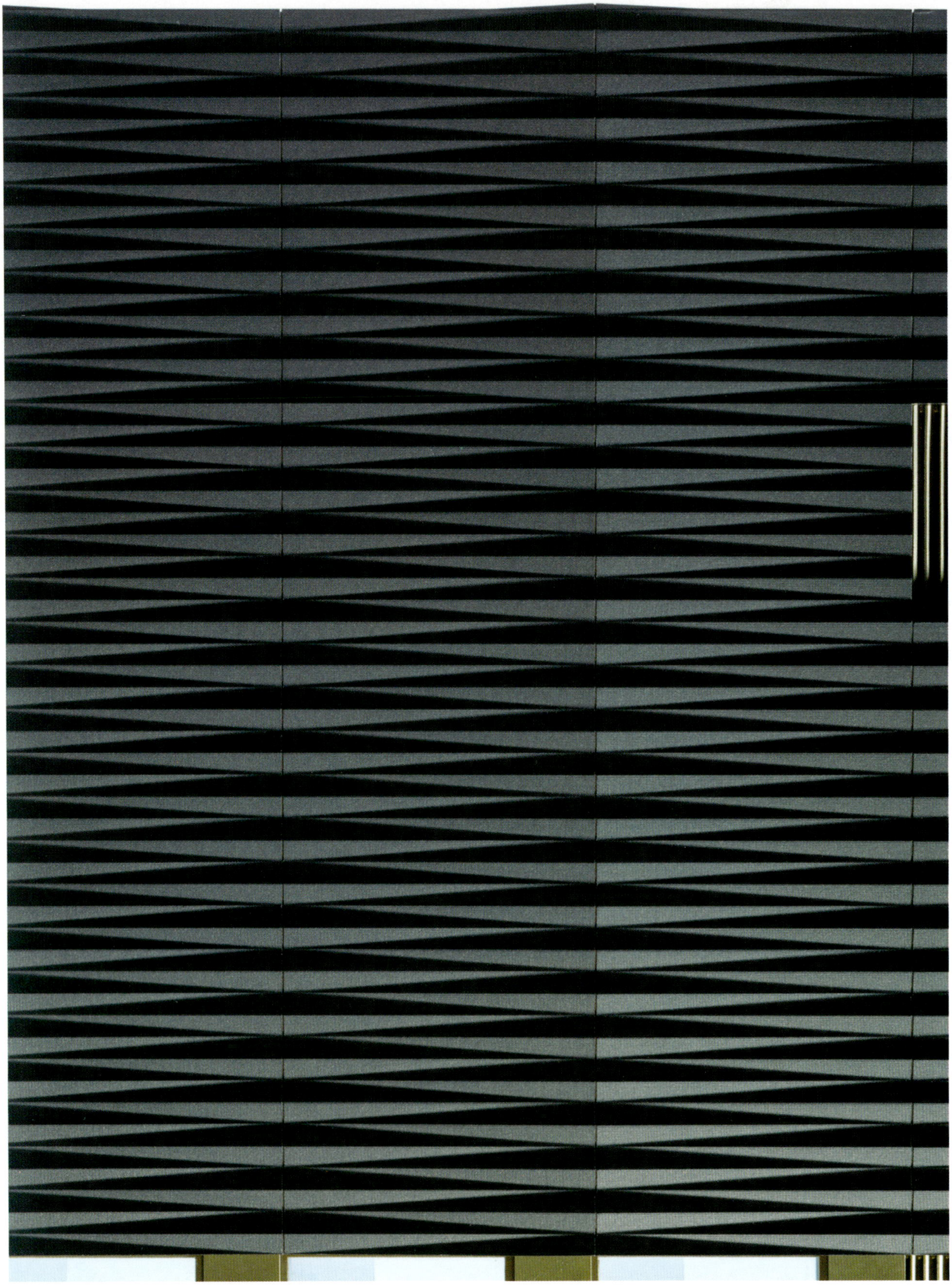

CHAPTER 3

A FIRST EXERCISE IN ARCHITECTURAL MODEL MAKING

This first exercise gives a basic understanding of the practices that underpin architectural model making. Through practical methods you will identify and explore the process of producing simple shapes. You will be able to identify the core parts of a scheme and these simple building blocks will allow you to explore the basic skills of making, evaluate materiality, and make conclusions regarding time and budget. From this first basic exercise the questions of scale, purpose, and level of detail and abstraction are first recognized; then through practical workshop techniques you will aim to produce other projects.

This exercise, followed by the other exercises in the book, will allow you to develop the core content of practical techniques, which will give you a solid grounding in many aspects of model construction, covering a wide range of materials and processes. Where applicable, laser cutting and CAD drawing will be outlined, affording you the guidance needed to achieve the desired result. These exercises are generally office- or home-based but will for the more adept have workshop elements; the aim is to give you the confidence to design, construct and finish your own scale models to a level good enough to approach virtually all of your model possibilities.

An understanding of how to create basic shapes will give you experience for making virtually all architectural models. If you can make a cube, a four-sided pyramid and a cylinder then you already have the required basic ability to create a house with a pitched roof and a chimney. This may seem simplistic, but getting to grips with the production techniques for these will give you the best grounding for building your own more complex projects later on.

Basic elements

For this exercise the aim will be the production of a square, a circle and a triangle. Good use of your equipment and materials will ultimately be the essence of any build – making these shapes adeptly out of cardboard will teach you an understanding of your model-making equipment (scalpel, square, steel rule, material card, veneer). Creating these shapes in a range of materials (paper, foam board, veneer and Perspex) will define levels of difficulty.

After this has been mastered, creating these shapes in three-dimensional form – making a cube, making a cylinder, making a pyramid – will be covered, again in a range of materials: card, foam, solid timber. The project also introduces how to finish a model: straight lines, sanding, measuring and so on.

Materials

This project could be undertaken using a range of materials – thin or thick card, timber, MDF board or Perspex – but to replicate this exercise, 2mm-thick cardboard and maple veneer are the materials used.

Equipment

Pencil
Circle cutter
Cutting mat

LEFT: **CNC machine elevation finished in pearlescent paint.**

■ A FIRST EXERCISE IN ARCHITECTURAL MODEL MAKING

Steel rule
Steel square, 3 inch and 6 inch
Scalpel
Glue – this is dependent on materials being used; consult the section on glues on page 26.
123 block

Note: timber blocks (cube, pyramid, cylinder) can be produced, but if you wish to advance to this level then experience of woodworking machinery will be needed beyond what is available in this book. An evening course in model making or woodworking will supply you with the necessary experience with which to work wood safely.

Before starting this exercise, check that you have enough material for the sizes of shape that you wish to make. It's always preferable to have more than you need rather than be left needing to buy more. If you're using veneers of timbers this could become particularly problematic because getting different leaves of veneer to match can be virtually impossible. (Part of the beauty of wood is that no two pieces are the same so grain and colour will vary between leaves of veneer from different trees.) If you don't have enough your model can look ill-conceived or scrappy; remember that part of the art of the model is in creating a considered item that has been thoroughly thought through.

It is worth creating a cutting list of material to work out the amount of material needed; this can be drawn out to dimension on paper, or (more easily) as a sketch with dimensions written on.

Having printouts at size of components, if you have designed your kit components, is a good habit to get into. Although with these initial projects the components are simple, later more complicated kits of parts can be very confusing if you don't have a drawn-out plan. The CAD drawing shows you the dimensions worked out for this project.

Square: Figure 1.

Square: Figure 2.

2D shapes: square, triangle, circle

Square

1. Take your sheet material (hereafter this will be referred to as card for these exercises) and check that at least one corner is square from two sides. This can be achieved using your 6-inch square and a ruler as a guide; if it is not square then, using your ruler and square, scalpel the one side to create a 90° corner. The 90° corner is the side of the card that you will now work from.
2. Using a propelling pencil, measure out from the one side horizontally with your steel rule the dimension of one side of your square (in this case, as the above CAD drawing represents, 100mm).
3. Make a small mark at 100mm.

A FIRST EXERCISE IN ARCHITECTURAL MODEL MAKING

Square: Figure 3.

Square: Figure 4.

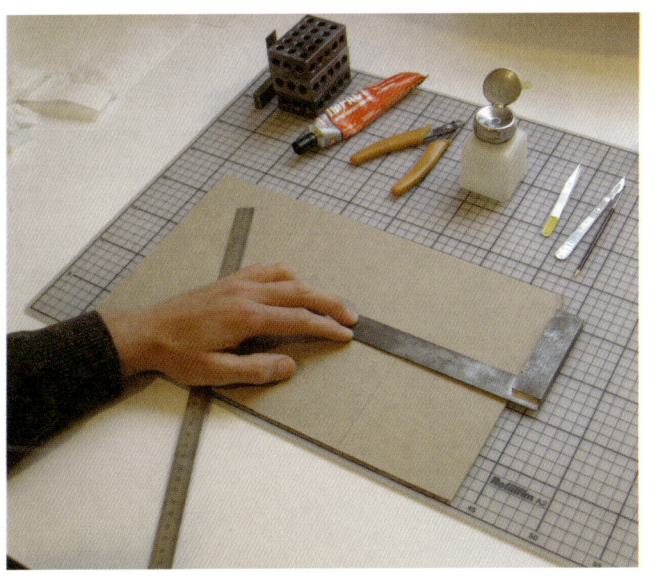

Square: Figure 5.

Square: Figure 6.

4. Repeat this process vertically, making another mark.
5. Using your 6-inch square, draw a line that corresponds with the mark made on your horizontal.
6. Repeat this with the vertical mark and draw a line. You should now have a perfect square drawn onto your card that is 100mm by 100mm. (Note: it is worth at this point checking your measurements again. It's a cliché but the adage 'measure twice, cut once' is always true and a costly lesson to ignore.)

7. Place the square onto the bottom of the card and the upright of the square to the vertical line that you have drawn. Applying controlled pressure, cut from the intersection point of the two lines out to the edge of the card. You may need to make several cuts to get through, depending on the thickness of the material. (Over time you will learn to make this cut probably in one or two motions as your strength and control increase.)
8. Turn your card clockwise by 180° so you have easy and

51

■ A FIRST EXERCISE IN ARCHITECTURAL MODEL MAKING

Square: Figure 7.

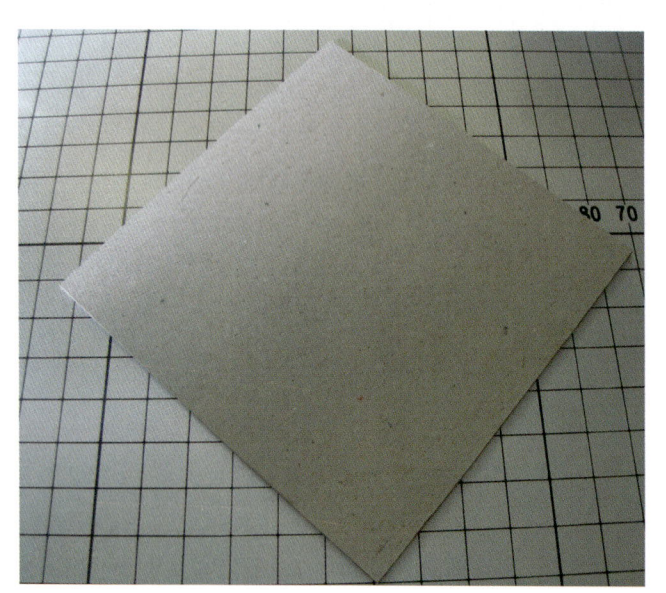

Square: Figure 8.

Square: Figure 9.

safe access to make the next cut.
9. You now should have one square of card.

This exercise is worth practising a few times to get used to making precision measurements and cuts, and handling a scalpel. Getting a feel for the weight and strength that you need to put behind a scalpel can mean the difference between avoiding lots of cuts, broken scalpel blades and, most importantly, shaggy cuts to your material. The weight, cutting angle and control of your scalpel will make a big difference to the quality of your work.

Triangle

1. Following the same approach as the square from the first exercise draw out a square with the long dimensions of the triangle that you want to make (in this case 100mm is the dimension to use again). Along the top side of the square measure 50mm (half way) and make a small mark with your pencil.
2. Place your steel rule diagonally from the bottom right corner of the square up to the 50mm mark as drawn on the top side of the square. Draw a line joining the two points.
3. Repeat this process diagonally from the bottom left-hand corner of the square up to the 50mm mark. Draw a line joining the two points. You should now have a triangle drawn to your dimensions.
4. Taking your scalpel and steel rule, using the techniques you developed from the previous exercise cut along the drawn line to produce your triangle.

52

A FIRST EXERCISE IN ARCHITECTURAL MODEL MAKING

Triangle: Figure 1.

Triangle: Figure 2.

Triangle: Figure 3.

Triangle: Figure 4.

53

■ A FIRST EXERCISE IN ARCHITECTURAL MODEL MAKING

Circle

Circles can be produced with the use of a circle cutter. These can be bought from most craft shops and work in the same way as a compass, but instead of a pencil lead on the outer arm there is a scalpel blade. This should allow you to create almost any sized circle.

If you do not have a circle cutter then a rudimentary compass can be created using a pin, a piece of string and a pencil. The circle can then be cut with a scalpel following the pencil line; this is an effective and simple solution – but not usually as accurate as a circle cutter or a laser cutter!

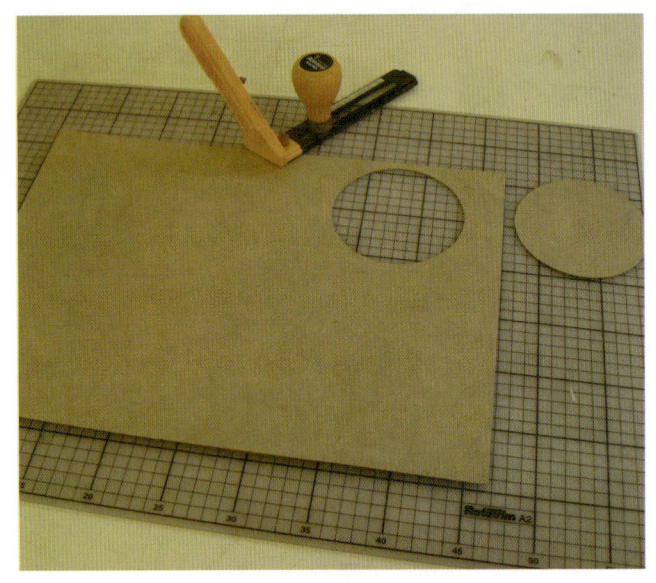

Circle: Figure 1.

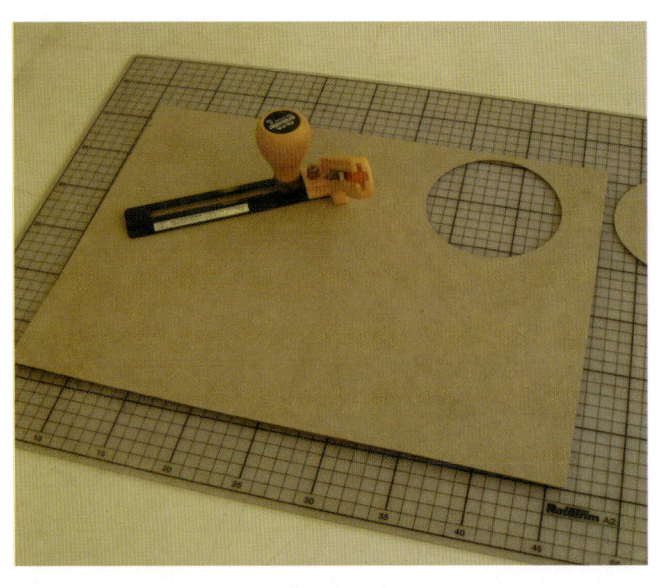

Circle: Figure 2.

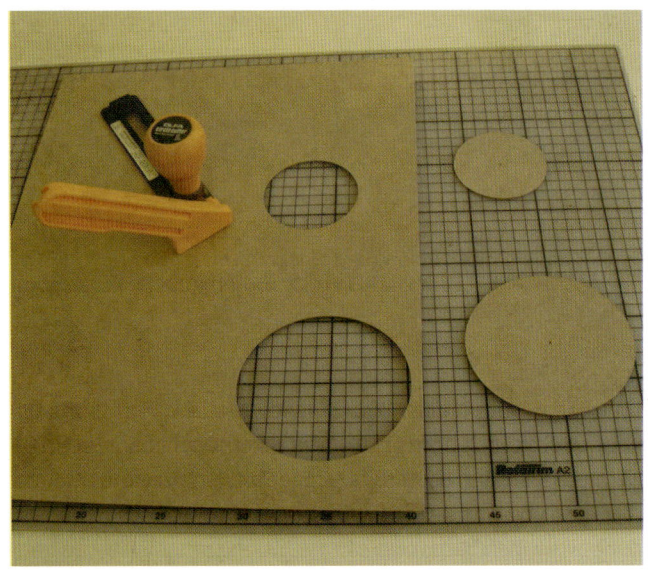

Circle: Figure 3.

3D shapes: cube, pyramid, cylinder

Now that you know how to create these basic two-dimensional shapes this process can be repeated to create the building blocks of the next exercise. Once again it is a good idea to make a cutting list for the components; this is especially important as material thickness will have to be taken into account in the assembly of parts.

Cube

1. You should now be able to arrange a series of squares ready for assembly (as has been stated, it is important not to get confused by the different sizes of components which have been offset for material thickness). *Note*: sometimes it is worthwhile having a dry-run assemble which can be held together with tape, which is a useful way to double check offsets. Although only a cube in this

54

A FIRST EXERCISE IN ARCHITECTURAL MODEL MAKING

exercise, if it was a series of complicated elevations that have taken time to draw, cut and assemble, then the wrong offset can cost a lot of valuable time and materials or seriously compromise the overall finish of your model. As a model maker you work in millimetres and tolerances of fractions of a millimetre; this can make the difference to the neatness and accuracy of the eventual model.

2. Using a 123 block (square block) set up for your first gluing scenario. Check you have all your component pieces in the correct places and the 123 block tight up against the base square. For more delicate or flimsy elevations it may be worth using double-sided tape to hold down the 123 blocks to restrict movement during the gluing process.
3. Apply the glue to the surface to be bonded.
4. Hold together in place then using a small metal square check that the first side is at a 90º angle to the base plate. Keeping the sides square is essential as all four sides go on.
5. Once the glue is dry, repeat this process for the next side, applying glue to the two sides to be glued.
6. Again use a small square to check the accuracy of your work.
7. This process should be repeated for the third and fourth sides. All the time check for the straightness of your work.
8. If the original layout of the components and offsetting of material has been done correctly the four sides should all have gone together on the base plate.
9. Apply glue around the four sides of the cube and carefully place the final square on the top. This should complete the cube. This is a good point at which to check for accuracy.
10. You should now have a perfect cube that measures 100mm on all surfaces. This process is as complicated when including offsets as the basics of any elevated building; with a little practice a five-, six- or multi-sided shape of building can be constructed. If the box shown in the sequence of photographs had been built in Perspex then this could be the glazing line of a building with the addition of elevations – then a sophisticated architectural model is created.

Cube: Figure 1.

Cube: Figure 2.

A FIRST EXERCISE IN ARCHITECTURAL MODEL MAKING

Cube: Figure 3.

Cube: Figure 4.

Cube: Figure 5.

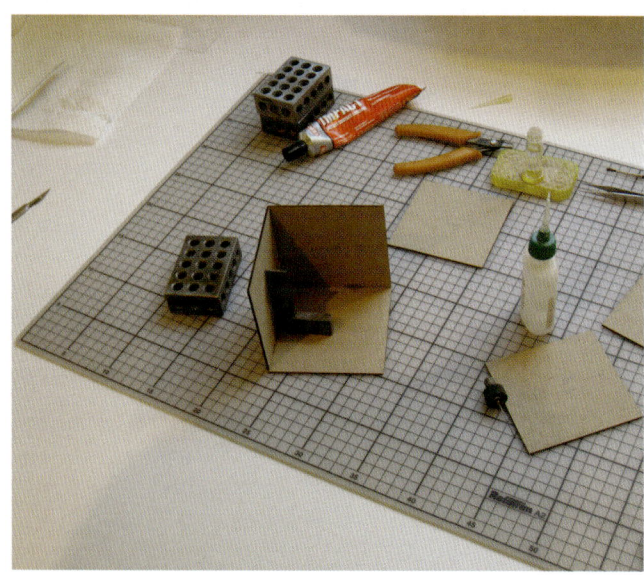

Cube: Figure 6.

A FIRST EXERCISE IN ARCHITECTURAL MODEL MAKING

Cube: Figure 7.

Cube: Figure 8.

Cube: Figure 9.

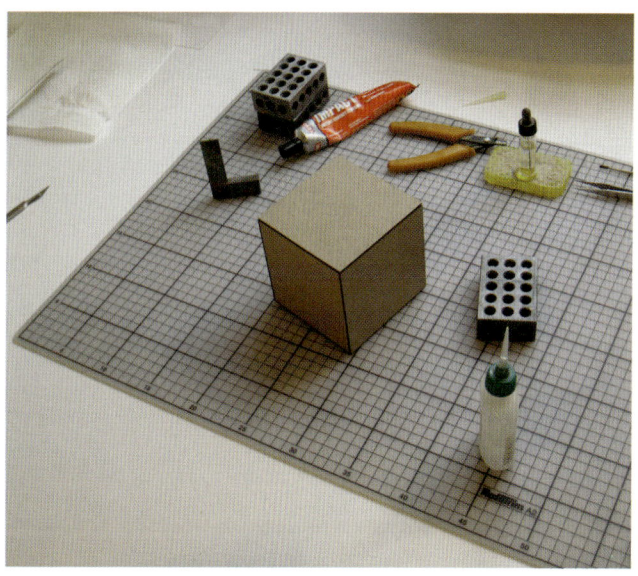

Cube: Figure 10.

57

■ A FIRST EXERCISE IN ARCHITECTURAL MODEL MAKING

Pyramid

1. As with previous exercises start by arranging your components.
2. Offer the two smaller offset sides up against each other across the base plate.
3. Apply glue to the bottom of one side and hold in approximately the correct place while the glue sets.
4. Apply glue to the bottom of the other side and hold into position until set. A spot of glue can be used to tack these components into place at the apex of the pyramid.
5. More glue can be applied to the inside of the joints to strengthen the bond.
6. Glue should now be administered to the open sides ready for the overlapping sides.

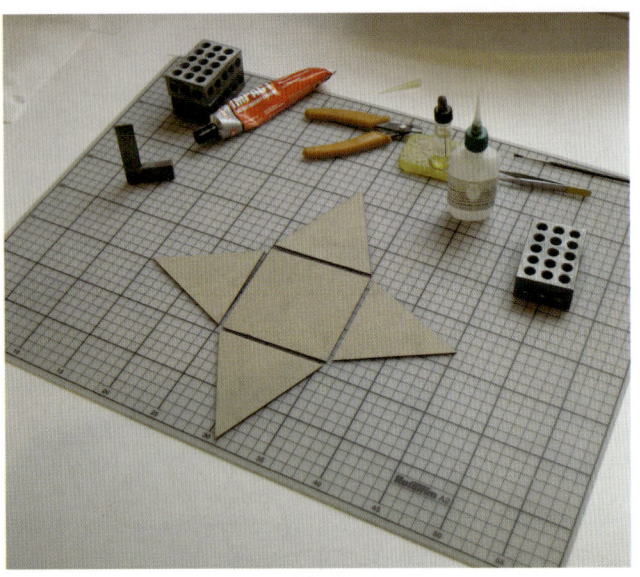

Pyramid: Figure 1.

Pyramid: Figure 2.

Pyramid: Figure 3.

Pyramid: Figure 4.

A FIRST EXERCISE IN ARCHITECTURAL MODEL MAKING

7. Carefully fit the third overlap side, lining the glue edges through and adjusting the leaning sides that are already tacked into place (this is potentially a good point at which to offer up the fourth side as well, to check that your overlaps have worked out).
8. Dribble glue inside the three sides of the pyramid to strengthen existing bonds, then glue the last edges and mount the last side. The finishing side attached completes the pyramid. As with all models, the finished article should be looked over for possible errors, even if for no other reason than to look for minor discrepancies; these lessons will enable you to improve your next build.

This is the basic principle behind the production of most

Pyramid: Figure 5.

Pyramid: Figure 6.

Pyramid: Figure 7.

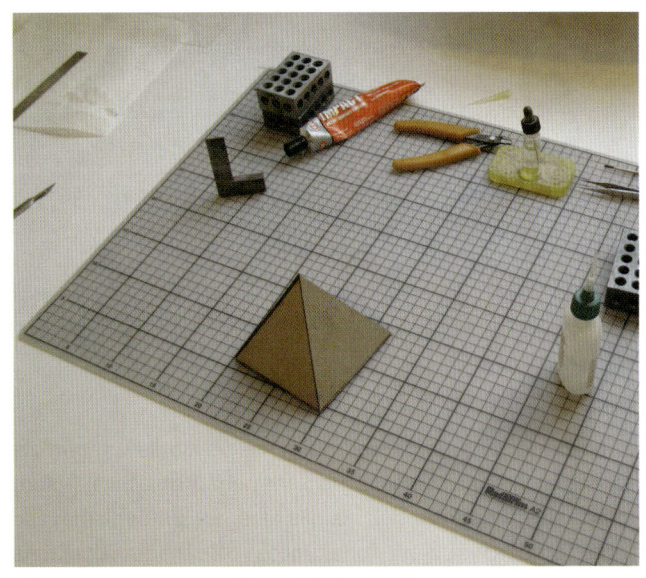

Pyramid: Figure 8.

59

A FIRST EXERCISE IN ARCHITECTURAL MODEL MAKING

pitched roofs. More complicated roof structures can be undertaken by either using ribs that act to support the cladding above (much as a real roof is constructed, using rafters and beams) or a blocked-out mass that can be constructed in timber or chemiwood to create the underlying shape. This allows for a stable structure from which to clad your finished top surface and can often be the best way of arriving at a neat, accurate finish, but will often require access to a machine shop. The rib system is often the best way, especially if you have access to a laser cutter (although this is not essential).

Cylinder

For the production of a cylinder the choice of materials is essential to the success of the exercise. If using cardboard the circles created in the initial exercises will act as a top and bottom. These should be made of a thicker material that is stiff, to act as a gluing surface. (Consult the CAD cutting list for the components needed.) The wrap material that creates the side cylindrical surface should be made of a much thinner material. For the purposes of this exercise I have used a veneer.

1. As should always be done when taking a new sheet of material, check that two sides for one corner are at a 90° angle. Always try to ensure squareness of the material that you will be working from; this will avoid a lot of

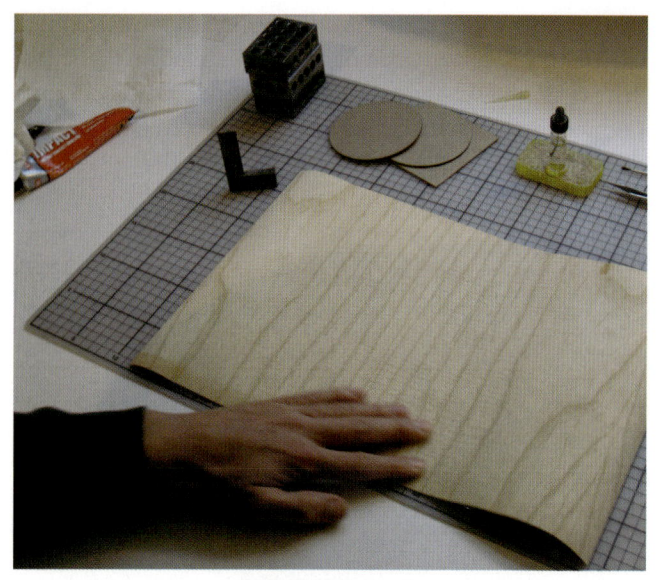

Cylinder: Figure 1.

Cylinder: Figure 2.

> **VENEERS: GOING AGAINST THE GRAIN**
>
> When using veneers the direction of the grain must be taken into account: trying to bend a veneer against the grain around a tight circumference will probably crack or tear the wood. The bending of veneer against the grain can be achieved, however – very few things are impossible – but do not underestimate the amount of work that has to be put in. If you have to wrap veneer against the grain then soaking in water and massaging the veneer around the bend will eventually get you the desired finish. This is a time-honoured method that woodworkers have been using for centuries.

mistakes and complications later on, allowing you to trust your materials.

2. If not a clear 90° angle, use a metal 6-inch square and steel rule to mark and measure for squareness.
3. Using one side as a master, use your rule and 'square up' the vertical side, drawing a line from top to bottom.
4. Using your 6-inch square, cut the vertical line; this should now give you a 90°-angled edge to work from.

A FIRST EXERCISE IN ARCHITECTURAL MODEL MAKING

Cylinder: Figure 3.

Cylinder: Figure 4.

SCALPEL BLADES

Bear in mind that scalpel blades are far cheaper than veneer, so it is worth changing the scalpel blade a number of times during these exercises. Although the blade may appear to be still sharp (it can easily cut your finger), it will become blunt; replacing the blade will make a real difference to the ease at which you make cuts and improve the quality of your finish.

6. Wrap the newly-cut length of veneer around one of the circles; approximately mark the circumference of the circle (it is worth marking this a good 20mm over the required amount).
7. Taking your 6-inch square, place it tight to the long side against the veneer and over the mark with the upright of the square.
8. Using a scalpel, cut down the line, applying enough pressure to cut through the veneer, preferably in one cut, but initially two cuts will be fine.
9. Arrange your components on the cutting mat: two circles 100mm in diameter and a spine rectangle that is 100mm length by 96mm high. (This has been offset to take into account the height of your cylinder: the circles that form the top and base of the cylinder are made from 2mm thick card, so when both these thicknesses have been subtracted from the overall 100mm desired height we are left with 96mm.)
10. Making sure that the 96mm side is the vertical length, offer up the spine rectangle across the diameter of the 100mm circle of card.
11. Making sure the surface is clear and clean, glue along the bottom of the 100mm side of the rectangle.
12. Using a metal square to guarantee a 90° angle, glue the rectangle to the base circle of card. It is essential that the rectangle sits with its sides flush to the diameter of the circle and is at a 90° angle from the base circle.
13. Once the glue has set, holding the rectangle, apply glue to the opposite side of the rectangle.
14. Again, using the square to ensure a 90° angle, the rectangle can be glued accurately to the circle ensuring that it sits within the diameter of the circle. This is

5. Ensuring that you are using the 90° squared side, measure down the veneer, ensuring the grain is vertical so that you can perform the wrap. Mark at the 100mm measurement on your ruler (the 0mm mark should be at the top edge of your veneer). Repeat this mark at a few points along the sheet from your square side. Using the marks as a guide, lay the ruler over them, and using your scalpel, cut horizontally across the grain.

61

■ A FIRST EXERCISE IN ARCHITECTURAL MODEL MAKING

Cylinder: Figure 5.

Cylinder: Figure 6.

Cylinder: Figure 7.

Cylinder: Figure 8.

62

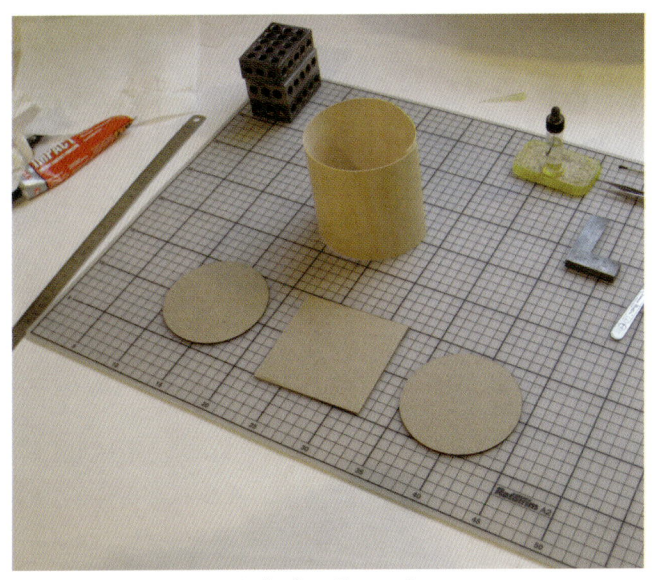

A FIRST EXERCISE IN ARCHITECTURAL MODEL MAKING

Cylinder: Figure 9.

Cylinder: Figure 10.

Cylinder: Figure 11.

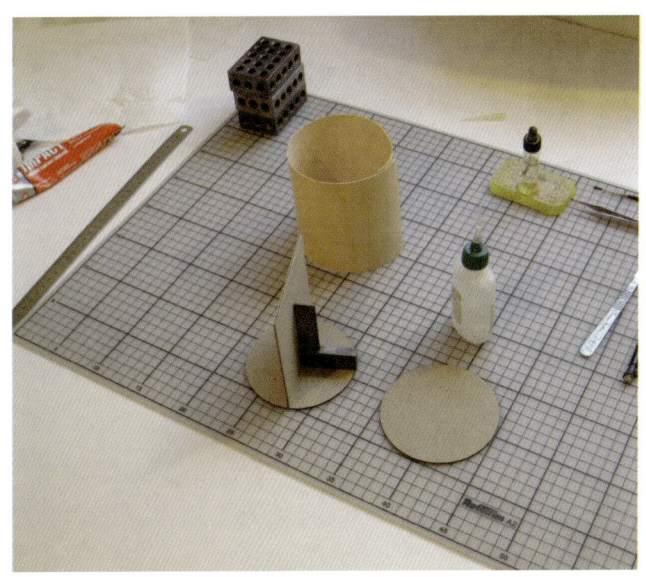

Cylinder: Figure 12.

63

■ A FIRST EXERCISE IN ARCHITECTURAL MODEL MAKING

Cylinder: Figure 13.

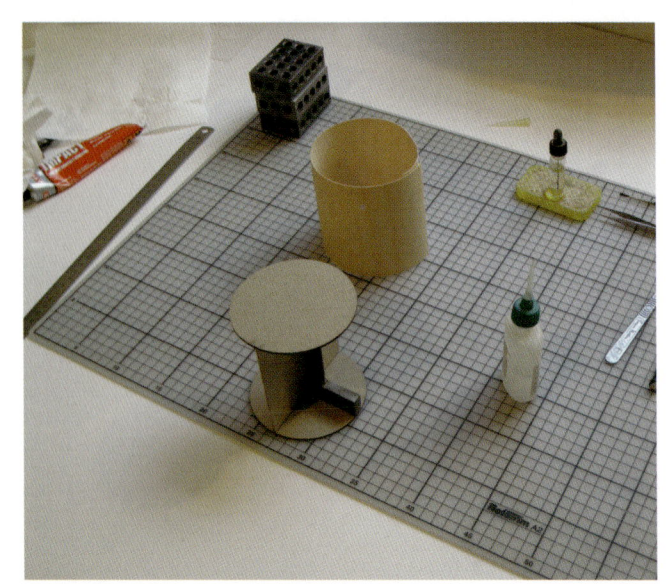

Cylinder: Figure 14.

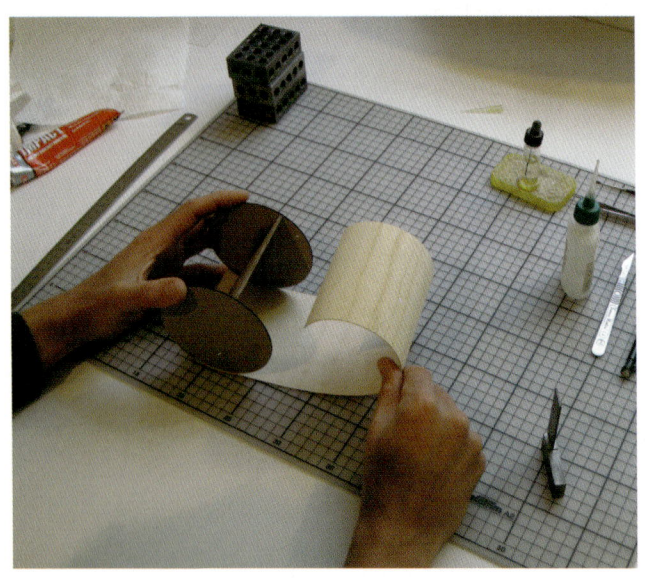

Cylinder: Figure 15.

Cylinder: Figure 16.

essential so that when wrapping the cylinder it fits. The entire circle edge should be in contact with the veneer.
15. Check that the veneer is the correct length to circle the frame that you have constructed.
16. Use a square to make a pencil mark at the corresponding points on each circle (this will ensure that as the veneer is wrapped around both circumferences there is no twisting). Tack with glue to wrap the frame at the same points of the circles, top and bottom.

17. Applying small amounts of glue to the edges of the circles, roll the veneer carefully around the frame.
18. If this is done correctly you should finish perfectly where you started, thus completing the cylinder.

The finished cylinder, depending on size, could be used in a rotunda; smaller cylinders could be used for chimneys; a semi-circular cylinder could be used for bay windows, to be attached to a building, or as an extension or conservatory.

A FIRST EXERCISE IN ARCHITECTURAL MODEL MAKING

Cylinder: Figure 17.

Cylinder: Figure 18.

Cylinder: Figure 19.

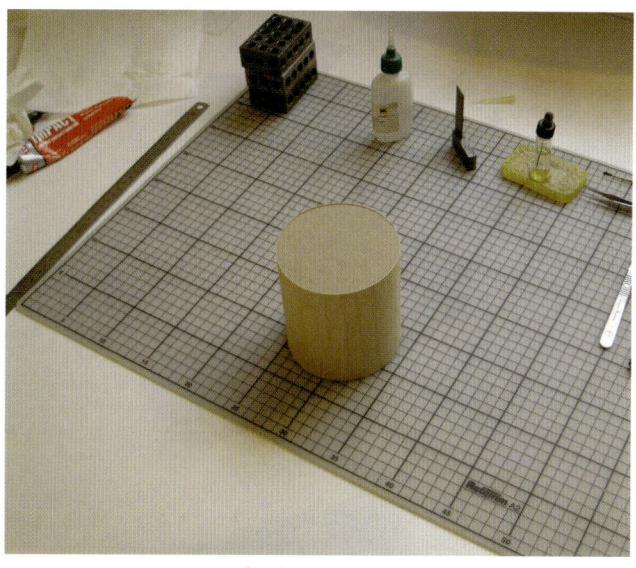

Cylinder: Figure 20.

Using your new techniques

The simple shapes that you have produced allow you as a model maker to produce the vast majority of the shapes and structures needed for an architectural model. The techniques learned here will allow you to elevate a building, create massing forms and use spines to create far more complicated shapes; and with practice your hand-eye skills will develop, enabling you to master most projects.

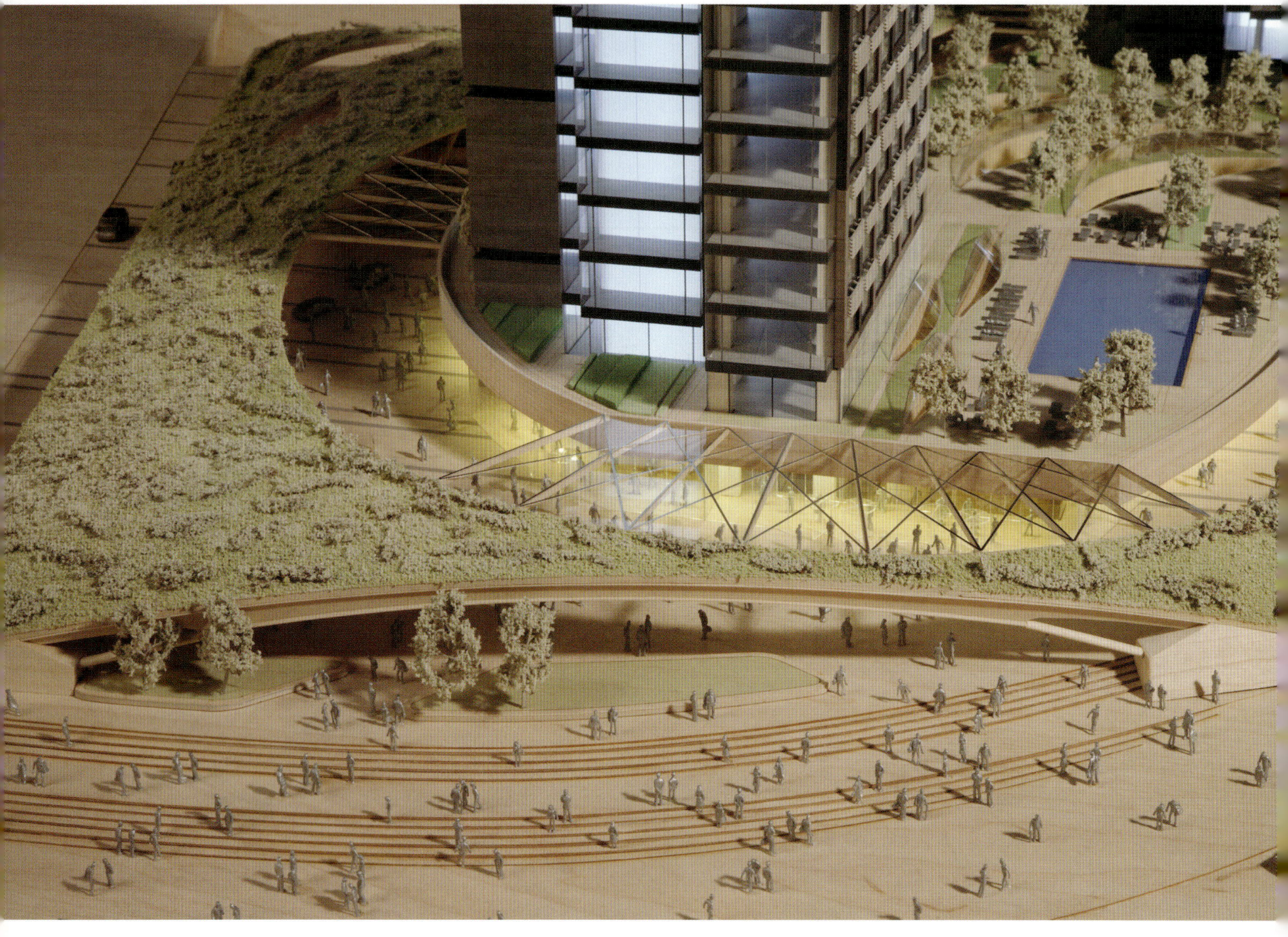

CHAPTER 4

APPROACHES TO MODEL MAKING

This chapter explores through case studies the processes involved in the construction of models, looking at past projects in various styles and formats in order to gain an understanding of the outcomes that may be achieved through your own models.

Having already discussed in brief the subject of abstraction, we need to investigate in greater detail the principle of conceptualizing a model. If the required level of information (plans, elevations and so on) is not available, or the time frame or budget isn't appropriate, then an abstract model will be a sure way to impress a client at an early stage of a competition, without getting into an in-depth analysis of material finishes and building detail. All architectural models by definition have some level of abstraction: the materials used and the reduced level of detail, for example, will always create this. Abstracting a model to a conceptual point can be a truly impressive way in which to approach a model while really making the best of the primary aims of a design.

Mass

Revealing the basic forms of your building as a block can be a very successful way of investigating your subject. However, to create real impetus to the aesthetic qualities, correct selection of materials is required. Generally speaking, a massing model can be built at any scale; the 2012 Olympic athletes' village shown in this chapter is a large-scale (1:200) massing model, ideal for when garden areas, site landscaping or the flow of pedestrians or traffic are being investigated. This type of large-scale model is also useful for development of elevation. The models can have elevation stuck to the faces of the blocks from paper prints – a highly cost-effective way to develop the design of such a large site. The model shown is constructed to be lightweight: the entire model was built from card and paper, and was transportable (the model breaks down into manageable portions) and easily updated. It was used initially as a massing model (numerous architects brought their buildings to be mocked up within the model), and later for the investigation of the elevation detailing. The model's lifespan had to be factored into the build process: it was used during the design process for the athletes' village over a number of years, being altered and updated continually as the development progressed. The sheer size of the model, covering an area of 3 metres by 2.5 metres, was also ideal for the design process, allowing as many as twenty architects to gather round the model during meetings and presentations.

Most such models will be built at a relatively small scale, as the exploration of mass is often linked intrinsically to the context of the surrounding buildings. It is usually also quicker and more cost-effective to build the model at a smaller scale; quick studies of the initial mass allow an architect to change the shape and update the design quickly, and it is often the case that many small models are built as the inspiration of the surroundings affects the development of the building. Massing models are an invaluable tool for the early developmental processes of a model's form. It is good practice to build the context and base levels of the model in more finished, stable material; these would be called the fixed elements, while the study of mass and layout go on within the site.

LEFT: **Timber, acrylic and three-dimensional printing model produced at 1:150 scale in conjunction with Millennium Models. (Photo: Andrew Putler)**

67

■ APPROACHES TO MODEL MAKING

Figure 1: a large-scale working model used for design development of the site early in the building's evolution.

Figure 2: early study model at 1:1000 with the scheme buildings massed in foam.

Figure 3: the scheme now resolved. This same 1:1000 model has been modelled with frosted acrylic blocks fitting into the original base and context. (Photo: Chris Edgecombe)

Figures 2 and 3 show 'before and after'. The first model (Fig. 2), at a small scale of 1:1000, was developed over a period of a month, produced in conjunction with the design process. We can see that while the contextual elements were modelled in traditional materials to a finished standard, the scheme itself, built quickly out of Styrofoam, could be played with, allowing for continual changing and updating. (This process can go on for long periods as the mass and layout of buildings

APPROACHES TO MODEL MAKING

Figure 4: in this 1:750 model with sprayed timber base, no fewer than six different varieties of wood are used to colour-code the different building types.

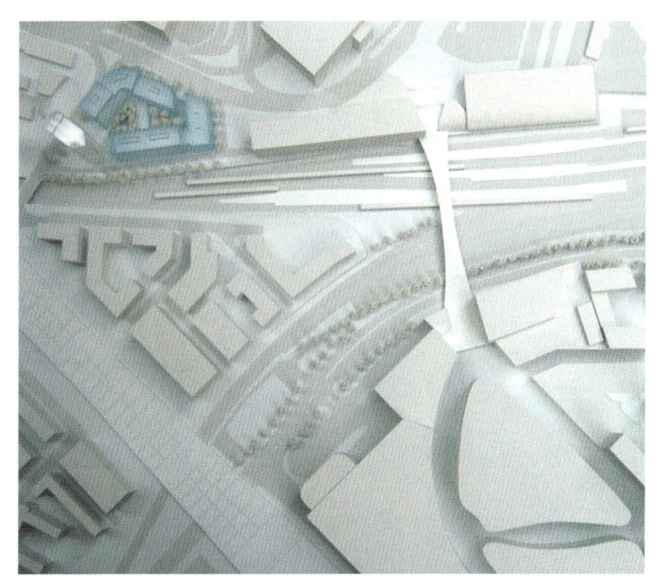

Figure 5: 1:750 sprayed and acrylic model for a potential bid.

are refined within the scheme, and it is a good idea to design the model with scheme insets: this is the process of having the ground within the site boundary on a separate plate that can be removed and updated as the design develops.) The initial designs of the site mass and layout became more solidified, then a more sophisticated, 'polished' scheme was produced (Fig. 3). The difference between Figures 2 and 3 is a world of detail and interest, but the context and base are the same model: the first used hot wire cut foam to develop the mass and was changed numerous times; the second (final) version was modelled out of Perspex layered 3mm acrylic and frosted with matt lacquer, a more sophisticated spray-finished ribbon landscape, and the final planting schedule. This model was then used for presentation and competition entry. The obvious benefits of this process were that the context was developed early on to help with the design process, and time (and ultimately money) was saved when the final insert could be made to fit into the model. This process has become more prevalent since the use of laser-cutting technology. The insert shape is simply one drawing file that can be cut countless times with accuracy; the model maker knows that each one will fit perfectly.

Depending on the message that a model is attempting to portray, the materials used for a massing model can be as simple or sophisticated as the model demands. We can see in Figure 4 that the coding of different elements through the use of different timbers is a useful way to show variation in building types. Here, six timbers are used to show different types of housing (key worker homes, apartment blocks, three-bedroom family homes and luxury apartments, for example). This process develops a graphic response to the brief whilst remaining compatible with the boards that will be used for the presentation.

The choice of material or colour can also be used to describe the phasing of the project. In Figure 5, although the materials used for the buildings within the scheme are the same, the buildings have been colour coded for the phasing of the development in terms of timescale. The clusters of blue buildings were to be developed initially and the transparent towers (*see* Fig. 6) were planned for later development. These buildings were made from layered acrylic slabs to show mass and floor volumes, and were set within the context of a mono-

■ APPROACHES TO MODEL MAKING

Figure 6: the scheme in acrylic slabs colour-coded with tinted lacquers.

Figure 7: timber master plan in lime and maple.

chrome background. This type of model allows the opportunity not only to see the scheme within its context, but also enables full focus on the new development without being caught up in the outlying contextual buildings. We can see from Figure 5 that although the contextual buildings are present the focus remains on the two sites at either end of the model. The addition of colour has a dual purpose: to describe the phasing and to draw attention to a key area. (Note, however, that drawing attention isn't always the desired effect, and in some situations a scheme may need to be nestled into the model and not 'shout'.) This model was one architect's scheme proposed within a massive new development area, the existing buildings being the proposals from other architects – it was therefore important that this development had a voice amongst many other new and exciting buildings.

Smaller scales will normally allow an opportunity to build a larger number of contextual buildings. Figure 7 is an example where we can see the use of a small scale: in this proposal for new buildings within an established university town the appeal of a sympathetic timber was used to show building heights and major architectural features. The same materials were used for surrounding context and to show the integration into the site of potentially contentious buildings for the locality. Feature buildings were accented in acrylic to best represent the progress that the new building would bring to the area – without dominating the existing buildings in the locality.

Using a plan in creating a massing model

The key element in making a model of this nature is a plan printed to scale from which model buildings can be built. We can see from Figures 8 and 9 that the building should be

70

APPROACHES TO MODEL MAKING

Figure 8: a timber model still being produced sits on its plan.

Figure 9: contrasting timbers of pear wood and walnut being used during a build. The buildings are located on a plan.

denoted on a plan. Often the client can give a standard height or intermediate sketches to produce the roofscape; the buildings (as in this case) can be machined out of timber to fit the printed plan and then have some elevation detail applied to the mass. As the balcony detail to Figure 8 shows, this type of conceptualized detail adds an intricacy to the building; there is no need for worked-up elevations to achieve a clear idea about the articulation of the building.

Figure 9 shows the working of the model maker's thoughts on paper. The plan drawing has been marked out and colour coded to express the different types of timbers to be used. It is also worth transferring relevant information – floor layout, heights and so on – to one drawing; this prevents confusion and gives a master copy that the building 'stays with' until the last moment before the building is attached to the model base. (It may sound strange, but this method also provides a written history of the task: if changes need to be made during the build or if there is uncertainty about what has been discussed with your client, then this master plan ensures everything works, and when the stick down onto the base happens, you have a visual reference of where each building sits and the orientation of the buildings.)

Floor stack

Using floor plate stacks and floor thickness slabs is an effective way to reveal the intricacies and sense of scale of your building, through height and slab shape. Another use for the floor slab technique is in the construction of surrounding buildings. (How a scheme is set within its context is an important aspect of model making.) Figure 10 shows how the floor slabs surrounding this 1:500 scheme give relevance to the scale of the proposed building while showing it in its context. The slabs are frosted to pull them back from focus, giving a ghost-like impression which doesn't dominate the overall model composition. The architects' intention was to build a model that had forward-thinking appeal, while being clean and unfussy – the building was a hospital – and this clean but soft approach, reinforced by the colour scheme, was used to present the relationship of the hospital with the important function of its gardens. All models should tell a story that best represents the main principles of an architect's design, but they should also contain sub-plots on different levels, giving the model a depth of interest that keeps people looking.

APPROACHES TO MODEL MAKING

Figure 10: 1:500 acrylic sprayed model of a hospital. This model was produced at competition stage.

GLUING A FLOOR STACK MODEL

When designing a floor slab model it is essential to avoid messy glue marks; the models are very often transparent or at best translucent, so the model footprint should have an offset score-line of 1–2 millimetres inside the cut line (as the diagram shows). This line acts as a barrier to the glue and prevents it from travelling inside the rest of the area between slabs. Use chloroform with great care; then the model, once stacked up, can be glued around the outside. Glue travels only in the channel that the score line creates between the edges of the model. This technique, once mastered, will allow for almost seamless gluing and not detract from the model's finish. When gluing a model down to the base, it is also worth spraying the bottom of transport buildings the same colour as the base, allowing you to use liberal amounts of glue and guaranteeing a clean, invisible join.

Model project: the 'Gherkin'

This is a great practical project to build and teaches valuable lessons about materiality, scale and the conceptualization of a building. The model is of Foster + Partners' Swiss Re HQ building (the 'Gherkin') in central London, and although built using only floor plates it is without doubt still recognizable. This lesson is an important one to learn: through the reproduction of shape the clear acrylic stack is still easily recognized, and it explains the mass without the need of elevations.

The CAD drawing provided is at scale to the model; these floors and combs were drawn and then laser-cut, but if you want to build this model then they may be cut out of the book and spray-mounted on to thin card, styrene, or other appropriate material, and cut out using a scalpel. Alternatively you can use the drawing, which has important dimensions as a guide. Draw these components up and get them laser-cut out of any material you want (the slots for the combs should be adjusted for your material thickness or the model will not slot together correctly). This process also introduces how to finish a model – straight lines, sanding, measuring, etc.

APPROACHES TO MODEL MAKING

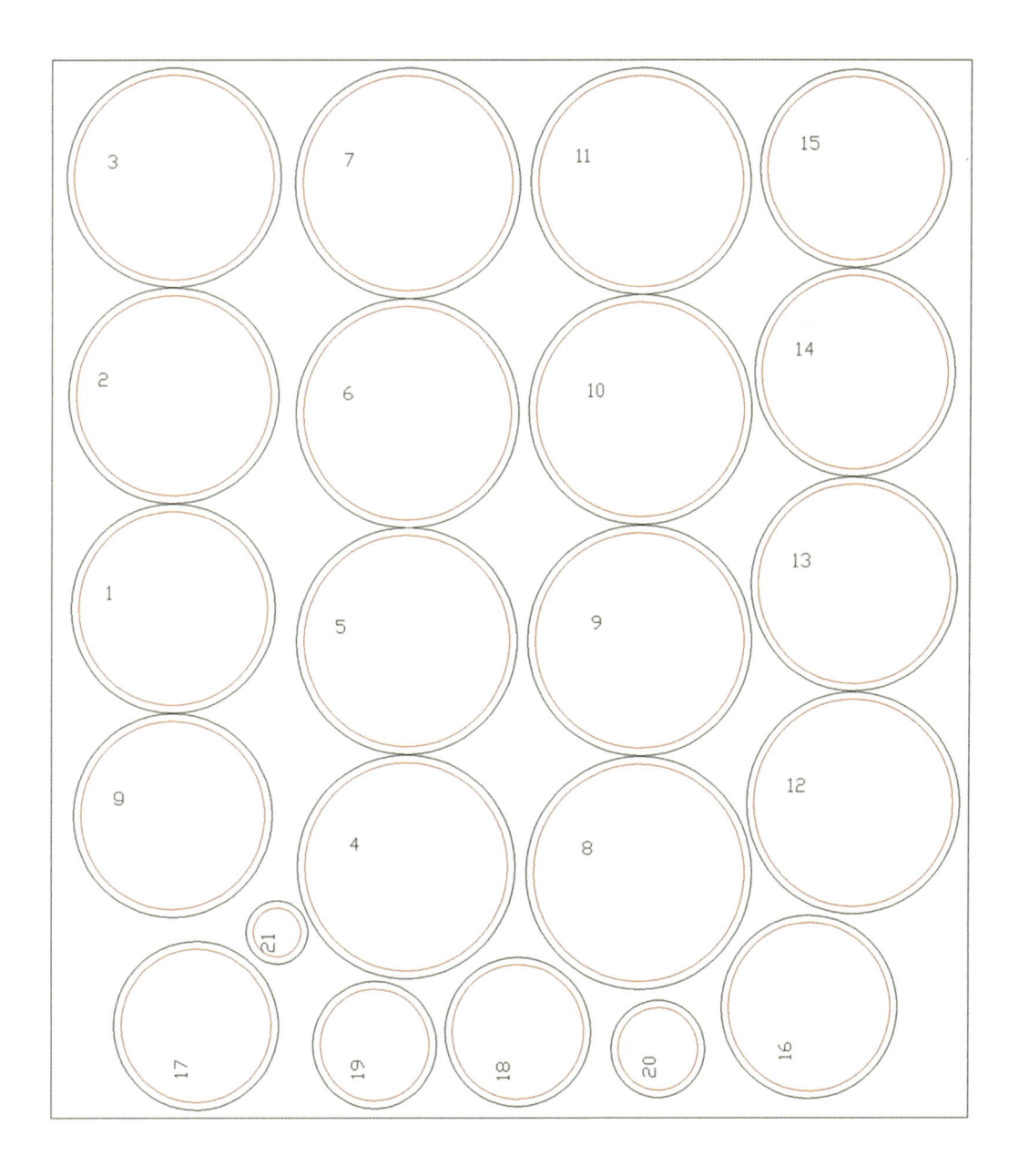

CAD drawings for Foster + Partners' 'Gherkin' model in both floor plate and floor slab form. These drawings are to scale (1:1000) and may be copied and cut out.

73

■ APPROACHES TO MODEL MAKING

APPROACHES TO MODEL MAKING

Materials and equipment

A range of materials may be used, from thin or thick card, timber, 3mm MDF board, veneer or acrylic. To replicate this exercise precisely, use 1mm acrylic. (*Note*: if you are producing the model by hand, 1mm acrylic will be time-consuming and difficult to cut; 0.5mm acrylic can be more easily scored and snapped, but thin card, styrene or veneer are preferable.) The photograph shows the model being built in clear acrylic for aesthetic reasons and to demonstrate the conceptual nature of the model design. It has been laser-cut.

Pencil
Cutting mat
Steel rule
Steel square, 3 inch and 6 inch
Scalpel and 10A blades
Glue: chloroform (dependent on choice of materials)
Chloroform dispenser
Sable brush
Tweezers
123 blocks
Lighter fluid

If, as suggested above, you have decided to use the provided drawing as a template to cut out the components yourself, then spray mount, circle cutter and lighter fluid are also required. Spray mount the paper copy of the components to your material sheet.

1. Have a paper copy of your components printed out at scale to help you organize them.
2. Placing your components on top of the printout prevents confusion when constructing your model kit, especially in this type of build where all the components are of a similar size. They must be assembled in the correct order or the model will be the wrong shape and ultimately won't work (you would have to break the model apart and reassemble; the model would never look as clean and crisp again and would probably break whilst being dismantled).
3. Clear enough space to build the model on your mat; a clear and organized work space will reduce the likelihood of mistakes, and help keep the quality of your work to a good standard.
4. Taking one of your combs, place it on the mat following one of the mat's vertical lines. Trap the bottom of it

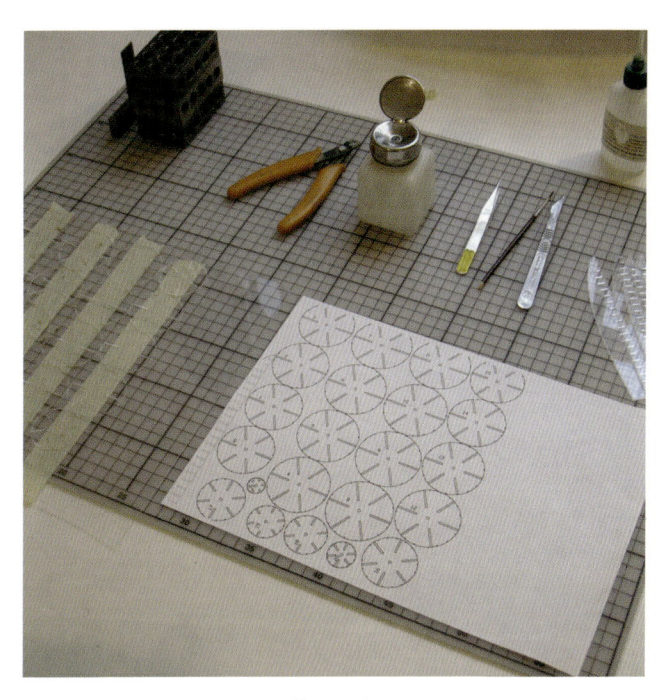

Figure 1.

Figure 2.

■ APPROACHES TO MODEL MAKING

tightly between two 123 blocks.

Note: consider securing the 123 blocks into position with double-sided tape to limit movement during the build process. If you double-side them down, do it in a position where you can easily access all sides of the model. (Note that in these photographs the model moves; this is to show the process as clearly as possible.)

5. Take the first floor, circle B (see drawing).
6. Place in the corresponding slot on the comb, at the bottom of the building (circle B should be placed into slot B). This process then can be repeated up through the slots.
7. Check regularly that the circles are going into their corresponding slots; it can become very confusing later on if not.
8. As you move up through the floors, the circles get smaller. Model makers are generally quite dexterous, but tweezers may be used if necessary for the smaller circles to avoid dislodging the lower circles.
9. Once all the circles have been placed on the first comb you can place the second comb on the opposite series of slots so that the combs now carry through the full diameter of the circles. It is now that you will be able to see if you have put all the circles on in the correct order.
10. You can now start to insert the other combs around one side of the model. It may be tricky to feed the slots

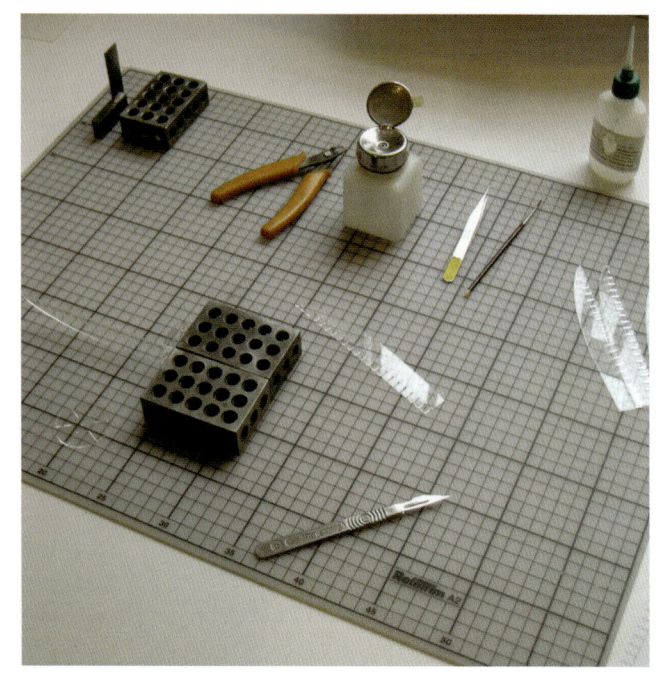

Figure 3.

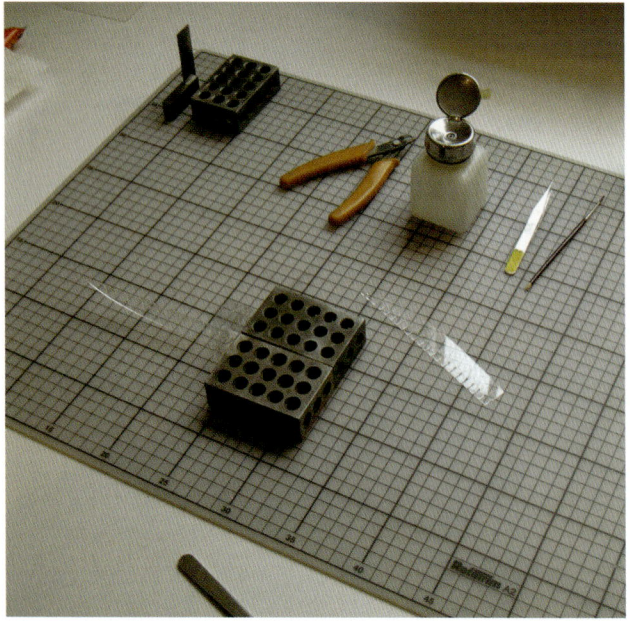

Figure 4.

Figure 5.

76

APPROACHES TO MODEL MAKING

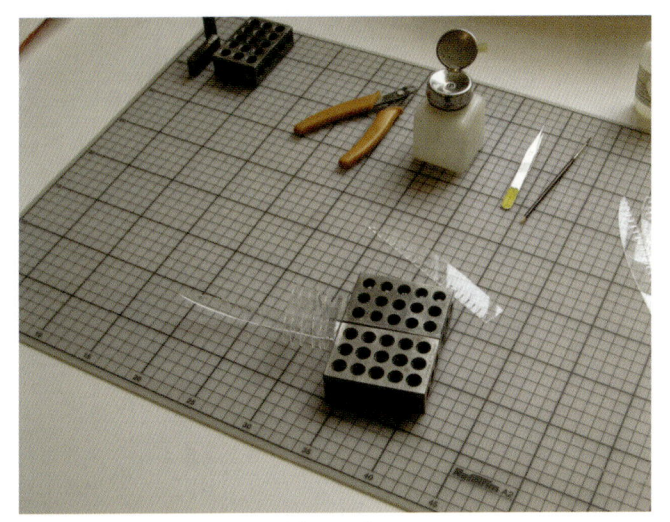

Figure 6.

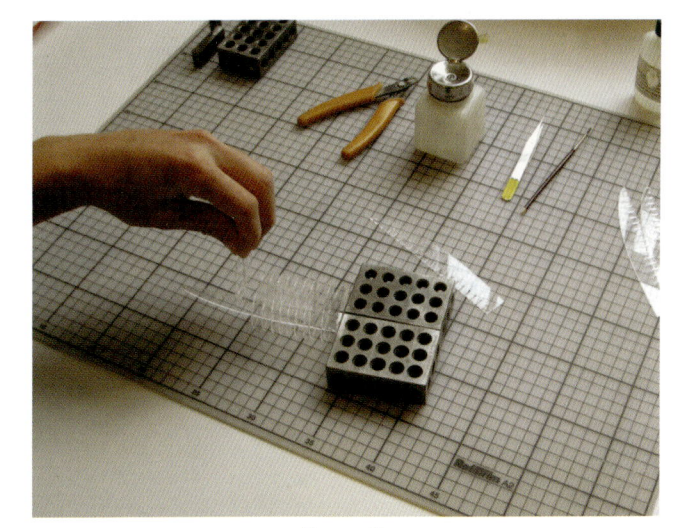

Figure 7.

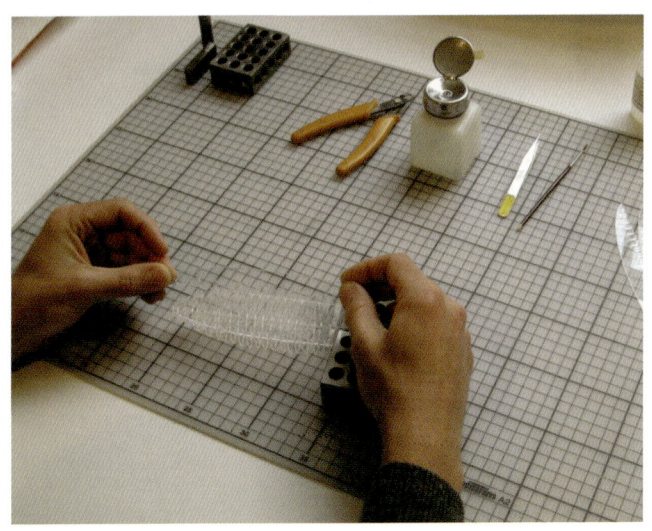

Figure 8.

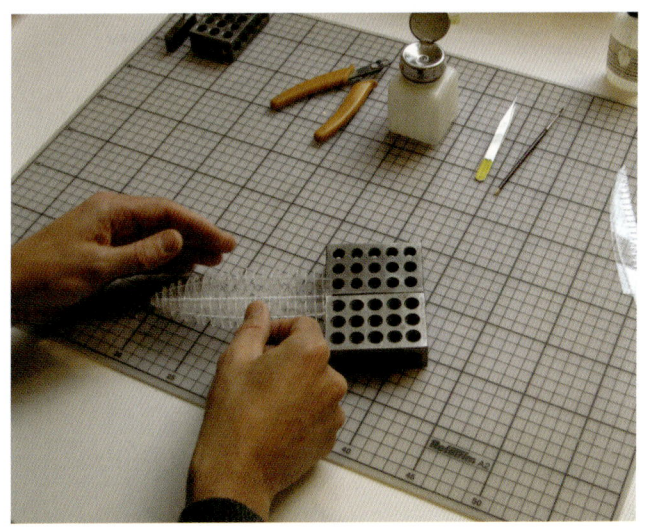

Figure 9.

through their corresponding inserts; take your time and try not to dislodge any circles and they should slot into place.
11. Without moving the model you should be able to get four of the six combs onto it. They should get progressively easier to insert, as the circles start to find their positions.
12. Holding the combs that are already in place firmly (if you are unsure of doing this then a small amount of chloroform can be used to tack the combs in place). Lift the model and rotate it in your hand.
13. You should now be able to slot in the next comb.
14. Placing the model down on the cutting mat, the last comb can be slotted into place.
15. Carefully holding the combs in place it is now time to stand the model upright and trap it between two blocks, to guarantee the squareness of the combs to the circles.
16. Once you are happy with the positioning of the circles, they will probably need tweaking to get them visually square, and then the model can be tacked together with chloroform.
17. Working from the top of the building down, administer the chloroform by touching the brush close in to where the combs meet at the centre of the model. The chloroform will run along the joint automatically – you don't need to use an excessive amount of chloroform,

77

APPROACHES TO MODEL MAKING

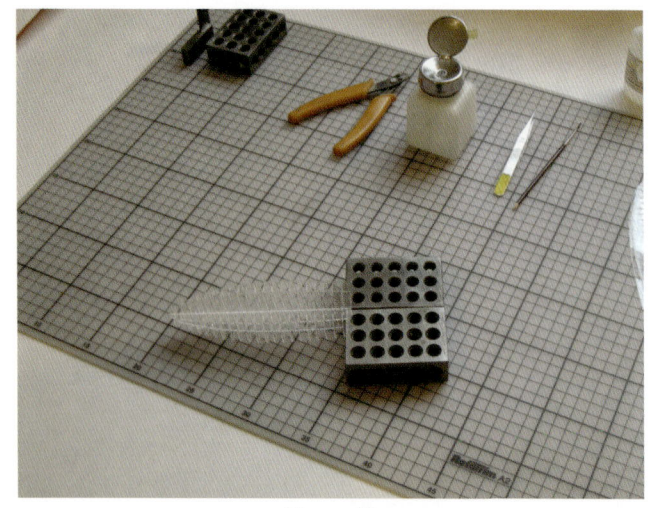

Figure 10.

Figure 11.

Figure 12.

Figure 13.

which will help keep the model clean and sharp. (*Note*: it is worth investing in a chloroform dispenser as this chemical is particularly pungent to inhale. A dispenser will limit the amount that you can breathe in or spill by drawing a small amount into a dish. Dip the brush into the dispenser dish and remove excess from the brush on the side of the dish.)

18. Once one comb has been glued to the circles you should be able to remove the blocks and start to glue around the model.
19. Having worked around the model, touching the brush to the centre points where the combs and the circle meet, you can now (checking visually that your model is square all the time) run your brush from the centre back to the edges.
20. Give a few minutes for the glue to dry; then the base of your building can be fitted. Lift up your model; the ground floor circle (A) should clip onto the combs which have their slots exposed.
21. With the application of some chloroform the ground floor is now attached to your model.
22. Once given a little time to dry, the finished model is quite sturdy and robust, despite appearing delicate and fragile.

This technique is a relatively quick way to produce the form of a building, keeping it abstract while revealing a considered amount of intricate detail. The process that you have learned here can now be used to produce any number of floor stack

78

APPROACHES TO MODEL MAKING

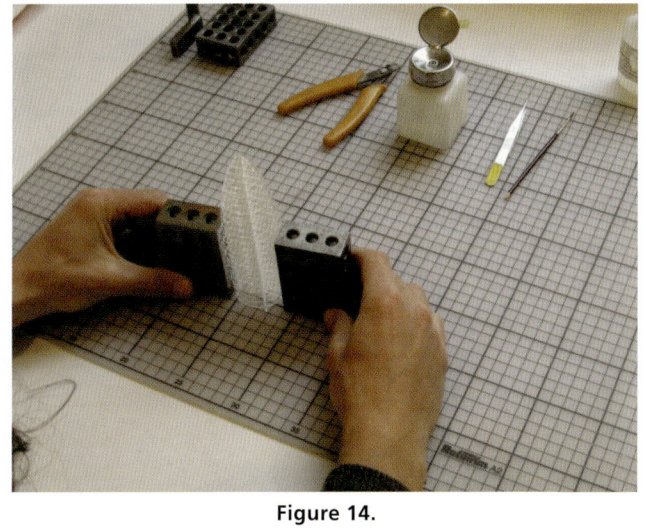

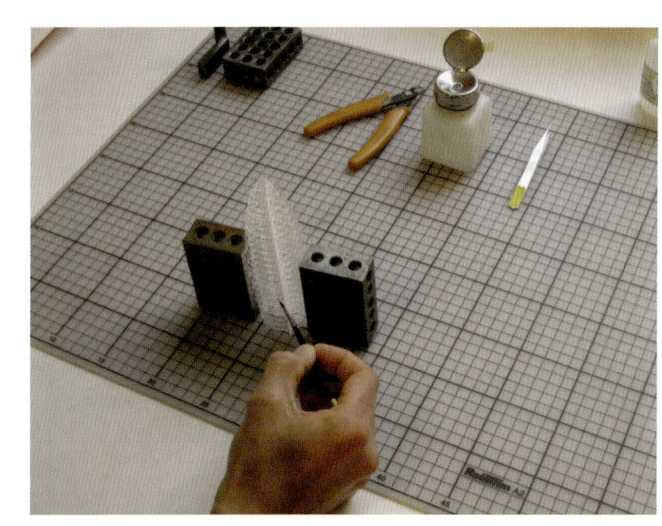

Figure 14.

Figure 15.

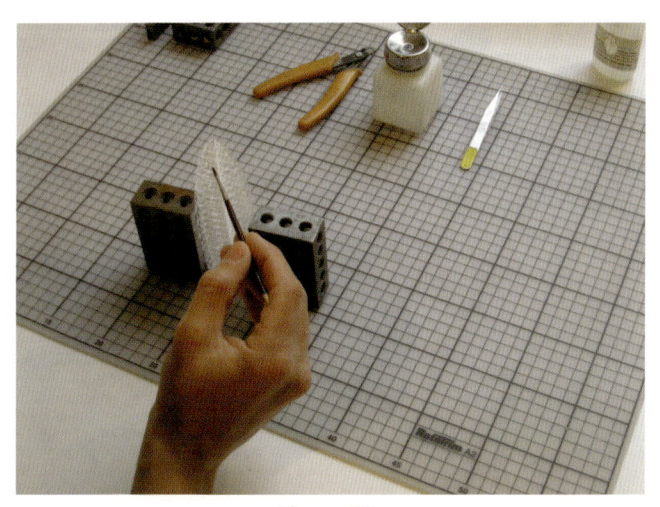

Figure 16.

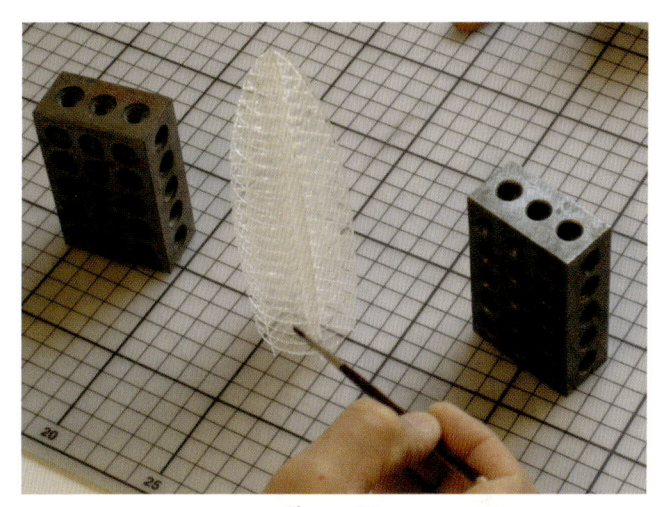

Figure 17.

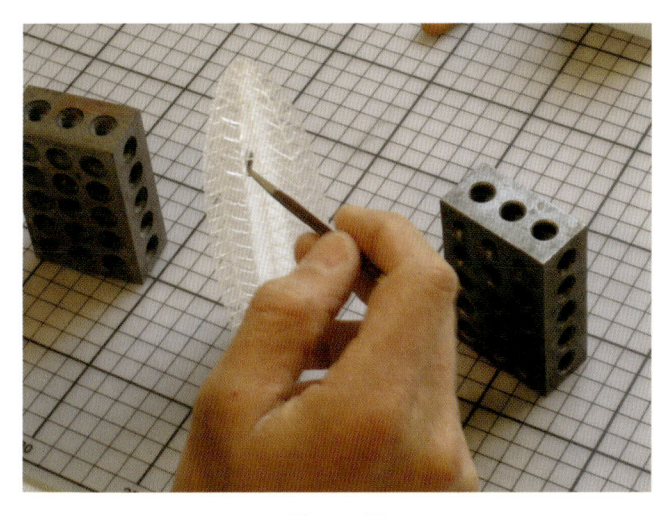

Figure 18.

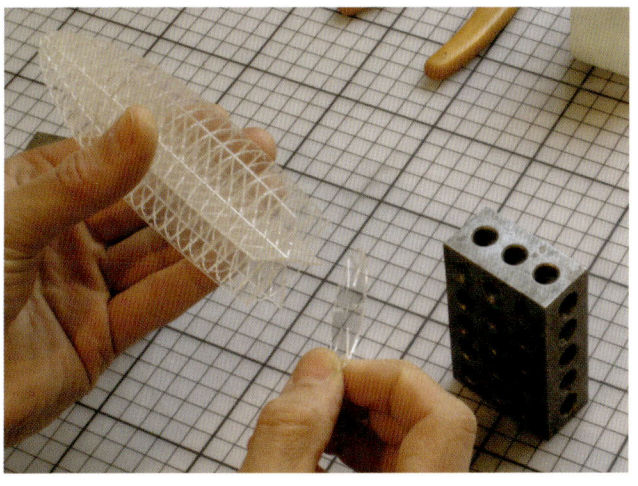

Figure 19.

79

■ APPROACHES TO MODEL MAKING

Figure 20.

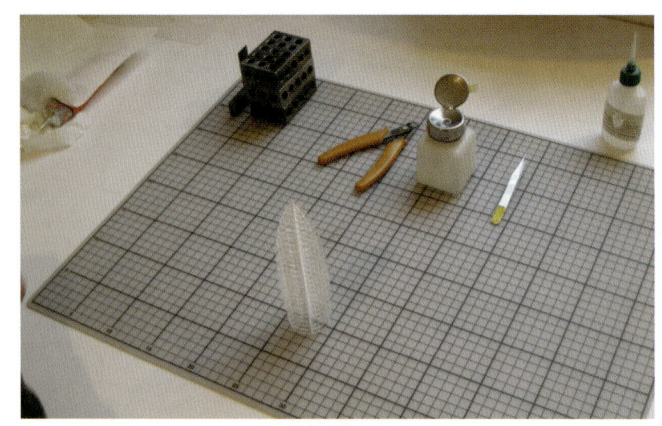

Figure 21.

models. The comb system can also be used as a construction technique for elevated floor stack models. The process is largely the same, but if for example it is a square building floor stack, the combs may be removed as each side of the model has an elevation glued to it. This allows you to build a model that shows floor levels but without using walls to build it up.

Elevation studies

Elevated models are normally produced from the scale 1:500 up to 1:1 for sectional pieces of buildings. At 1:500 the elevations are normally reasonably simplified but can still hold quite a lot of detail. Usually elevated models work at their best when produced at a larger scale – 1:200 or 1:100, for example. The layering of an elevated model can be seen below. Various materials can be used, depending on the effect that you are aiming to achieve. In the sample photos the models have been produced with a glassing line, window depth line, brick line and fenestration line. An elevation is shown in timber and grey card finish (Fig. 11) and the difference is shown between a glass line and a blind reveal (Figs. 9 and 10). From the drawing below we can produce an elevation study; this elevation has been broken into four layers. To replicate this process you can use your own elevation or cut and replicate this one.

Materials and equipment

The elevation has been made from a maple veneer, 1mm acrylic, 1mm grey card and oak veneer to show a variety of materials and their possible effects. The model has been glued together with a contact adhesive. (The glue chosen will depend on what you use to make the model; see page 26.)

The equipment needed is virtually nil: a cutting mat and the

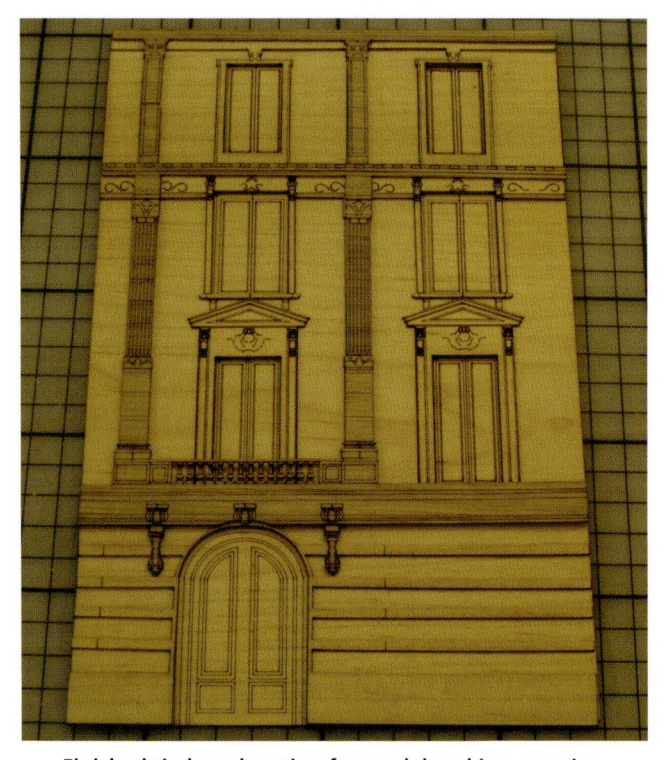

Finished timber elevation for model-making exercise.

APPROACHES TO MODEL MAKING

contact adhesive should be all you need but it might be worth having a scalpel handy to clean and tidy any edges. If you are making the elevations from scratch then the tool kit needed for the exercises in Chapter 3 is adequate to get the job done.

1. As at the start of all model builds, arrange your components and equipment on your work surface to avoid confusion once you start making.
2. Turn over the first brick layer and using the contact adhesive create small circular motions with the glue, covering the entire gluing areas. Be careful around window and door apertures not to let the glue spill over onto the front face side. Place the glued surface onto the glazing layer, then pull off; the gluing marks that have remained on the glazing layer will show you where to apply the same circular motion gluing on this layer.
3. Having given a few moments for the adhesive to dry off, carefully place the first brick layer on to the glazing line (make sure the layers go together in the correct place, as it will be hard to peel them apart once together – contact adhesives stick quickly). Use the corners and the sides of the elevation, or the window and door apertures as a guide when placing the elevation.
4. This process should be repeated with the stone layer onto the brick layer, gluing onto the stone layer first then placing it onto the brick layer and removing it quickly. Again, use the remaining glue to show you where to apply glue on the brick layer. This way of doing it makes more sense with this layer, and is a good habit to get into so that you don't apply too much glue to the wrong areas. When sticking more complicated areas together, this way of working will be invaluable in keeping a clean, accurate build.
5. You should now have a three-layered elevation. It's worth noting that if you have made any messy glue mistakes these can be removed: wipe away the excess with a rolled piece of towel or rag, then use a small amount of lighter fluid to remove the rest with a light rubbing motion. You may need a few applications of lighter fluid to remove all of the adhesive; if using veneer then a light sand all over will remove any remaining marks.
6. Repeat the gluing process for the column layer and the elevation is now built. Weight the elevations with a few 123 blocks until the glue is completely dry.
7. Sometimes you may wish to use different materials in the layers to draw attention to certain layers. In these photos we can see that the column layer has been replaced in Figure 9 with an oak version; this gives the model extra depth, gives added interest and may be used to create relevance to a specific part of the build.
8. In some cases the blind reveal (glazing line), instead of being made from the same material as the other layers, can be made from acrylic, as seen in Figure 10. This might be desired by your client as a way to view the inside of the building or in some cases to get a view from the inside of the building, to understand spacing of the model's surrounds and context – or just to give lightness to the model. The window frames can be engraved to give relevant detail.
9. Figure 11 shows the 1mm grey card version, mixed with the maple veneer at column layer and using the acrylic glazing level. This photo acts as a reminder that different

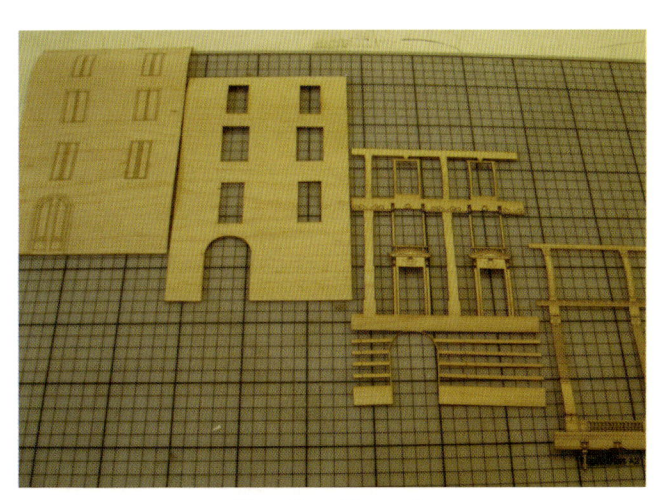

Elevation: Figure 1.

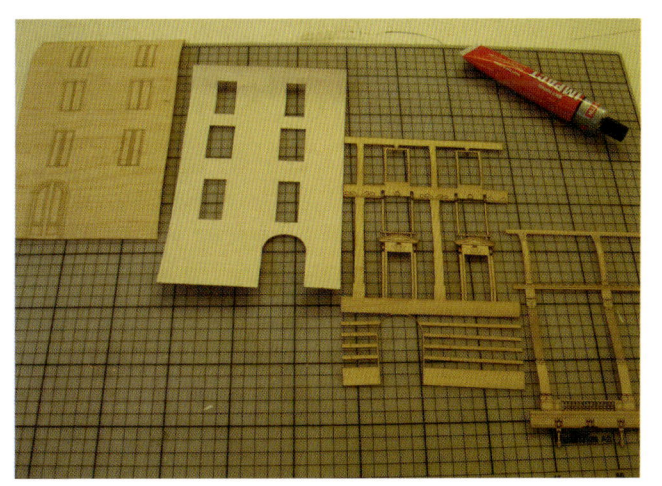

Elevation: Figure 2.

■ APPROACHES TO MODEL MAKING

APPROACHES TO MODEL MAKING

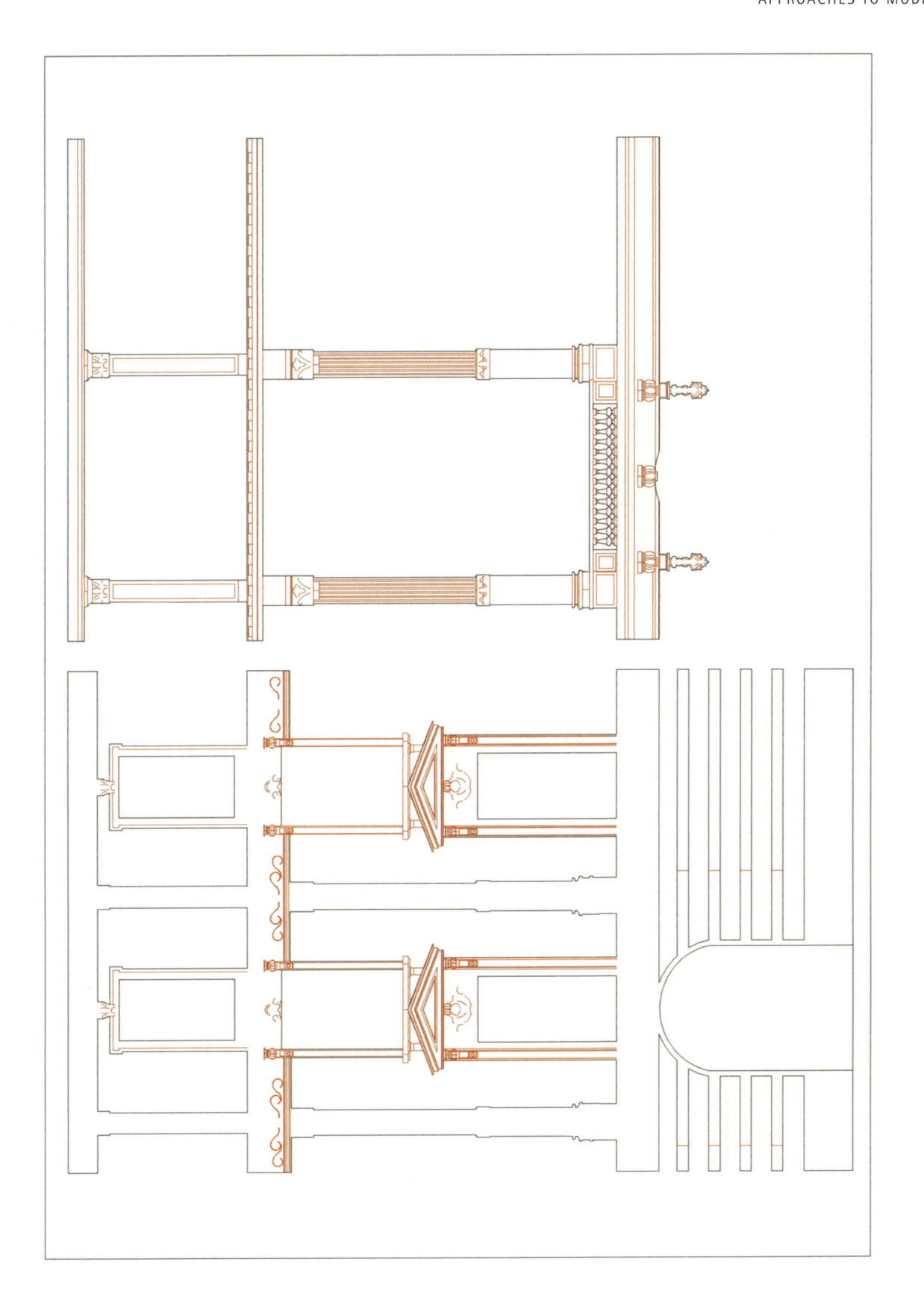

CAD drawings to aid in the production of the model exercise. Each drawing is a layer needed to produce the elevation, the material choices are flexible; a good exercise with which to experiment and have fun with.

83

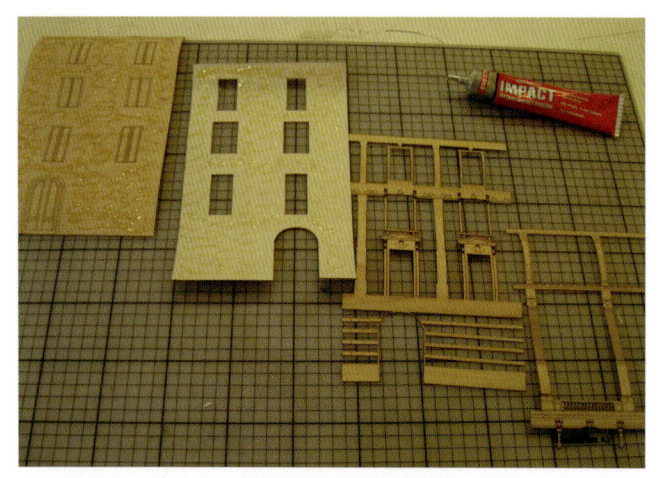

■ APPROACHES TO MODEL MAKING

Elevation: Figure 3.

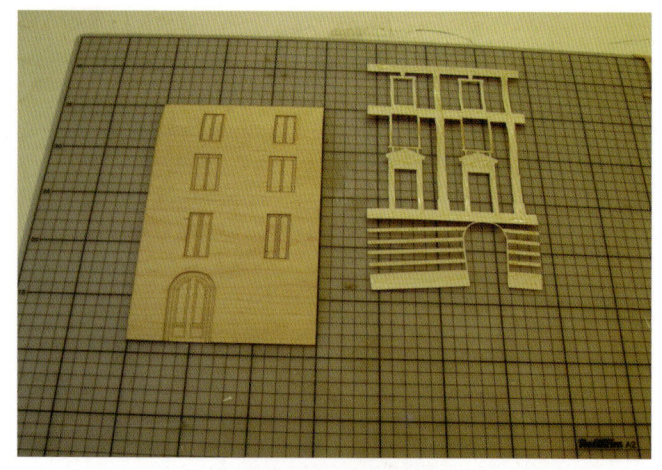

Elevation: Figure 4.

Elevation: Figure 5.

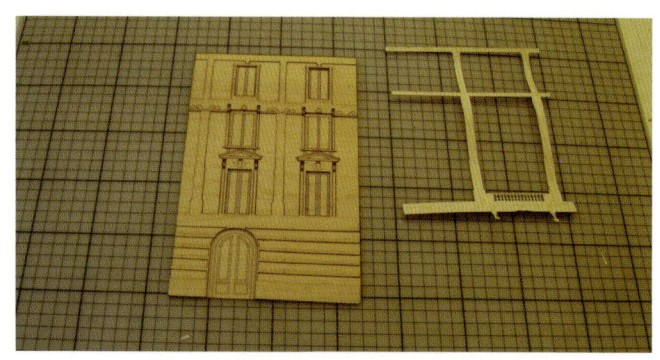

Elevation: Figure 6.

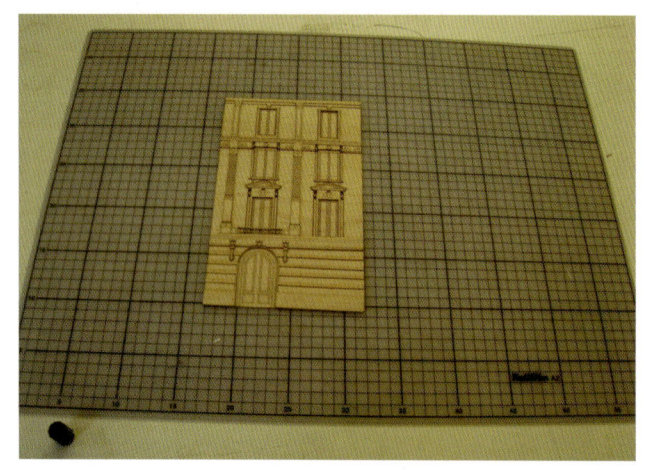

Elevation: Figure 7.

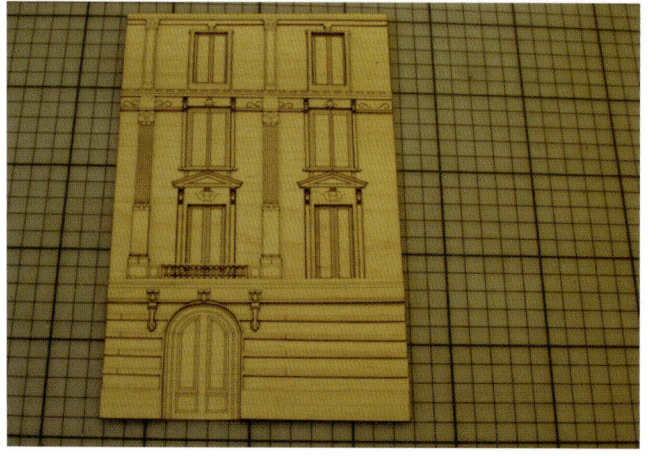

Elevation: Figure 8.

84

APPROACHES TO MODEL MAKING

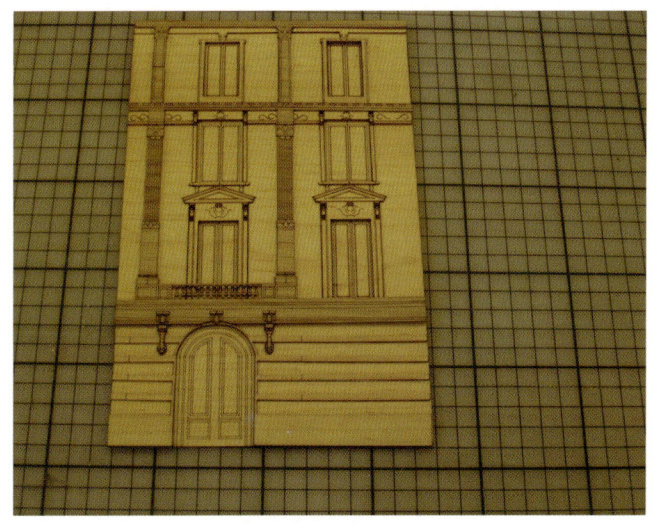

Elevation: Figure 9.

Elevation: Figure 10.

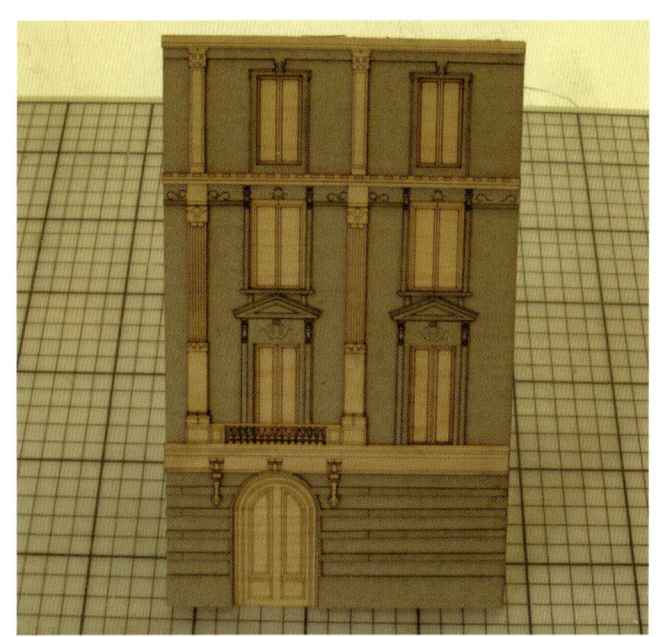

Elevation: Figure 11.

materials and the mixing of materials can give a completely different sense of the design. It is worth experimenting with lots of different materials and colour finishes to explore the variety of outcomes achievable. This type of research and development will give useful experience of how different materials behave, and how they interact with each other at different scales and for different designs. The design used was of a classical building so the natural look of the timber and grey card was sympathetic to this type of design, more so than if using metal or bright colourings, which might be more appropriate for a modern design.

■ APPROACHES TO MODEL MAKING

Sections

This style of model works incredibly well when you want to investigate the properties of a model in detail. A sectional model is most useful when produced from 1:100 in scale upwards; depending on the size of the building to be modelled, 1:50 is often a great size – big enough to investigate but still manageable in size.

One such investigation can be seen in Figures 1, 2 and 3. The photos show the design progression: Figure 1 was the early concept into the model, the aim being to understand the space internally with reference to the window apertures and by proxy the external frame of the elevation. This early, crude design was then developed into more of a rectangular form (Fig. 2), keeping the pop-out box aperture but developing the structure of the cladding to the building. This investigation now begins to explore the material finishes with realistic colouring to the frames, cladding systems and pop-out rectangular boxes in particular. The third photo (Fig. 3) has now developed the articulation, further purifying the view and solving the problem of revealing enough glassing while still having light protection and screening. The three models together represent effectively how a model can aid the devel-

Sections: Figure 1. A 1:50 elevation section. This is the first of three sections of the same building as the design develops.

Sections: Figure 2. The second of three sections of the same building.

APPROACHES TO MODEL MAKING

opment of a design and show the changing initiative of a design throughout its development.

The animation of the offices in Figure 4 helps to give a sense of scale while also presenting the sense of space in the building's interiors – very important when presenting the design to clients.

We can also see from Figure 5 that the detailing and colour reference matching at scale has allowed for a true sense of what the building would look like when it is complete.

Cross-sectional models

Sectional models can be produced to reveal the internal building as well as the exterior elevations. The model below shows the elevation detailing to the main entrance of a building. This study explores the materiality, fine detailing and general fenestration – essential elements of the cross-sectional model.

At a big scale the model incorporates a sufficient level of detail to answer questions or to show particular features in their most descriptive lights. The courtyard elevations enable the viewer to see out onto the courtyard gardens and understand the spaces and how they work. It is also possible to view the intricacies of the internal spaces, people flows, reception areas, and ceiling heights. When building smaller-scale models, where a flavour of the elevations needs to be represented, there are numerous possible ways in which to represent the building design. This type of model conceptualizes the design and represents it through a level of abstraction, relying to a

Sections: Figure 3. The third of three sections of the same building.

Sections: Figure 4. View into a 1:50 sectional model, to see the internal spaces.

Sections: Figure 5. Louvre condition on a 1:50 model in realistic spray finishes.

An exploration of internal spaces and landscape: 1:200 section model through a building in sprayed acrylic. (Photo: Andrew Putler)

■ APPROACHES TO MODEL MAKING

great extent on the light-handed approach of the model maker to choose sympathetic materials to tell the story.

Figures 1 and 2 show how a model can still be elevated at a small scale, once again using the insert approach, but without getting too fussy with detail (which might have overshadowed the main theme of the model). The use of a solid acrylic block at the glazing line and a white random window elevation that shows the variety and sizes of window (with smaller windows lower down and winter-garden style double- or treble-height windows in the upper storeys) allows the language of the towers to communicate the theme of the design. The low-rise timber creates a softness and expresses a change in material from the towers; the windows strive for a more uniform, tighter expression of architecture. Just showing the mass would not allow this design to be communicated – but a larger model would either cost a lot or need an unrealistic level of detail at the design/drawing stage. Conceptualizing the model down to these main expressive themes allows the story to be told while not interfering with the broad concept that the architect is developing. Very often, 'less is more'.

Choosing material colour and scale are the key factors in conceptualizing your design. The use of metal, acrylic and timber can be used to great effect when abstracting and conceptualizing a design. Returning to a basic materiality in a model will often allow the purity of a design to be represented through the simplistic choice of material. The models shown (Figs. 1 and 2) are a conceptualized section of a building, showing two different elevation designs. One side of the building faced the river; the other side faced gardens, and the designs were created to reflect the stimulus of the building's surroundings. The first followed the wave pattern of the river; the second reflected the gardens, the design of the model

Cross-sections: Figure 1. A 1:1000 insert model constructed from textured, sprayed acrylic and timber.

Cross-sections: Figure 2. The view down onto the towers and winter gardens.

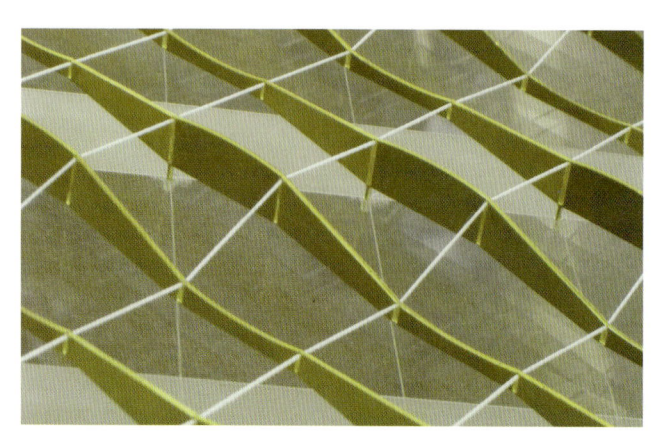

Conceptual investigative front elevation condition modelled from brass etched metal with acrylic and elastic.

Conceptual investigative rear elevation condition modelled from brass etched metal with acrylic.

being pared back to reflect this basic concept. The acrylic backing worked as a glassing line; frosted bands reflected the floor plate behind. This simplified structure gave the continuity with which to present the two designs, modelled in brass, thus creating a unique but abstracted understanding of the building's concept. The models work on two levels: they create an understanding of the design whilst the abstract use of material and colour realize the building to great effect.

An interview with Sam Morgan

Can you give me a breakdown of what the job entails?
My job title is Project Supervisor, which sounds fairly self-explanatory. I liaise with the architects and organize and instruct my team. This can range from creating CAD work to showing members of my team how to make, spray or assemble something. I also have to make things as well! We make the model happen within the time frame that the project allows. This can range from a few days through to a few months but ultimately we try to best realize a model that represents what the architect is trying to say with their design. We are a service within the company along with the graphics, visualizations and 3D computer modellers who support the design proposition.

Can you tell me about the history of Foster's model shop, the size of the practice and how long it's been in existence?
Foster's architectural practice is approximately forty years old. I'm told it grew quickly as a practice, with the in-house department being established over thirty years ago, but then it was organized using freelance model makers as opposed to permanent members of staff. It is in the last quarter century that the model shop has been as it stands today, and has started to take shape with a system that uses teams of model makers (each team working on different projects) and a management structure that allows for the breadth of what is undertaken. When I started ten years ago there were about twelve model makers in the department with one Manager, three team leaders, and a pool of eight model makers who moved around jobs. Foster's in-house Model Shop Manager supervised a small number of team leaders, with a pool of staff under them, who rotated between different projects. There was also a Sketch Model Supervisor (usually working in paper and card), whose role was to facilitate architects who wished to develop their own models.

MODEL MAKER'S PROFILE: SAM MORGAN

Sam Morgan is an Associate at Foster + Partners. After gaining a BA (Hons) in Model-making at the Kent Institute of Art, Sam Morgan worked as a freelance model maker before joining Foster's model shop as a junior model maker. Sam Morgan has now been with Foster's for over ten years and in his capacity as an Associate he runs teams and oversees the making of complex models for some of the most prestigious architectural projects happening around the world.

How then has the model shop changed in the time that you have been at Foster's?
The model shop has gone through a prolonged period of growth and expansion that underpins the importance of the model to the architectural practice. Within a few years of my joining the department I saw it grow and with around twenty staff it was decided to alter the organization of the teams. We moved away from the pool of makers who rotated between projects, towards more structured teams with a hierarchy, which means that during the build process we have project supervisors overseeing mid-level and junior model makers whilst communicating with the model-making management team above. This arrangement allows us to create relationships in which team members can learn and develop within a structure where the supervisor is keenly aware of everyone's strengths and weaknesses in the team. We rotate the team members every six months or so to maximize the learning experience for the team members.

In the last three years the company has supported the advantages of having a progressive model-making department, with major investment going into additional new premises with a full complement of model makers also remaining at the original space. The importance of the model in the design development to communicate a vision was always an integral part of how Norman Foster presented and rationalized his own design process, and this is key to why the company has arguably the largest model shop in the UK today. Foster's now has over forty staff spread over the two sites as well as the 3D printing departments, a dedicated CAD support team and the five-man team that is still in place to facilitate the architects' self-led sketch model investigations.

■ APPROACHES TO MODEL MAKING

What advantages do you see to the production of models by working in-house?
The benefits can probably be broken down into three key points:

- The relationship that model makers can build with the architects: although Foster's offers large model-making facilities, one of the important aspects of the service we provide is to have good communication with the architects requiring the model. It is essential that we can fulfil the specifications required by everyone involved at the architectural practice, and this can mean catering for over one thousand architects. Having good relationships and communication with key staff and project heads allows us to engage in a good knowledge of projects. Developing this understanding over the years has assisted us to achieve the best results. The company ethos and a feeling of togetherness are always important when working in a pressurized, deadline-based environment.
- Information regarding the design can move efficiently between the architects and model makers. The fact that we are an in-house part of Foster's and that we are physically there with them allows for a freedom of conversation. Information regarding the design can move efficiently from the architects to the model makers and questions are far easier to get answered in the 'to and fro' of in-house, rather than if we were a separate company. With this deadline-based industry the fluid nature of design progression has to allow for the models to change during the process to keep up with fast pace of the design progression.
- Costs can be kept down. Due to design alterations, it can be costly and difficult to liaise with an external company. Foster's can avoid the expense that changes can incur when dealing with separate model-making companies. The in-house approach, although within a budgeted financial structure, does permit quick movement to allow for the changing face of the design process; outside companies probably wouldn't be in a place to handle this with the same speed.

How do you decide, with an architect, the direction a model should go, such as the scale and style of the model?
The model specification has normally been decided upon by the time I get introduced as a project supervisor. The Model Shop Manager will have a briefing up to six weeks before the model starts. It's at this point that the specification of the model is decided. In that meeting the needs of the model are discussed. Models are often created to bid for a contract or for a competition and the specifications for these types of models are often prescribed at source. Scale is often decided on by considering what the model is intended to reveal to its audience. For example, a 1:500 model may not be big enough to represent the desired needs of the model, say if the purpose is to examine a glazing condition or understand the internal spaces, but a 1:100 model will adequately represent these needs. Alternatively a 1:100 model could be deemed to be too large if the model is exploring the building's relationship to its context or is a master plan of a town or city.

Any completion requirements given to Foster's (if the scope of a model is dependent on some key pieces of information, for example) are rationalized at this early meeting. We ask for a 3D CAD model and a realistic breakdown of the drawings that will be available when the job starts – reference images of past projects from our catalogues and any 2D visual information such as renders and computer models. This information allows us to take an overview on the time frame, team size and budget that will be allocated to the model. We will use a catalogue of previous Foster's models to allow us to find the style that best suits the project along with any input from the architects. If we are not fulfilling a specific competition brief this is where the decision of style is made.

What styles of models do Foster's use, and what are the benefits of developing a palette or style?
To keep within Foster's style we refer to the past catalogue of projects, which assists us to determine the type of model we will produce. At Foster's there are three main types of model that cover most possibilities: we use white models, blonde timber models or coloured-up models which use a colour palette created by Foster's. These three model types or palettes provide a safe set of criteria within which to explore the design. Everyone within the workshop knows the palette and can safely fill in the blanks when some variables are not in place. We know through experience what colours and finish work well with a blonde timber model, or in simplistic terms what colour grey spray finish to a building works with the green we will use for grass. We understand what the ben-

efits and limitations of the materials are, because these styles have been honed over time. Within the model shop there is an understanding of what to do, which allows cross-over within teams and shared vision of what the model will look like.

The other important factor beyond this system offering the model makers a controlled set of variables is that the palette allows continuity for the architects. The models will often go before internal design review panels; having a set, clear palette allows them to focus purely on the design.

Does the practice size and its demands affect the workshop environment?
As the practice grew, so the model shop has grown. With the size of the workshop increasing, this also means that there is capability for larger and more extravagant models. To fulfil these larger projects we maximize the capacity of our workshop. We tend to go as big as the workshop and staffing numbers allow, and so over time, the workshop and staff numbers have increased with the size and demands of the models.

Another reason for building large models is the demands of International projects, especially in the Middle East and China, where the fashion for very large models has developed due to models needing to show vast areas and buildings in context where whole new districts and sometimes entire cities are included in developments.

Models can take hours of work and the deadline nature of the project can sometimes mean it is necessary for staff to undertake long working hours to produce models. In the past, day and night shifts have been discussed to get the size and scope of models completed within specific time frames.

Looking at your career, have there been changes in architecture which have changed the type of model, the technology used in production and the expectations of the architects?
When I started in model making, the majority of technology available to us was already set up. CAD was already in place; so was CNC and laser cutters – we have perhaps become more adept at using these machines but the general way of working hasn't changed. How the architects use CAD has altered how we receive drawings and generally makes for better working practice. The introduction of 3D CAD has allowed them to build the model on screen and then pull it apart to give us 2D drawings of floor slabs and face elevations. This has made for a far smoother transition of information for the models. Elevations work better with floors and there is a greater understanding of what the building is likely to look like. This also lends itself to an appreciation of what is needed from a computer model to produce a 3D print of a building, component roof or organic shape.

The integration of 3D printing has and will continue to be the biggest changing factor in how we design and build architectural models; we have 3D printing departments with dedicated staff and computer modellers. Because of the advancements in design, complicated shapes have become easier to manipulate and of course building practices are always advancing to allow for greater imaginings. 3D printing has made it possible to accurately and quickly deal with the challenges that these design leaps have made to producing a model. This obviously has led to greater expectations from architects and their clients in what is achievable in the time frame of a model build. Due to all of these advancements, it is possible to produce bigger, more complicated models now in less time than we did ten years ago.

What do you see for the future in architectural model making?
There is a demand to see buildings in 3D before they are built. I think this will always be important to how people are able to visualize something that isn't there yet. Until the way we perceive a 2D drawing and how we interface with a computer model on screen changes, then the need for 'physical models' will always be there.

3D printing is a 'new technology' influencing model making and it will continue to take a larger, more integrated role in the industry. This development, I believe, will reduce the number of model makers needed to 'finish' a model. As 3D printing progresses the crispness and detail achievable will eventually allow for a more complete article being printed, as opposed to only components being produced and hand finished at the moment. Ultimately it will become cheaper and quicker to 3D print the bare bones of, say, a tower (floors and walls) already stacked, than a person manufacturing them. I believe, though, that dealing with different materiality, colour and finishes will remain within the model makers' domain and the possibilities of an integrated approach with 3D printing are far-reaching if properly thought out. It is, after all, another tool.

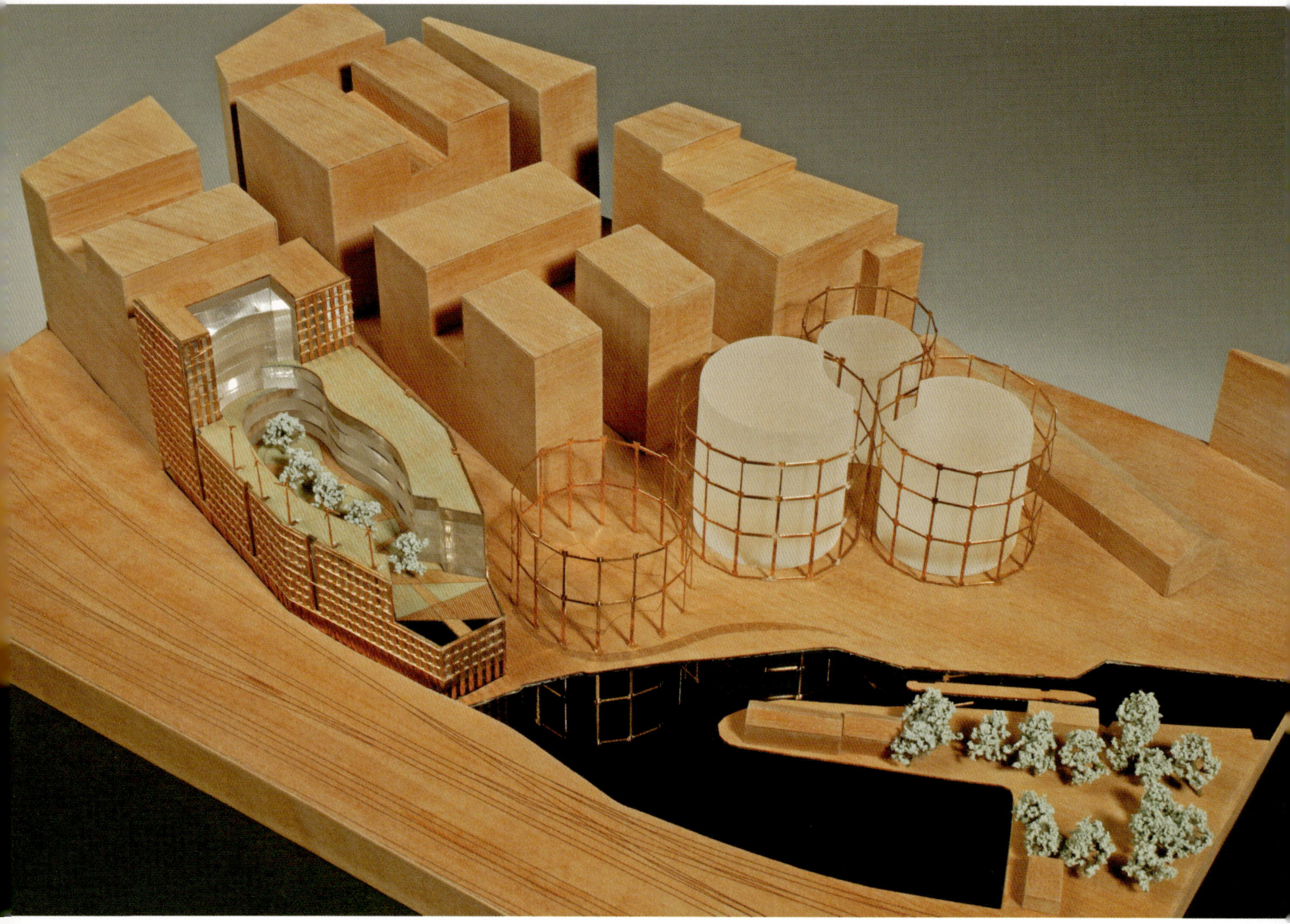

CHAPTER 5

UNDERSTANDING BASES

The aim of this chapter is to develop an understanding of the importance of the base board: how the composition and style of a base enhances the quality of the building scheme. Base boards back up the detail and development of your site through the correct management of the landscape and ground works. The base can do more for a model than just be the plinth for a new design; if developed correctly, it will give context and develop a greater understanding of the design while allowing the design to be viewed in its best possible light – after all, the design of a building is often all about how it is seen in relation to the world around it. For a model the base board is the world within which a building will exist.

Understanding the extent of your model: context, information and scale

The extent of the model needs to be thought out at the beginning of any job, and the nature of the base board will usually be affected by numerous factors. What are the important details that the base can add to your scheme or building? This will usually take the form of landmark buildings which can be used to put your building in context. There may be features that help to explain the purpose of your building, such as location close to a river or the sea. If this can be shown on a base then the design can be explained by this context, or the desirability of the site expressed. The use of water, cliff edge, hill or slope can sometimes just help with the composition of the model. If the base allows the inclusion of such features then dynamism can be added to the overall appeal of the model. It is usual practice to situate the building itself in the centre of the base, using the base and context buildings to frame the new building or development. Using this approach, and deciding the relevant context and landmarks that need to be represented, then a rough estimate of the size of the base can be worked out.

Using reference material

Gather as much information as possible when deciding the scope of the model's base board. Use resources such as Ordnance Survey maps to gather a sense of the contouring of the site; websites with satellite photography are also useful for identifying important buildings. This will help to show you the natural extent of your base.

The distance that these variables are from your building can help to decide the scale of the model. If the model's purpose is massing, then the key surrounding buildings are an important aspect of the model; therefore, building the model at a smaller scale to envelop the entire key outlying buildings and landmarks is worthwhile.

There will always be a certain amount of compromise when working out the scale to include these important features while still having a large enough scale to detail the building. If you have the responsibility of deciding the base extent then it is always worth discussing the decision you have made with

LEFT: **Swiss mountain pear, acrylic and metal-etched model, scale 1:750.**

■ UNDERSTANDING BASES

colleagues, or getting the extent signed off by your client. It is often the case that later on someone will question why the model is oriented this way or that, or why a particular building has not been included. It will be expensive to extend the base and add more offsite buildings later, especially if you're working for a fixed price, so make considered decisions. As a general rule, people tend to react to what is in front of them, as opposed to visualizing the outcome at the start. Checking these things early on will save hard work later.

SETTING THE DATUM

To build any base the ground levels need to be worked out right at the start, usually in metres above sea level. (Without an understanding of these levels the building could, in an existential sense, be floating anywhere in space!) In order to work out these ground levels accurately, you need to set a datum, from which everything else is built. In its simplest terms, a datum provides a base reference for measuring locations on the earth's surface.

Usually when working out a datum you will need to look for the lowest ground measurement. Remember to look at the lowest levels that can be found across the extents of your base, then also look at the lowest level that your building will go down to – you might have basement or sub-basement levels that need to be modelled. Once the lowest level is found it is a good idea to go a few metres below this. This figure is the datum for your model.

The CAD drawing will help to visualize the following explanation. Let us say that the model's scale is 1:200 with a basement and shows some context of the surrounding area. The lowest spot on the sloping site is 14 metres above sea level; the basement ground level is 12 metres above sea level. The lowest point is therefore 12 metres above sea level, and this would be the datum level.

The model of your building will need to include the ground floor as part of it, so it is essential that this has something to sit on. Taking the datum down to 10 metres above sea level will give you a tolerance (or 'wiggle room') if all the calculations aren't exactly correct or you do need to make alterations to the design. This is the model datum from which the following calculations can be worked out. The building can, when fitted to the model, have support blocks placed between the base board and the underneath of the building to bridge the tolerance gap to allow it to sit at the right height. There is nothing worse than the building sitting at the incorrect height; it is often a sign that a model has been poorly executed (however beautifully made) when the ground butts up to the building and is running through the middle of a door.

Calculation: the lowest land height was 14 metres. 1 metre at 1:200 scale is 5mm. The datum level (10 metres) can be taken from 14 metres, i.e. 4 metres (at scale, 20mm). From a flat datum point across the base board the first ground level can be put in place, adjusted for material thickness.

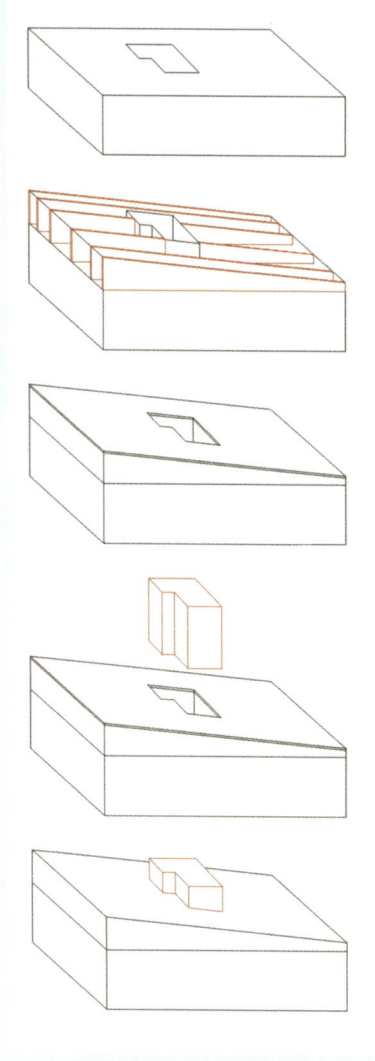

A CAD diagram explaining the key steps for the production of a smooth contour base.

94

UNDERSTANDING BASES

Styles of base

Two main styles of base can be constructed, according to the style of the building that you are producing and your chosen materials.

Smooth contours

This type of model can be built out of any material you wish: timber veneers, styrene and acrylic sprayed sheet are the most common. The basic system works by producing struts or ribs that are shaped to height (as explained in 'Setting the datum' above). The drawing shows how this is achieved with different spot heights on the drawing being transferred to the ribs; these heights are joined together to create the different slopes and land falls across the base. Remember when working out the calulations for these heights to subtract any material thickness that will be stuck on top of the ribs to form a skin.

If working to a large enough scale this first skin will act as road, and subsequent pavement pads are applied onto this, so giving the landscaping and layouts of the base. The same principle carries if the roads and pavements are engraved onto one sheet (e.g. acrylic or timber veneer).

Sometimes, if you are working with a sketch model, a base print can be coloured up and applied using display mount or double-sided tape. The print quickly allows for detailing of pavements and printed textures of grass and landscaping.

Contour stack

This type of base relies on using the contours from Ordnance Survey maps and layering these on top of each other to create a three-dimensional interpretation of the land masses. Although stylized, these can make for some of the most dynamic and interesting interpretations of the landscape of your base. A range of sprayed and timber finishes can be seen in the photographs. A description of the most appropriate way to achieve this is given below.

Contour step model, scale 1:500, constructed using black back sprayed acrylic to represent water and Swiss mountain pear veneers to create the contours.

Large, timber, smooth contour base in production.

Contour step model, scale 1:750, in sprayed and clear acrylic. (Photo: Andrew Putler)

■ UNDERSTANDING BASES

How to produce a contour model

This base-making exercise works on the principle that the site is flat but has rises that are man-made: retaining walls and other hard ground works, such as the railway bridge. In many cases a model will demand some level of contouring; the illustration shows how best to break down a drawing to produce a contour step model.

You can see that the original drawing has been copied to give you three identical drawings. Starting at either the highest contour or the lowest (this is important for the process to work) select every fourth contour line as a colour (in this case, green) on the first drawing. On the second drawing select the second contour line and every fourth line, and designate the line as blue; repeat this process on the third drawing, designating the third line as yellow. You should now, over the three drawings have all of the lines designated with a colour. These will be your cut lines. All three of these drawings will be laser cut and the component contours from the three drawings will allow you to stack the contours on top of each other, producing a three-dimensional contour stack model from just three base-sized laser-cut pieces of material. This process saves large quantities of material and because all of the drawings are from the same master, they will be guaranteed to fit. If during the selection process you select the first green line on drawing A then the corresponding contour line on drawing B should be coded red as a scribe or engrave line; likewise if choosing a blue line on drawing B then the corresponding line on drawing C should be set to red as an engrave line. This means that when you come to stack the contours there is an engrave line to stick the above contour onto. Although this method sounds complicated, it will guarantee accuracy later on.

In this making exercise we will look at the layers that are required to produce the levels of a base board, and going on to complete the model in a conceptual clear acrylic stacking of existing buildings and scheme buildings. Finally the trees will be planted to finish the model.

Materials

The materials used in the base are 1mm to 2mm grey card. The model is at 1:1000 scale. The material thicknesses are essential to make an accurate model: at 1:1000 scale 1 metre is equivalent to 1mm. The card thickness allows us to build height through ground layers; using the material thickness to achieve this is a simple way to gain the desired ground heights. For this model build, a simplified layering will get us the relevant ground layers we need.

The CAD drawing provided at scale to the model is shown here. These base layers and acrylic buildings were drawn and then laser-cut but if you want to build this model then they

Contour step model, scale 1:500. Almost complete, the use of the contouring style can now be seen in reference to the scheme buildings.

Contour step model, scale 1:500, in sprayed and clear acrylic. The model is built using 1m steps, so creating 2mm steps on the model – a bold approach.

UNDERSTANDING BASES

Contour CAD drawing: a guide to 'top hatting' a model, a cost-effective technique in terms of time and materials.

■ UNDERSTANDING BASES

CAD drawing: what can be expected from a contour drawing?

can be cut out of the book and spray mounted onto card, styrene or the appropriate material and be cut out with a scalpel; alternatively you can use the drawing (all important dimensions are shown as a guide). Draw these components up and get them laser-cut out of any material of your choice.

Equipment

Pencil
Cutting mat
Steel rule
Steel square, 3 inch and 6 inch
123 blocks
Small snips
Tweezers
Scalpel plus 10A blades
Glue: chloroform (depending on materials; see page 26)
Chloroform dispenser
Sable brush
Contact adhesive
Glue nozzles
12mm model trees (these can be bought from all good model suppliers)

If you have decided to use the provided drawing as a template to cut out the components yourself, then spray mount, circle cutter and lighter fluid are also required. Spray mount the paper copy of the components to your material sheet. (Acrylic probably isn't the best material to use if producing the model by hand as it is time-consuming and difficult to produce due to the properties of the material. I would build the model out of layered card, styrene or veneer.) The photographs show the model being built in clear acrylic for aesthetic reasons and to demonstrate the conceptual nature of the model design. It has been laser-cut.

1. As stated throughout these building exercises it is important to lay out all of your components in front of you; this will limit confusion and the amount of error in the process of building.
2. Using contact adhesive, apply swirls of glue across the full extent and the edges of the gluing surface. As in previous exercises, place this onto the layer that you are gluing to. Remove and you should be left with a mirror

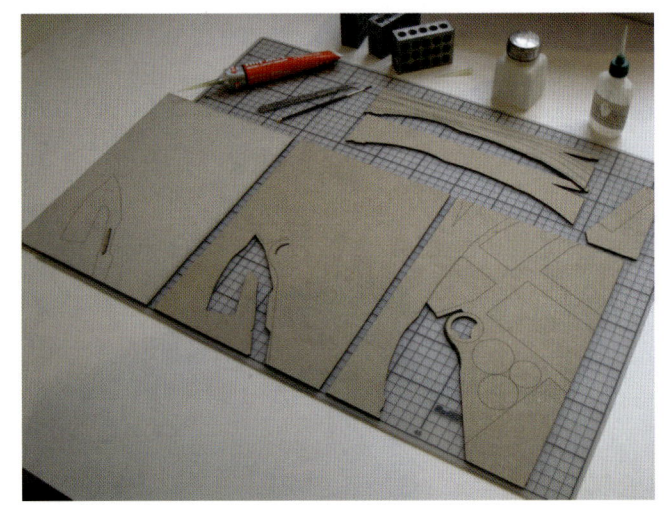

Contour model: Figure 1.

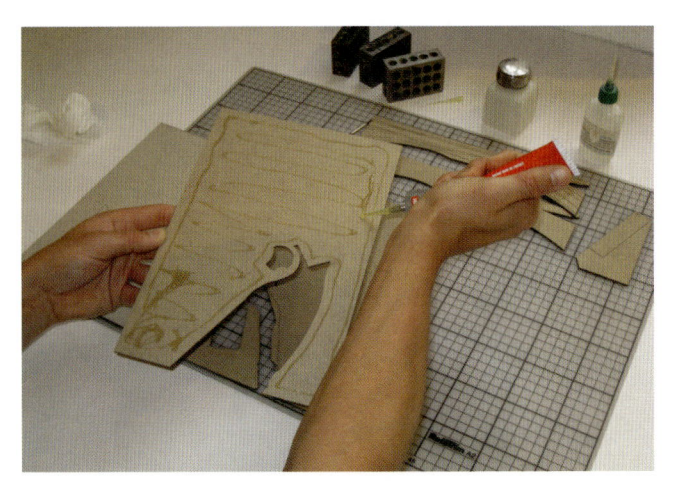

Contour model: Figure 2.

UNDERSTANDING BASES

■ UNDERSTANDING BASES

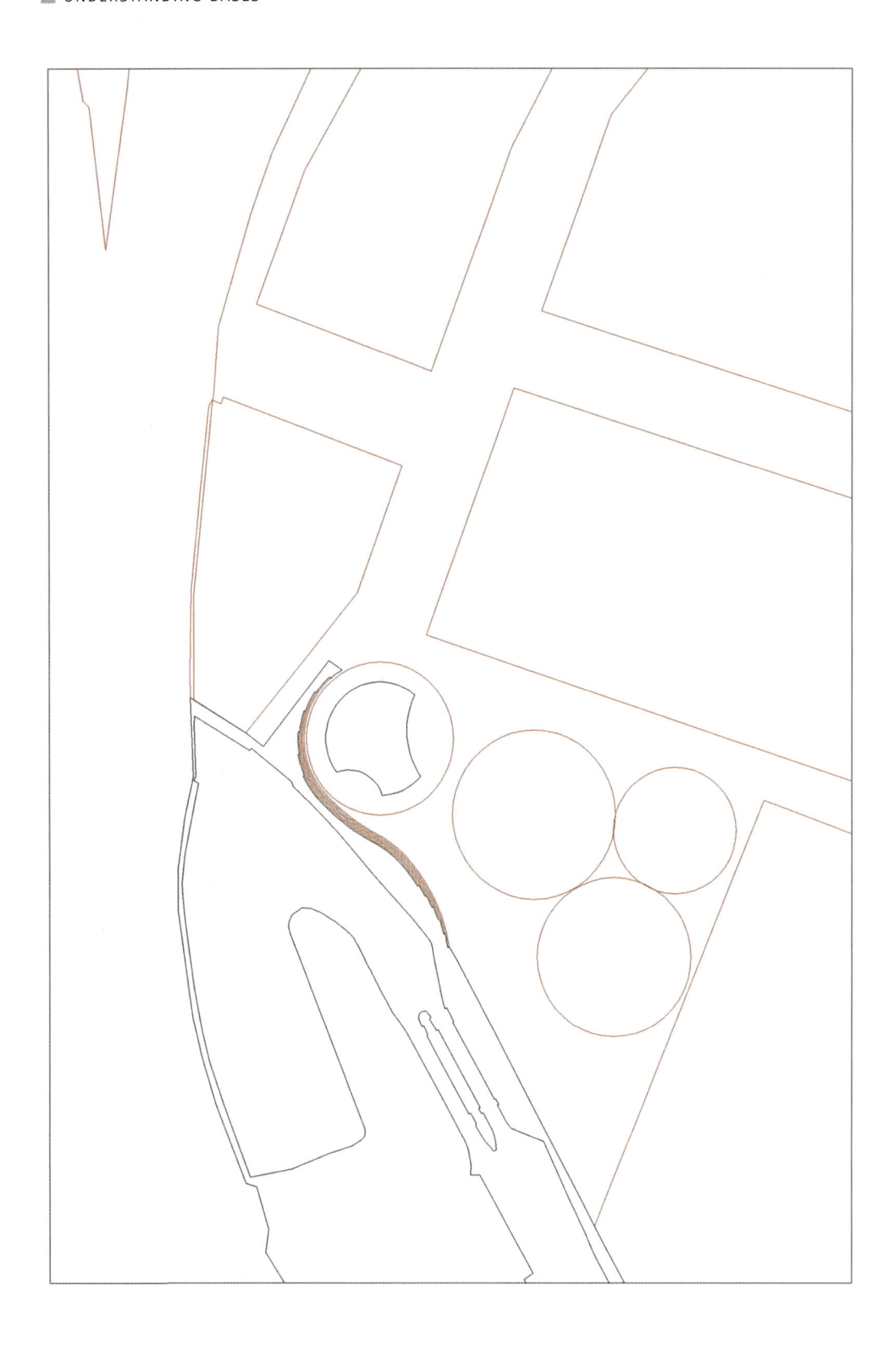

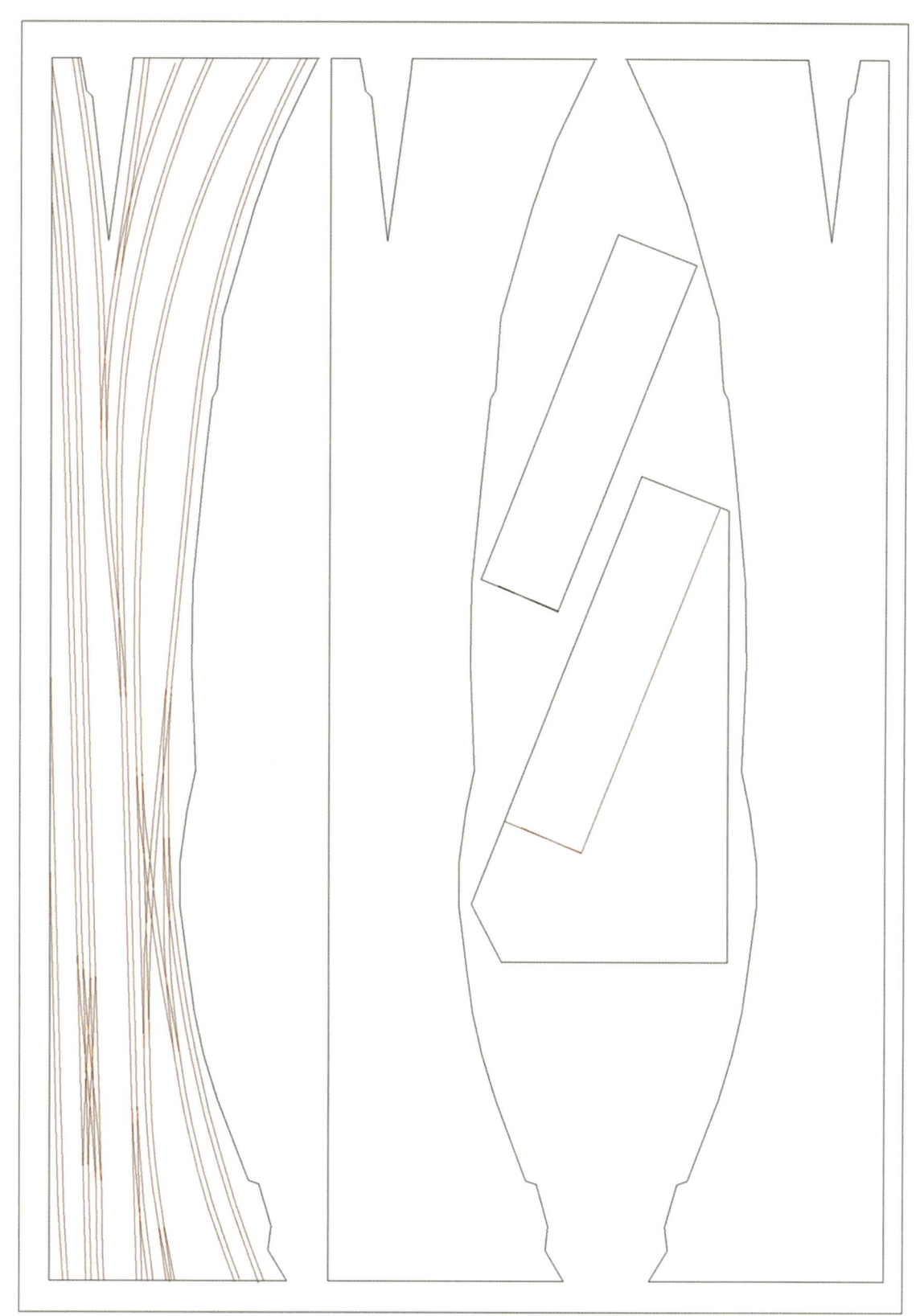

UNDERSTANDING BASES

The CAD drawings at scale to help in the production of the contour model exercise.

■ UNDERSTANDING BASES

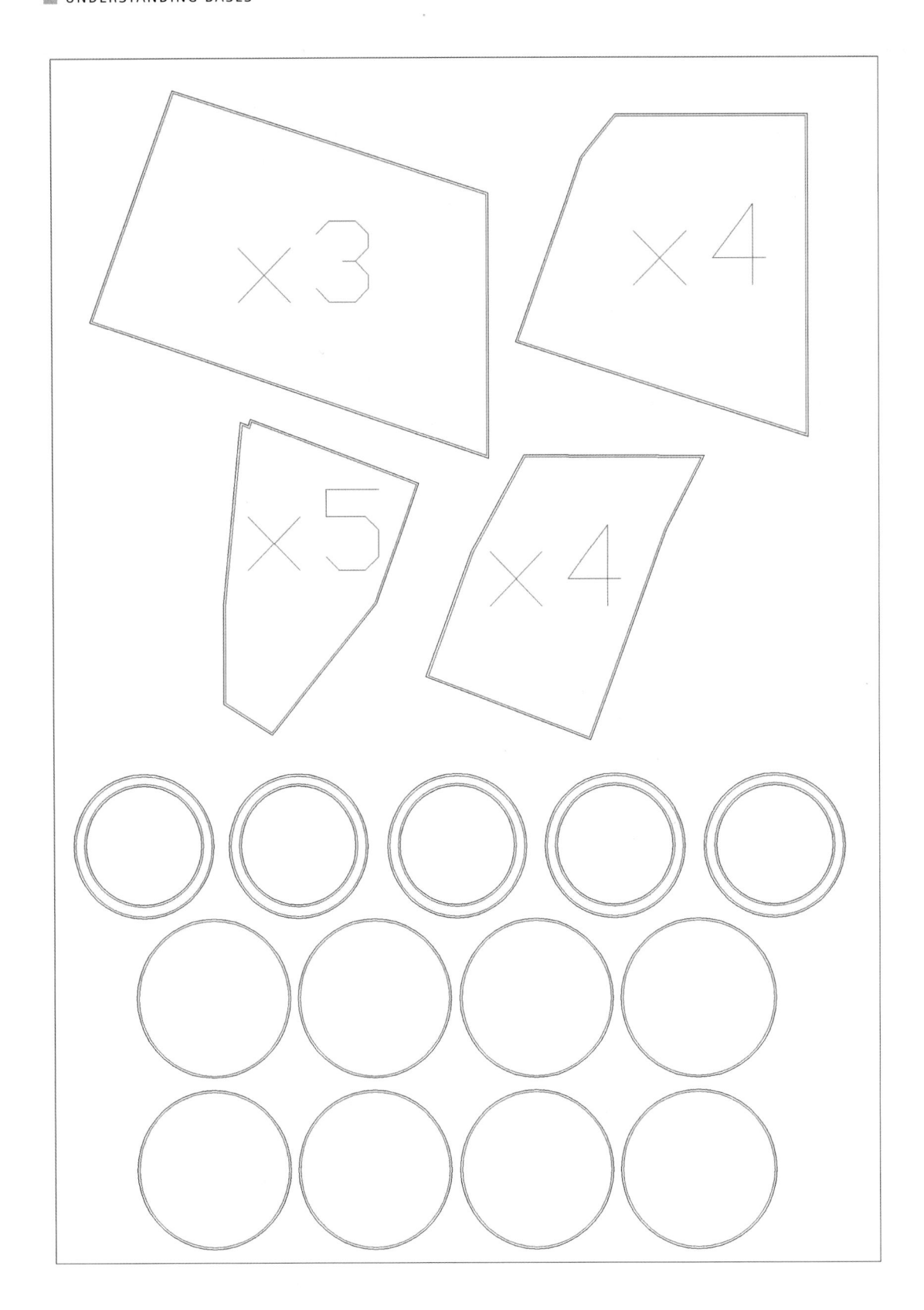

UNDERSTANDING BASES

glue residue on the other surface to be glued. Apply a liberal amount of glue to this surface and leave to tack off.

3. Using your 123 blocks as square edges to glue against, place the one layer (glue up) with at least two sides against the 123 blocks. Press down the two layers using the blocks as a guide and give time to allow the glue to dry.

4. While these two layers are drying, arrange your water layer using 123 blocks on at least two sides so when the ground layers are glued onto them you get a straight square edge on the sides of your base board. (You can use a variety of material for the water: clear acrylic can be back sprayed with a variety of colours, from realistic blue or conceptualized blues through to black or white depending on the type of model. Here I have used a pale grey card to keep with the language of the model.)

5. The two layers of ground that you have already stuck together should by now have dried. Glue should now be applied to the bottom of this, as described above. The same process of applying glue to the master level should also be followed.

6. Using your 123 blocks as a guide, the ground layers can be stuck down to the water level.

7. Use the 123 blocks now as weights to keep the layers in place while the glue dries.

8. In the meantime the smaller ground levels, in this case the railway raised level, can be stuck together using the same process as before. This way of working – organizing the process in which you glue things together

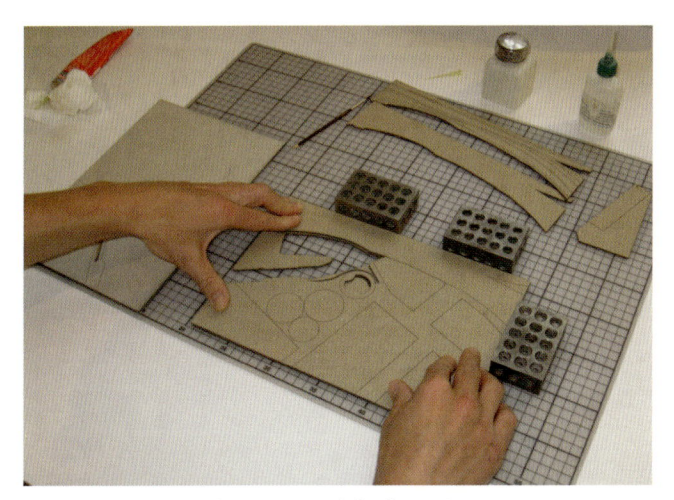

Contour model: Figure 3.

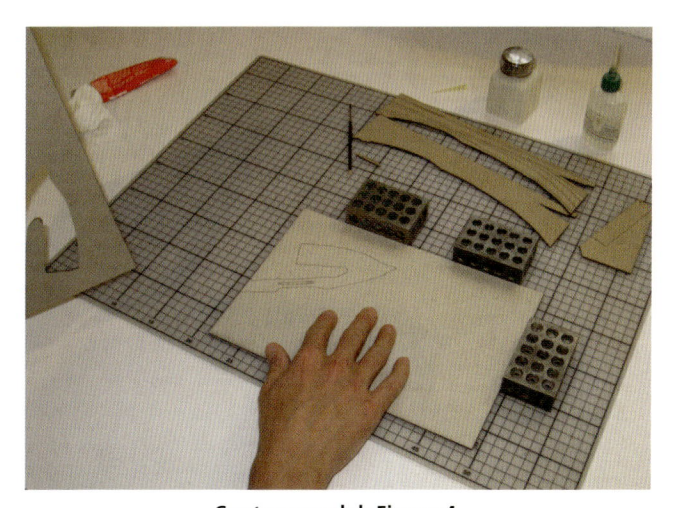

Contour model: Figure 4.

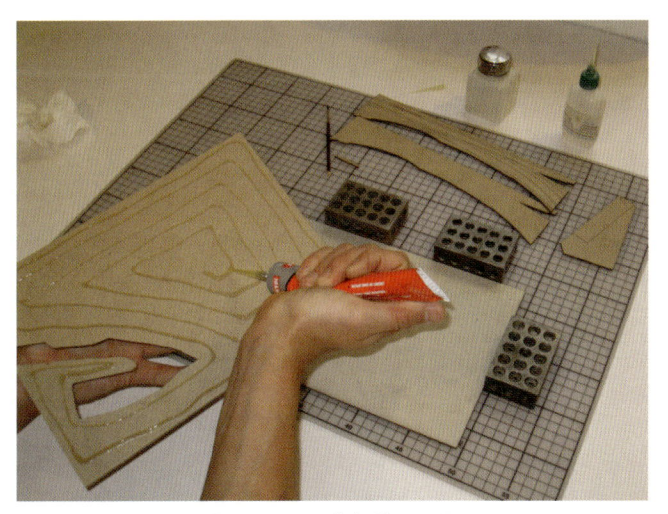

Contour model: Figure 5.

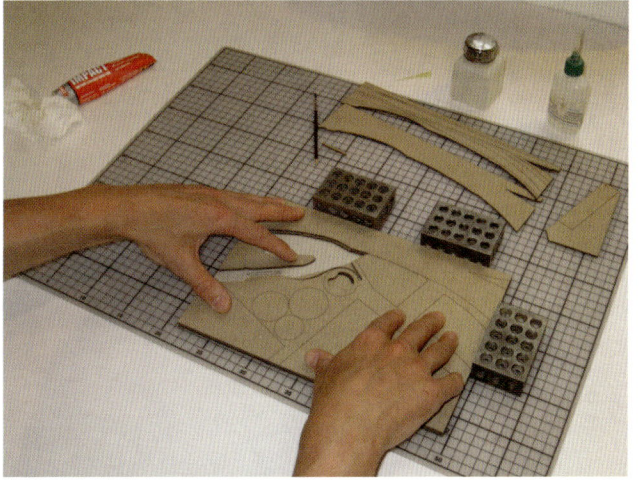

Contour model: Figure 6.

103

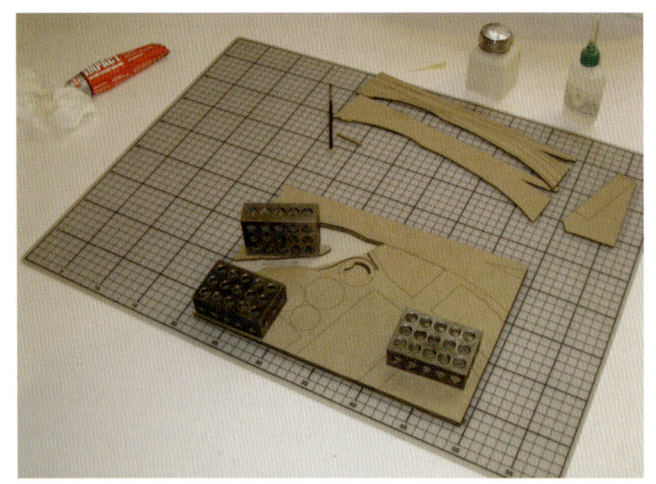

■ UNDERSTANDING BASES

Contour model: Figure 7.

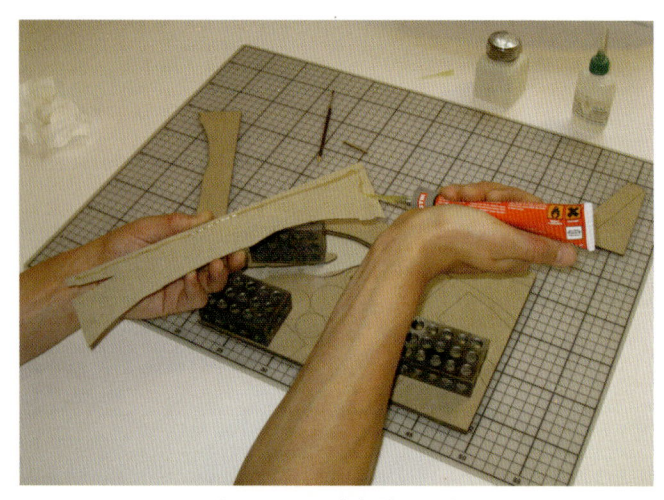

Contour model: Figure 8.

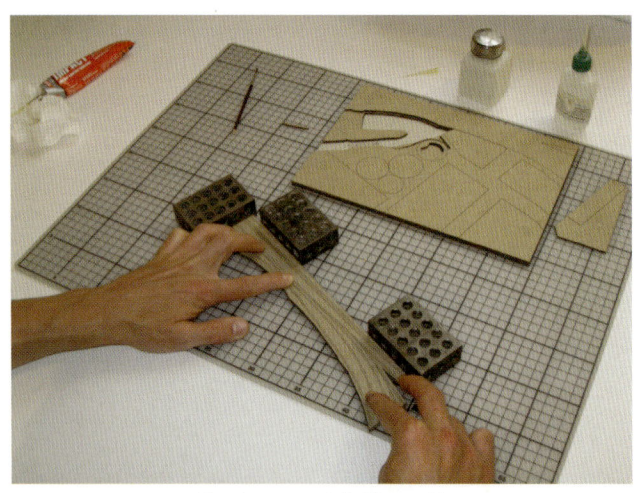

Contour model: Figure 9.

Contour model: Figure 10.

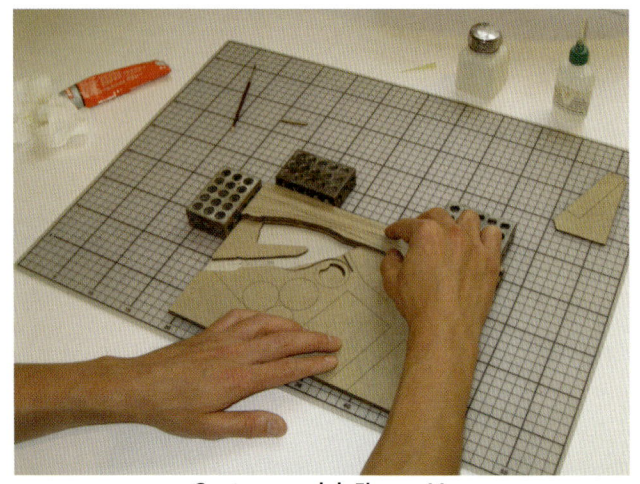

Contour model: Figure 11.

Contour model: Figure 12.

104

UNDERSTANDING BASES

to give adequate drying time to all your components – will eventually become second nature but is worth thinking about at the beginning of your build to achieve as much as possible during the build time. Also, trying to stick together component pieces that haven't dried properly yet will cause problems as the components can move, come apart and separate, leaving you in quite a mess. Remember that a large portion of model making is about accuracy, cleanness of finish and hitting your deadline. Thinking about what seem like small considerations such as this are crucial to the overall build time and quality of the model.

9. Once the glue has dried it is time to attach the railway bridge layer. Again using circular glue motions, repeat the technique of applying the glue firstly to the underneath of the bridge component and then transferring the glue to the main base.
10. Using the 123 blocks as a straight edge guide, stick down the bridge once the glue has become tacky.
11. Using the blocks to weight down the bridge as it dries, the individual islands of the mall can be glued down.
12. Repeat this gluing process for the last raised land mass.
13. The entire base layers should now be glued together, giving you the completed land masses. The thicknesses of the layers have combined to give you the accurate change in levels that is important to the outcome. This model has shown the ground level change, from water level, over two main land levels and a raised railway line, to a built-up land mass.
14. Putting the base aside, it is time to start the building stacks. These have been created out of 3mm acrylic, giving a floor-to-ceiling height (at 1:1000 scale) of three metres. Arrange the 123 blocks against two sides of the ground-floor slab. This will give you straight edges to stack the building against. Remember to have a dry run and arrange the floor slabs in the order that they are going to be layered. This is a simple shape to build, but for more complicated stacks it is worth getting them in the correct order because the shape and size can change as you move up through the floor levels. This will save you time and energy later on keeping your work clean and precise.
15. The slabs should, as the CAD drawing shows, have an engrave line approximately 1mm inside the cut edge all the way around. This is essential to produce a good gluing surface. After cleaning all of the acrylic components with lighter fluid, place the first floor on

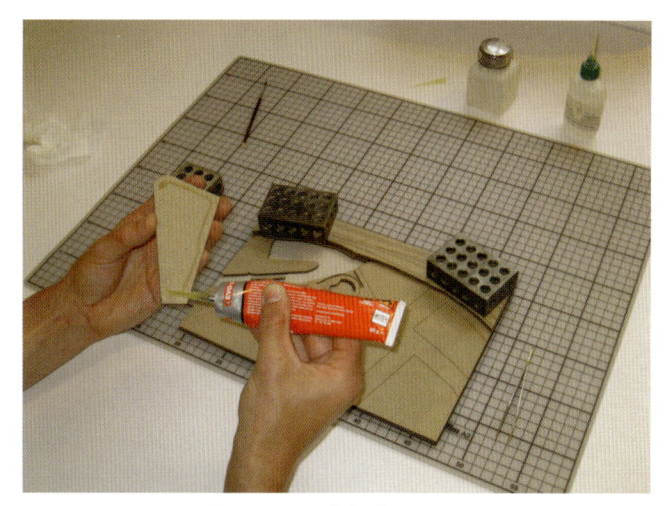

Contour model: Figure 13.

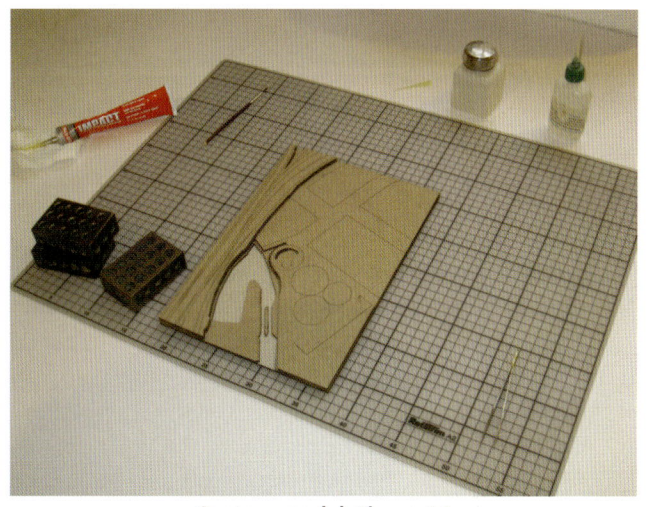

Contour model: Figure 14.

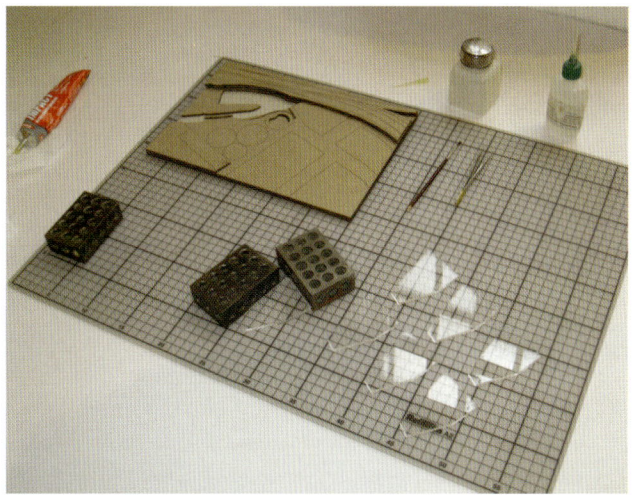

Contour model: Figure 15.

105

■ UNDERSTANDING BASES

top of the ground floor, get some chloroform onto your brush (removing any excess on the bowl of the dispenser) and touch the brush against the seam between the two floors. This is where the engrave line has its importance: it will stop the glue travelling past it to the centre of the slab. If done correctly the glue should travel around the edge of the slab between the engrave line and the building edge, thus providing a clean and almost invisible glue line that will hold the block together.

16. You might need to move one of the 123 blocks to get access to glue the other sides. This can be done with simple stacks, but with more complicated shapes (where you might need to double-side the blocks down) it might be worth waiting until the end – after the stack is built up and glued on the sides that could be reached.

17. Repeat this process of gluing for the remainder of the floors, stacking them up. Remember that there is no need to have the engrave line on the top floor as there is nothing to stick on top of it, and an engrave line would give an untidy finish to the model. Always check each floor as you assemble the slabs to make sure they are clean and smudge-free; this will make all the difference to the finished outcome.

18. Once the glue has dried a little, it is now worth moving the building away from the blocks to get access to the other sides and to apply glue around the block with a bit more confidence. Be careful, because this is where you could make a disastrous mistake at the last moment, don't become too confident and flood the model with glue. If in doubt and the model has sufficient glue to keep the slabs together then leave well alone.

19. The next stack can now be attempted. These buildings are the gas tower stacks; due to their slightly more complex nature (they have no flat sides) it is worth using the 123 blocks to create a 90° corner against which to build the circular stack.

20. With a little more confidence – having already produced one building – it may be worth stacking the components up before applying any glue. You may find it easier to keep the stack straight this way, but there is no hard and fast rule: the best solution is usually the one that works for you.

21. Having repeated the stacking and gluing process for all of the buildings you should have developed a little more confidence and the process that you have learned can be replicated for any stack model. The material thickness

Contour model: Figure 16.

Contour model: Figure 17.

Contour model: Figure 18.

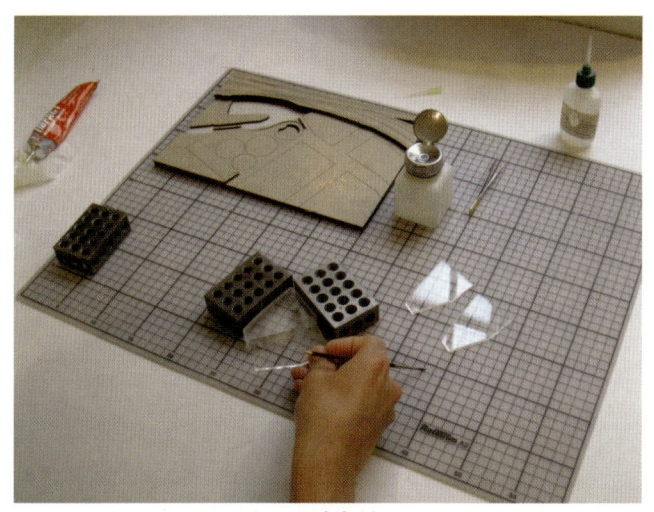

UNDERSTANDING BASES

Contour model: Figure 19.

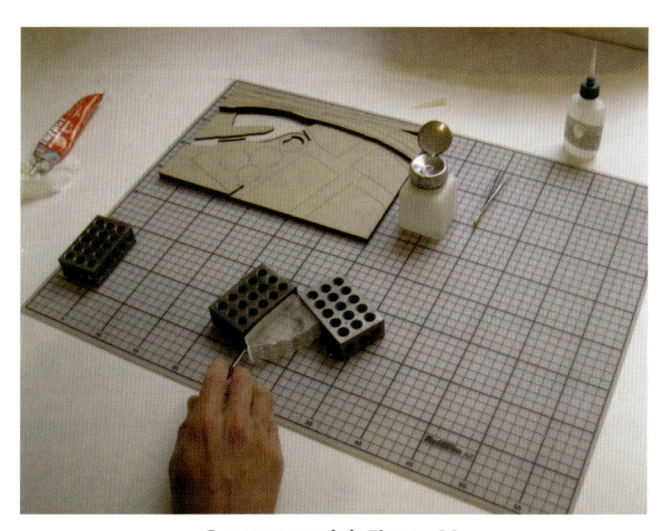

Contour model: Figure 20.

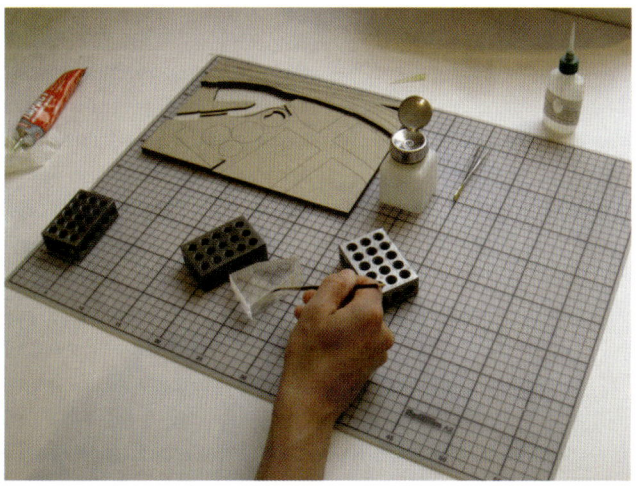

Contour model: Figure 21.

might change for different scales and the material and complexity of your shape might change, depending on the building that you are representing, but the core principles will remain the same for any floor slab stack. The slabs can now be glued down to the base. As stated previously, there are various ways in which to glue down clear slabs to a base: if the model has a sprayed finish

RECTIFYING MISTAKES WITH ACRYLIC

It isn't worth pulling apart the stack if you do get some glue past the engrave line. Depending on how much glue there is in the centre you may have to start again or more likely just live with it. Trying to pull the slabs apart now will leave a real mess and you won't be able to clean the acrylic to remove the glue.

Chloroform and dichloromethane are also known as 'acrylic weld' and the gluing process works by essentially melting the acrylic together to create a bond. Pulling the slabs apart will leave you with two melted surfaces that are ruined. If you really have to use these components, and you need to pull the slabs apart for other reasons than the glue travelling beyond the engrave line, then you will need to give the slabs time to finish curing (for a while the acrylic will still be soft from the effects of the chloroform). Once the acrylic has gone back to its hardened state you can sand the two disfigured sides, taking the grit of the paper down to at least 600 grit, and then polish them on a buffer if you have one. They will never look perfect but if the slab is low down in the stack then it may not be noticeable once the stack is completed.

It is worth noting that this process of sanding then polishing is the same process to use if you find a scratch on your acrylic; if you can, cut the slab, but if you really need to use it then with a bit of work you can remove the scratch. As stated above it won't ever look perfect again but if used within the stack it will be more than passable, and it will probably only be you who can see the blemish.

UNDERSTANDING BASES

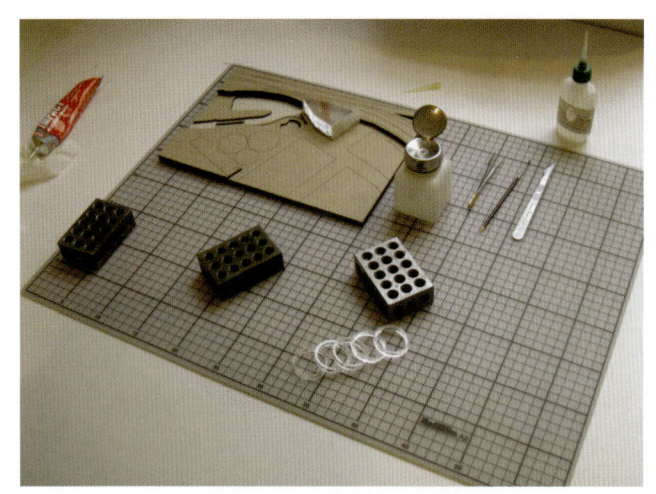

Contour model: Figure 22.

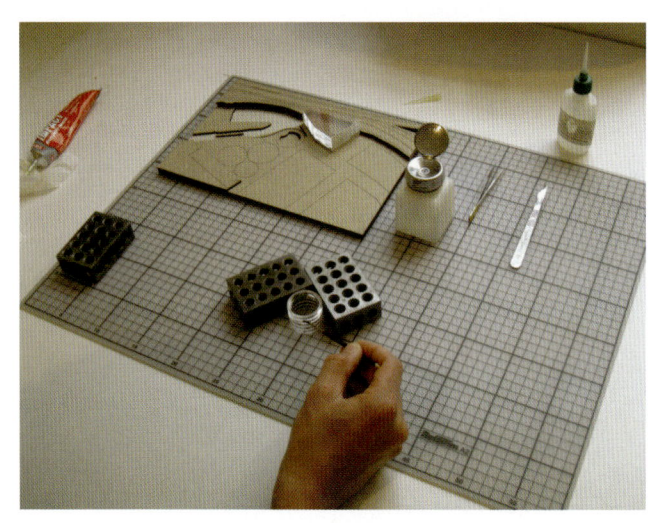

Contour model: Figure 23.

Figure 24.

then the best way to stick the buildings down cleanly is to spray the bottoms of the buildings the same colour as the base and use double-sided tape; or if the building's sprayed bottoms are then covered in masking or parcel tape, glue can be used to stick the buildings down. If using glue it is always best to cover the sprayed surface of the building bottom in tape, as glue will often react with the paint and the glue marks will come through – thus negating the point of spraying them. Where possible, strong double-sided tape is recommended. In this case, where the base surface is cardboard, then although colour-matching a neutral colour will work for spraying the building bottoms, the buildings can be glued down using strips of double-sided tape to the edges of the bottom slab. For buildings this size, two strips should be enough to hold the buildings in place against most reasonable knocks and bumps. If the building is bigger – or more importantly, heavier – then more strips around the edges of the slab will be needed or the bottoms will need to be sprayed too, to guarantee against movement once the model is completed. The base has the outline of the buildings' positions scribed/engraved on, so it should not be hard to situate the buildings correctly. A square is often useful, placed along one of these engraved lines, to be sure of sticking down in the correct place. If the base hasn't been engraved with the building positions, then a printed plan at the same scale can be placed over the base board and the corners of the building 'scalpeled' through to find the correct placement.

22. Trees usually come on a stringer of metal and need to be snipped off with wire cutters or sharp scissors. Pre-made trees can be bought at most good model shops in a variety of colours and sizes. They can be sprayed to adjust colour, or be tweaked and 'squidged' to create different shapes for types or species of trees. Normally trees are bought as deciduous metal-etched trees (the type used in this model); another type known as string and wire trees can also be bought and resemble conifer trees. These are cheaper and look it: unless they are needed for a specific type of tree or model I would try to avoid using these. Etched trees are more expensive, but for the overall finish and quality of your model it is worth spending a little more on them. The base plan can be again used to mark the layout of the trees onto the model, then (if the base is made from robust materials) a Dremel or small rotary drill can be used to drill holes to

UNDERSTANDING BASES

Figure 25.

Figure 26.

Figure 27.

plant them on the base. Because this model is cardboard, then a compass point or a scalpel tip can be used to make a hole in the base.

23. With this type of tree, the trunk widens out and a spur of metal attaches it to the stringer; this spur should be cut at an angle a few millimetres below the trunk. The spur will hold the model tree in the base with a little emulsion glue and/or superglue. The trees can be straightened up after the glue has dried. With the planting of small trees, or to tweak the shape or adjust the straightness of the tree, tweezers are useful tool.

24. You have now completed an entire model, putting together all of the techniques from this and previous chapters. These techniques are the basic skills with which to produce all bases and models that you might need.

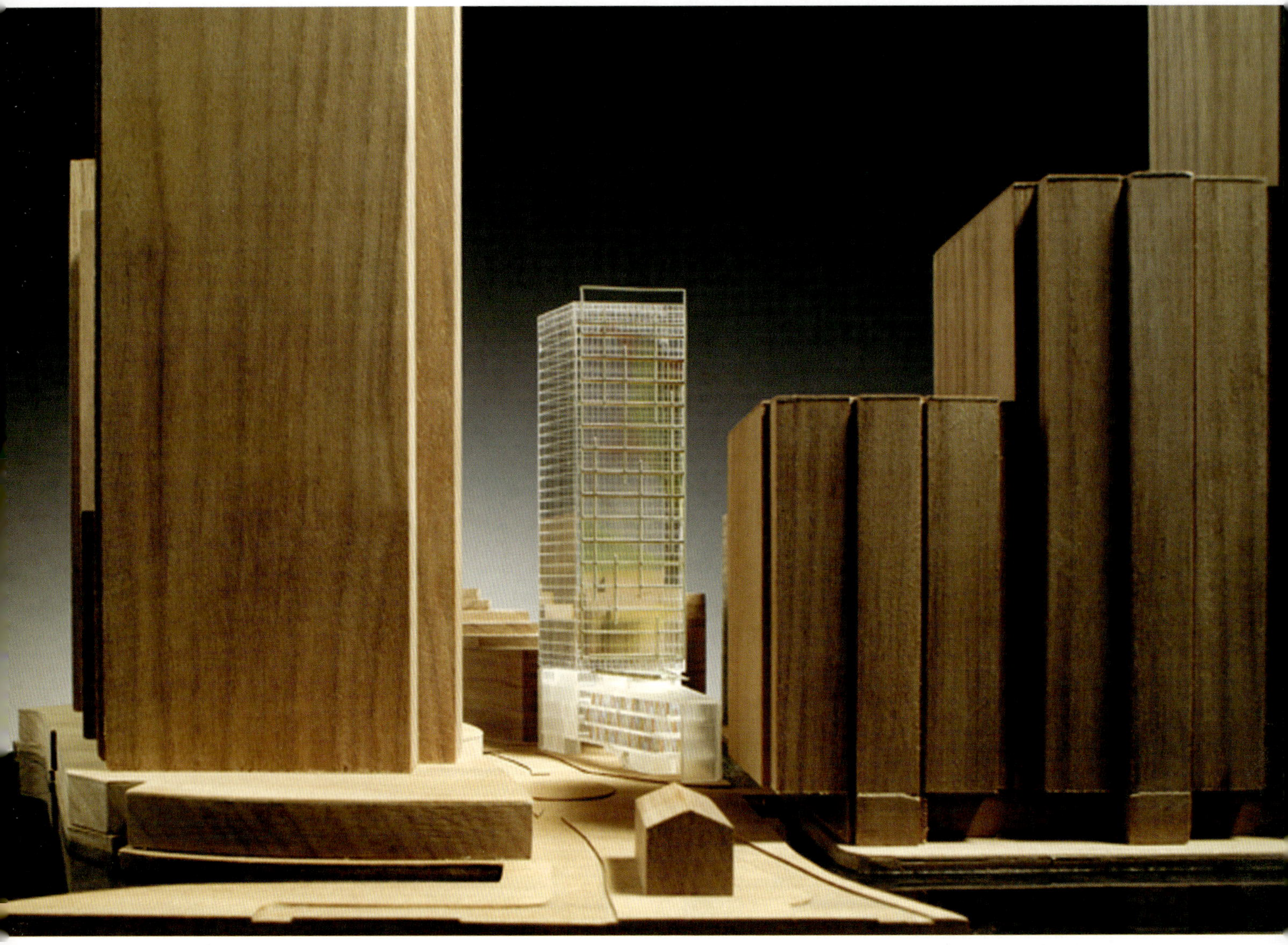

CHAPTER 6

MAKING OFFSITE BUILDINGS

Aerial photography and satellite mapping

In recent years an increase in resources has changed the research element of a model maker's job beyond recognition. With the onset of the Internet and free sites with satellite maps, aerial and street views, the investigation of contextual or 'offsite buildings' has become a quick and simplified experience. In the past, books with aerial photos and site visits were commonplace. Although it is still worth visiting a site to get a more rounded understanding of the environment that you are going to reconstruct, the modern experience of counting floors from Bing maps trumps the long process of squinting at aerial photography books or counting bricks on a survey.

Either way, the aim is to rationalize the architecture and estimate as accurately as possible the heights of the buildings that will surround the building you wish to model. Getting the heights and picking out the main architectural features of the context can make the difference between a successful, accurate model and a bland model that gives a false impression of its surroundings.

Online world satellite maps will offer either 'street view' (detail can be gleaned from eye level) or 'bird's-eye view' (for the roofscape and architectural features). These sites often offer a 'bird's-eye' icon, which allows you to see a three-quarter view of the buildings and enables you, with some accuracy, to work out the height of a building by counting the number of floors.

Floor counting is simple: the door is the ground floor and if there are three windows above that vertically, you can safely assume that it is a four-storey building. As a general rule, residential buildings are 3.5 metres floor to floor, and office buildings are 4.2 metres floor to floor. A four-storey residential building is therefore 14 metres high (4 × 3.5); likewise a commercial building would be 16.8 metres high. These measurements can be converted to scale to give you a reliable building height.

This can be elaborated on to get an even more accurate reading: for example, some ground floors on a commercial building might be higher – maybe 5 metres – and in an old cottage the likelihood is that the building is just 3 metres floor to floor. These are factors to bear in mind if the specific heights are key to the whole model (if, say, the purpose of the model is to convince planners that your building will not exceed the height of surrounding buildings).

Conducting surveys

If there is a need to conduct a full survey of the site then some of the more traditional ways in which heights are calculated may be used. To conduct a survey of the offsite buildings for modelling, with a camera and printed plan/map go to the survey area and photograph the buildings. So you know which building is which, mark an arrow on the map facing the direction of the camera shot and number the photo; this way you can move around the site photographing the buildings and specific architectural features that you may need to model. Remember that the photos don't need to be artistic composi-

LEFT: **Acrylic and etched metal scheme (scale 1:750) with walnut base and context. (Photo: Andrew Putler)**

MAKING OFFSITE BUILDINGS

tions but should frame whole buildings, landscapes, mounds and retaining walls. If some specific buildings need to be particularly accurate then measuring the size of a brick and its pointing can help; when back at your studio the number of brick courses can be counted from your photos and an accurate measurement of the height of the building can be calculated. Alternatively, especially for rendered or stone buildings, the use of a metre stick photographed against the side of a building will provide a height reference. The need for such detailed surveys is rare, but the practice of doing this a few times can help you to visualize building heights when using the Internet. (There was an incident many years ago when through inaccurate survey work an average of two storeys were lost on all of the contextual buildings for a development in central London, with the effect that the scheme building appeared two storeys too high. The impressive mass of the building overshadowed all of the offsite buildings around – it didn't go down well, completely negating the reason for the planning model in the first place.) Getting the height of offsite buildings correct may seem to have a low priority – the focus is on the scheme building itself – but it really can be the difference between a successful model and an outright disaster. All the component parts that make up an architectural model – scheme building, base board or offsite buildings – need to be thought through and made as accurately as possible.

Realizing your building's reference points

In many cases it is important to gather accurate information so that the reference points of your new building will marry with the surrounding buildings. If you are making the model for a client then an understanding of potential issues that the designer is facing will be invaluable when deciding on the important factors for the offsite build.

The model shown (Fig. 1) had very strict restrictions on the height of the building in relation to the existing buildings. One of the overwhelming reasons for making the model was to make sure that the design proposal would be accepted within the architecture of the existing High Street, so making sure that the offsite buildings were built to the correct height, presenting accurate elevation detail and considering roof levels were essential in portraying the relationship of the new building to its neighbours.

Figure 1: 1:100 Sprayed and clear acrylic model. The use of blind reveal windows is worth noting as a style for constructing detailed context.

Figure 2: 1:200 Maple timber and sprayed acrylic model.

It is essential to talk to the client and engage them in the relevance of offsite buildings. It is the model's job to communicate a design or function; the model quickly becomes redundant if the communication with your client doesn't delve into the important issues of the model that you are producing. Similarly, this same conversation should be considered if you are producing the model for your own design.

The best way to decide on the level of detail that you wish to put into a model's contextual buildings is to look at a range of models that have varying detail across lots of styles. By now you will have already decided on the scale and scope of your

MAKING OFFSITE BUILDINGS

Figure 3: a view down the street. The detail of the context buildings grounds the scheme in its environment.

Figure 4: 1:100 timber and acrylic model. The louvres have been metal etched and sprayed timber colour – a useful construction method when the components are too fine to build them out of timber. (Photo: Andrew Putler)

Figure 5: 1:150 building using sprayed acrylic and stainless-steel metal etchings. The context buildings are modelled with blind reveal detail and finished in a cool grey spray. (Photo: Andrew Putler)

■ MAKING OFFSITE BUILDINGS

Figure 7: 1:500 landscape model using various spray finishes to achieve the garden colours and tree variation. The context buildings have been constructed in acrylic slab and frosted so the main focus of the model remains the landscaped gardens. (Photo: Andrew Putler)

model and base to best represent your scheme building. Most offsite buildings will only need to tell the story that you wish to present – therefore further detail may be unnecessary apart from the main architectural features and roofscapes. The use of elevations to create a blind reveal effect to conjoining and facing buildings may be worth considering, especially if the new building's interaction is essential to the design or if the model is for planning (in which case elevating these buildings might reduce concerns).

Figure 2 is a 1:200 timber and white sprayed model where the scheme buildings (modelled in timber) faced out in all directions. The decision to elevate all offsite buildings was made to show clearly the environment in which the building was to be situated; concerns by residents in the surrounding houses and buildings needed to be allayed, and the best way to do this was to produce a detailed and accurate model, including parapets, chimneys and dormer windows. We can see from Figure 3 that the blind reveal detailing of doors and windows allows the observer to get down to street level and get a real sense of the impact of the new buildings on the street.

It is often the case that the main reason for a model is to represent the design, and the existing buildings are just a backdrop. We can see this in Figure 4, a 1:100 model built from timbers and sprayed metal etchings and acrylic. There is some interest in form and materiality – the existing buildings and base are built from maple veneer, and there is even a nod to the orientation of the building with recognizable buildings such as the church spire in the background – but the style of the context, with its blank façades, blends into the background. It is there for reference and to portray an honest depiction of the site, but allows all the intricacies of the new scheme to breathe and be the focus of attention.

At the other end of the scale, Figure 5 shows a model built from acrylic and spray finished. The contextual buildings and base were spray finished in tonal warm greys, so that they didn't overshadow the scheme building, but were modelled representing elevations and detailed architectural features and landscape. The use of colour allows the scheme to be the true focus but the relevance of its place in the landscape is fully acknowledged. This model fulfils the brief on many levels: it allows for an exploration and celebration of the building's design while representing its architecture in context and the influence this has had on the design. It also presents height and mass information and its orientation for the viewer. More models were made of this design at different scales and using different materials to truly extend all of the benefits of the building's location, representing a much wider contextual scope.

Showing the design in its context

The purpose of contextual buildings is just that: they should frame the scheme building's design in its context. The models in Figures 6 and 7 demonstrate this perfectly.

In the model in Figure 7 the context buildings give a sense

MAKING OFFSITE BUILDINGS

of the scale and act as a backdrop to a gardens/parkland model. The model is made from pear timber with accents of sprayed colour; a range of tree species represented through size and colour is complemented by the use of acrylic slab stacks for the existing buildings. This is a fine example of allowing the focus to remain on the area of study while still giving the model structure.

The model in Figure 8, again modelled in pear wood but at a larger scale (1:250), integrates the new build into its immediate context. The use of blind reveal elevations gives the new build structure within the model while also grounding it within its surroundings. The existing buildings that are not adjacent to the site have been modelled to a good level – presenting major architectural features in this way leads the eye towards the proposed building.

Major architectural features

What can be deemed as a major architectural feature is generally dependent on the scale of the model. A 1:1000 model will barely reference main pitches and flat roofs due to the small scale. In these cases, especially in built-up areas or cities where the roofscape is very complex, the trick is to look at the roofscape and make decisions about what to leave out. Even on a 1:500 model the simplification of these roofs will give the model a resolved finish, avoiding fussy and unattractive clustering and often saving valuable time and money. After all, if you look at the roofs of a built-up city block, the haphazard amalgamation of years of plant addition and development don't often make for a very resolved image; no one really wants to see a model of air conditioner units and chiller plant.

Figure 8: 1:250 Swiss mountain pear models. The scheme sits effortlessly in its context.

■ MAKING OFFSITE BUILDINGS

A 1:100 model, on the other hand, will encapsulate most aspects of a building, everything from chimneys and dormer windows through to mansard roofs, domes and plant blocks. Getting the level of detail right can be difficult and depends on the materials being used. If the context is for a study model and is built out of foam then a high level of detail is difficult to achieve: foam can be hard to shape in fine detail and the results can look crude and amateurish. Keeping the work simple with only broad gestures gives a more complete and confident finish. Likewise, large-scale offsite buildings built in acrylic and sprayed can often look light on detail and therefore look unfinished and overly simplistic. It is often then worth adding extra details to roofscapes and building articulation. If this information isn't available or the budget doesn't stretch that far, giving the contextual blocks colour or using a timber veneer can be a clever way of adding interest or creating a more appealing backdrop to the scheme building. Sometimes if the offsite buildings don't have any real relevance to the model then building footprints – the building floor plate cut from thin material and applied – may be enough to do the job.

Small-scale offsites

The level of detail and finish is essential when producing the work. Having an understanding of materials and how best to finish them will aid you in the choice of materials and subsequently you will be able to get the best results from them. Small-scale models usually benefit from the choice of light and clean materials. White or light sprayed block (from chemiwood) or blonde timbers usually give the best results. If you look into the distance then things obviously appear smaller but lighter as well; this preconception carries across to the architectural model. At small scale you don't want your materials to be too dark and risk a heavy, lifeless model. In some cases the model will demand strong colouring; in Figures 9 and 10, a 1:1250 model of southwest London, the material chosen was walnut, a dark-brown purplish wood. Although dark, the timber is known for its lustre and gave the model the quality of extravagance and exclusivity which worked in its favour.

The images are progress shots and also act as a reminder that when producing these type of models, the methodology is to have a printed drawing at scale with which to draw sim-

Figure 9: 1:1250 walnut context buildings on a plan.

plified roof layouts and mark building heights onto. This drawing will then act as a tool for the construction and assembly of the buildings. This will also be a master layout to tape the buildings down onto when complete, as it becomes quickly confusing when doing large areas of buildings for a model if you don't have a guide to where they all go when it's time to stick them to a base.

Large-scale offsites

Large-scale offsites should be lightweight and durable. The best way to achieve this is by building the mass of the buildings as boxes (earlier exercises in this book – cube, pyramid and cylinder –should stand you in good stead for the majority of buildings). These boxes, whether in MDF or high-impact foam board, can be clad in veneer or have joins sanded and sprayed. Elevations can be added and the roofs boxed out and attached.

If more elaborate detail or roof forms need to be created they can be produced in solid form. In timber model offsites in particular, it might be necessary to keep the grain of the wood going in the same direction or impossible to clad veneer onto complex or organic shapes. We can see in Figure 11 that the bulk of the building has been massed in boxed construction and veneered, while domed roofs and parapet detail have been machined out of solid lumps of timber. In Figure 12 the models are again boxed construction, clad in veneer, with detail and elevation (such as the portico and columns) being machined out of solid timbers. Small roofs and parapets likewise have been machined. No laser cutting or CAD elevations were needed to produce these models as a printed plan and satellite maps provided all the information needed. (The more traditional model-making skills, such as circular saw, lathe and milling machine work, are not covered in this book; a model-making or woodwork course is recommended to gain experience of these skills.)

Offsite building in any material will require a lot of machine

Figure 10: 1:1250 walnut context buildings on a plan.

■ MAKING OFFSITE BUILDINGS

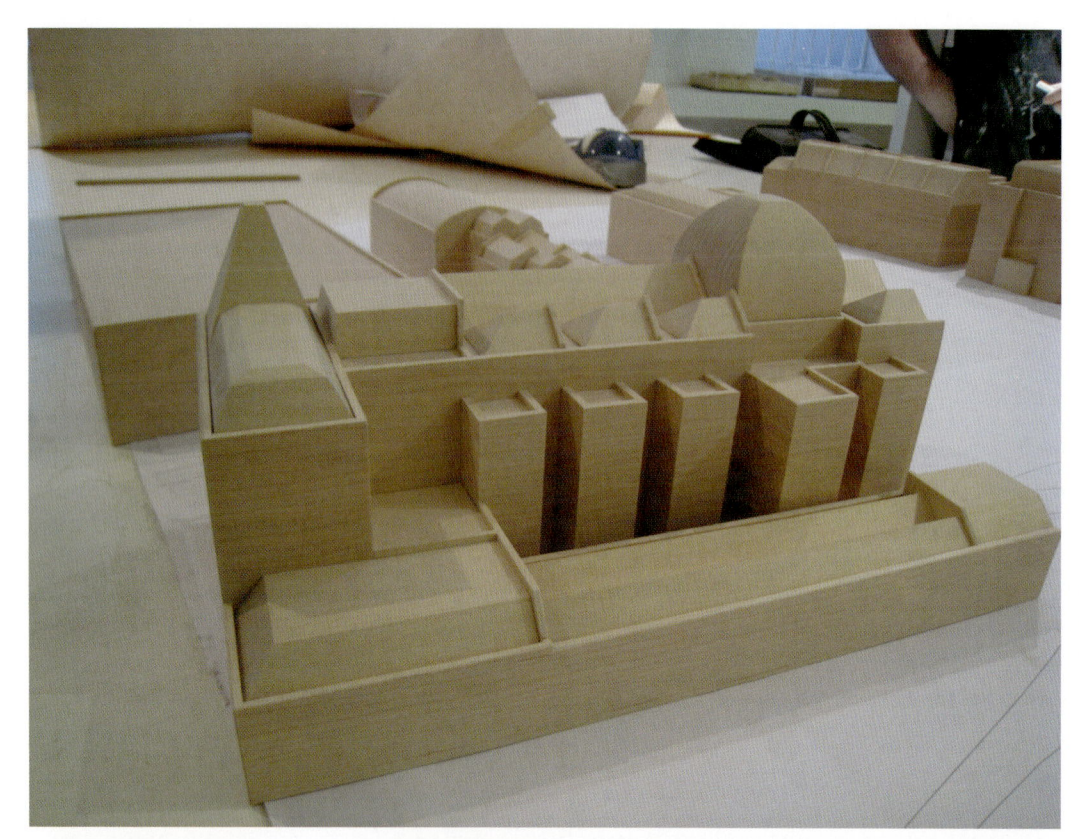

Figure 11: 1:150 lime timber block context model.

Figure 12: 1:150 lime timber block context model.

work and, ultimately, finishing work. To sand and finish most types of building the following equipment is generally required:

Superglue
Wood glue
Squares
Angle blocks
Sanding blocks
Wet and dry sandpaper grits 80, 180, 320
    (coarse/medium/fine)

Superglue is a 'wonder product' for making models and although many experienced model makers denounce it as an unprofessional product not to be used by experienced craftspeople, they are missing a trick. Used properly and with a little experience, it can stick almost anything to anything else, and it can be used as gap filler and as a weld; it truly is one of the most important substances in a workshop. When using superglue for sticking wooden blocks together, be careful: when sanded it will leave a black line in the joint that will look unsightly. When joining timbers it is preferable to use wood glue, which will take a little longer to dry but will dry clear and in most cases leave an invisible join.

Wet and dry sandpaper will finish your work to a high standard. Using double-sided tape, attach it to a hand-sized block, something like 9mm MDF or thick acrylic. This will make it flat and the block can be kept square when sanding. Make sure that the block is square-edged and the sandpaper is stuck down across the entirety of the block (this sounds fussy but will make all the difference to the quality of your work). Alternatively, sheets can be taped to a board for the sanding of lots of smaller components. Note: if you are sanding onto a board, sand in circular motions as opposed to side-to-side; this will give an even sanding. A side-to-side motion will limit the control and distribution of pressure, and may result in sanding an angle onto a piece of material; this is soul-destroying when long periods of time have been spent producing and machining the block.

Some may believe that the block will need to be sanded down through all of the grades or grits of paper to get the best result; however, the same results can be achieved using just three grits (80, 180 and 320, or coarse, medium and fine). The coarse sandpaper will remove all elements of the saw, the medium will remove the coarse paper lines, and the fine will smooth the block. If sanding Perspex for polishing then a 600 grit or ultra-fine sandpaper may be used.

Ground floors and cutting in

The process of cutting in the offsite buildings is the last part of the build of any offsite work. If the base is flat, the offsites can be stuck straight to the base. When producing contour stack bases, however, it is worth checking the location of offsites within the contours: the contours could be wrapped around the building or added in at the drawing stage to avoid having to cut through numerous contours to get to a flat base. In most cases the base will have slopes and land falls across it. Either the buildings will have to be shaped with the negative of the slope to allow them to sit flat (this is a difficult process only worth attempting with small-scale offsites that are on a gently sloping base – even then if not executed accurately the buildings will lean in different directions), or they may be cut in so that they sit flat on your base board. Obviously the way in which you are going to attach the offsites needs to be thought about before the base is constructed; extra height can be added to the buildings to cover the proportion of the building that will be below ground level. The offsite height should be built from its lowest level to guarantee that the building sinks into the base all around, otherwise on a sloping site the building will fit into the base on one side and be 'floating' on the other. Finally, make sure that the ribs of your base do not cross through the hole into which you are going to sink the offsite.

We can see from Figures 13 and 14 that the holes should be clear of obstruction. The photographs also demonstrate the time-saving technique of cutting a larger hole than the building needs in the substrate layer of the base, which also improves the finish of the model. We can see in Figure 13 that the base has not yet been veneered and the hole is larger than the offsites; the area can be veneered over (Fig. 14) and the model placed in position and just one thin layer of veneer needs to be cut through (rather than the veneer and a layer of 3mm hardboard). This process also works if the skin is the road layer: holes can be cut larger in this layer and the pavement pads can be stuck on top – hiding any number of sins underneath. When the building is in position, it can be scribed around carefully and cut in, using a scalpel and a steel rule. Note: if the hole you cut isn't as accurate as it could be, at least make sure that it's straight and clean; a small amount of shadow gap can be tolerated, but a crooked, shabby line will make the model look terrible.

■ MAKING OFFSITE BUILDINGS

Figure 13: 1:100 model production shot. The base in the foreground has been cut away before being veneered to allow easy fitting of the context buildings.

MAKING OFFSITE BUILDINGS

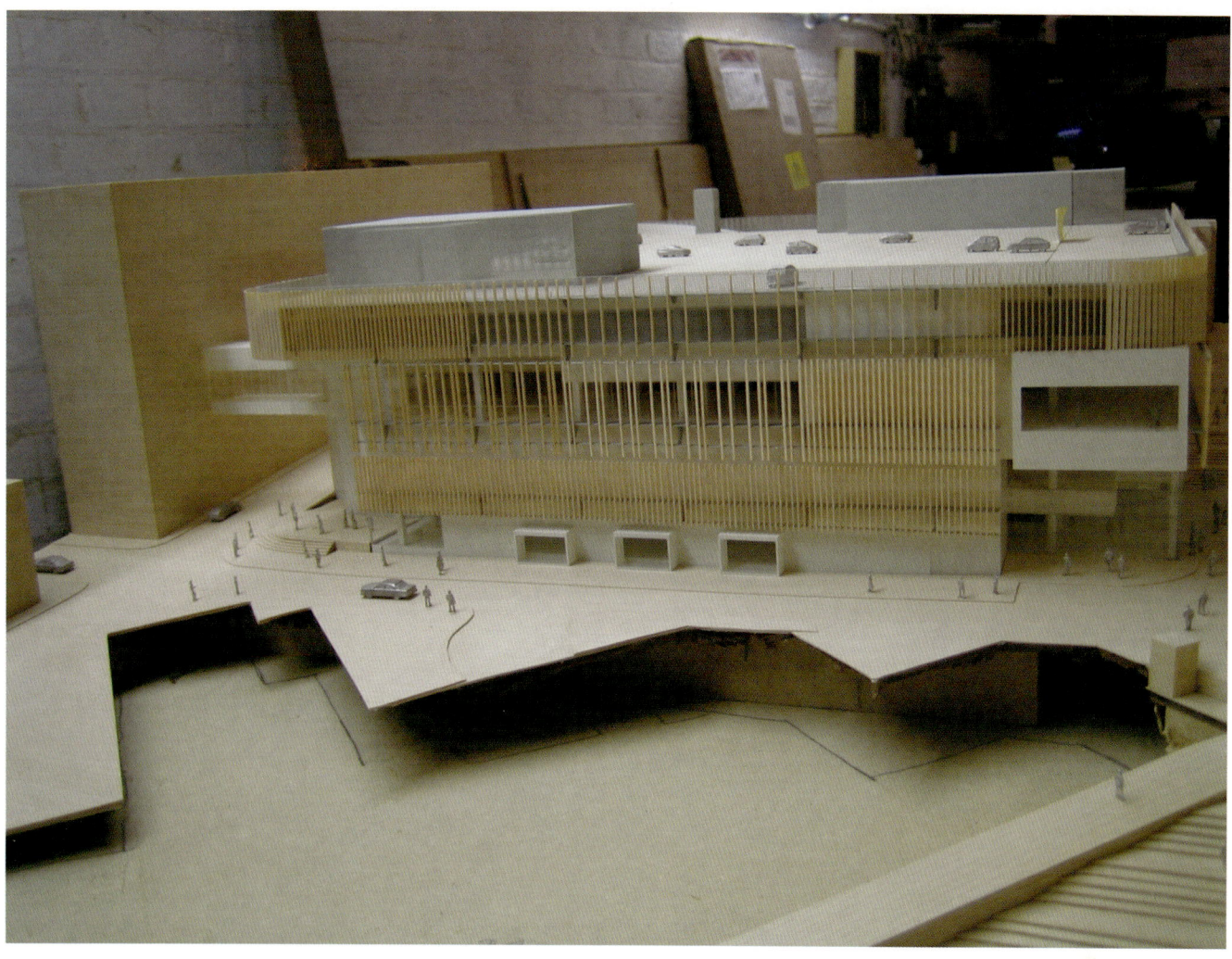

Figure 14: a further construction shot showing the same model with the base veneered. The void in the base allows easy and clean fitting of the context buildings.

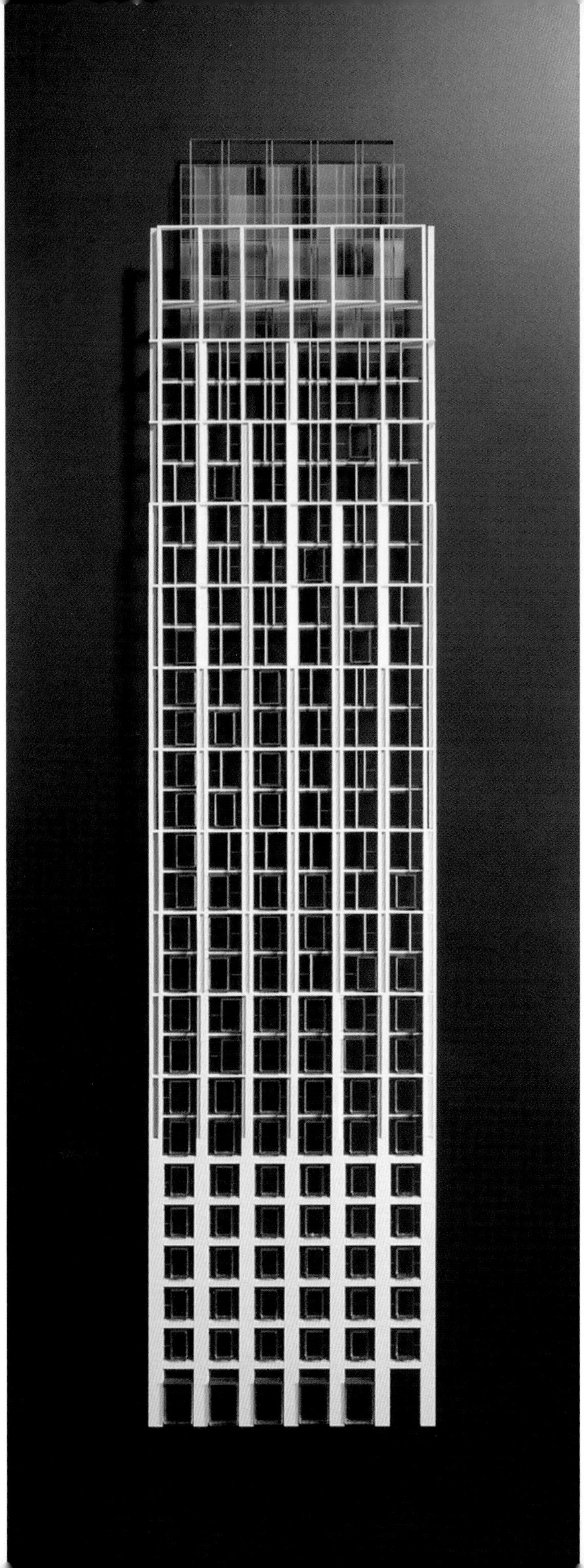

CHAPTER 7

COMMISSIONING A MODEL

Equipped with an understanding of the reasons for a model and the types of model that best represent your brief, you might find yourself in the position of commissioning a model from an independent model-making company. These companies will often have to be strict with the level of information required at the onset of a project: whilst they can often accommodate changes along the way, it is important to remember that they are an external company and are often working to a fixed price – it can become very expensive for clients when major changes are made to the design midway through the build. In the initial briefing, develop a clear understanding of what you want from the model and relay this to the model makers. Communication is the key, especially when it comes to the vision behind the model. With adequate levels of information a successful model can be delivered to a realistic schedule.

There is a substantial difference between an independent architectural model-making company and an in-house team on the payroll: their aims and goals differ. A polished model is often the reason for approaching a model-making company, while the role of an in-house team is much more design- and development-led. Both roles have many challenges, externally and internally. Aesthetically, a sketch model that is overworked will look like a bad presentation model, while a quick presentation model may start to look like an overworked sketch model; both can have a negative impact on how the overall building design is perceived, and a lack of confidence in the model can have ramifications in the confidence of the design overall (remember that this is often the first time a building is perceived in physical three-dimensional terms).

An in-house department is intrinsically organized to perform within these parameters, with the pressures of a deadline looming. It is often for this reason that in-house models are produced quickly, from inexpensive materials, while the design is still in a state of flux. This system of working in-house avoids the expense of halting a model in production. With an independent model-making company you will pay for extensive changes to a model that should have been made by an experienced in-house model maker. This can explain why the size of the workforce differs significantly between an in-house and an out-house workshop. Within an in-house system and with fewer members of staff the models rarely have the same level of finish. The models do not have the level of polish of an externally produced model, but are often concerned with development or communicating specific design ideas.

Traditional model-making companies are often called in when the design's evolution, budget, complexity and size call for a better resourced approach. This movement of the project's model from in-house to out-house can be flawed; a good communication of the required story, an understanding of how the project has evolved, and mutual respect from all parties can make the next series of models successful. Although having the same core skills, the interpretation and expectation from the two branches of the industry are often very different. Bridging this gap, especially when commissioning or receiving a commission, can make a difference to how the model is received.

LEFT: **Elevation study (scale 1:150), sprayed acrylic and metal etchings.**

■ COMMISSIONING A MODEL

Producing a quote

In most cases the first step in commissioning a model is to organize a time frame and schedule for the build. If there is already a standing relationship with the model-making company then a telephone enquiry or email will determine availability and timescale for the model production. If you know a model is coming up, it is worth informing the model makers so space can be cleared in their schedule for your build – or at least taken into account in their schedule. Even if the project isn't yet booked in, the model makers will be grateful if they can factor the possibilities into their timetable. To gain a successful model from a model maker it is good to foster a close working relationship with them. This also allows the model maker to develop a palette with your company, and have a greater understanding of the information that they receive. It may also allow for you to push through the occasional rush job with them: if the model makers are set up for the style of model and palette that you require, then they may have materials already in stock, and not need extensive briefings and meetings to discover the story that you wish to present through the model. Ultimately a model-making company is looking to build a reputation and long-term relationship with its clients – an architect, developer or institution commissioning a model will probably have future work to be bid for.

The information needed for a quote will usually come down to relevant drawings – usually at least a ground-floor plan and some elevations for the model maker to develop an understanding of the elevation treatment of the building. The level of information required will depend on the specifics of the model: overloading the makers with building details and material schedules for the building when a 1:1000 model is being proposed will only lead to confusion, potentially adding unnecessary costs to the budget. The point of a quotation is to get a clear and fair cost for the model; the best way to achieve this is to give a clear and fair view of the model that you require.

To gain an accurate quotation the model makers need to understand the vision of the designer, ideally at a meeting when the project and the design's story can be discussed. The important factors and details most relevant to the project can be communicated; this is often where fine tuning, scale and time frame for the model's production can be agreed. The model now becomes a realistic proposition. If a face-to-face meeting is impossible then the appropriate conversations can be made over the telephone.

Scale drawings on paper

The size of a model is often reflected in the visual language that an architect is familiar with, the sizing of a composition often conforming to the same criteria as drawing sizes. The sizes of drawings are usually those that can be conveniently transported – whether rolled, folded, laid out or fixed to a wall. The traditional drafting process imposes limitations on the size that is realistically workable, so the scaling of drawings within architecture is essential. When scaling and processing drawings, it is useful to understand and be able to communicate scale and detail. When looking at drawings digitally using CAD programmes, it is usual to work (or draw) in 1:1 scale, as this offers a true sense of the building's size and dimensions, and simplifies the process of transferring drawings between all the people involved in the project. A consistent paper size system is now used through all print industries, and in most modern architectural practices the largest paper size printed from a plotter is ISO A0 (841mm × 189mm), where the drawing size tends to represent the whole of a building plan or elevation; building details are usually described in A3 or A4 size. The paper sizes are chosen generally as a reflection of what can be represented onto them at scale. The scale chosen will reflect the required amount of detail; for example, a whole building can be drawn at 1:100

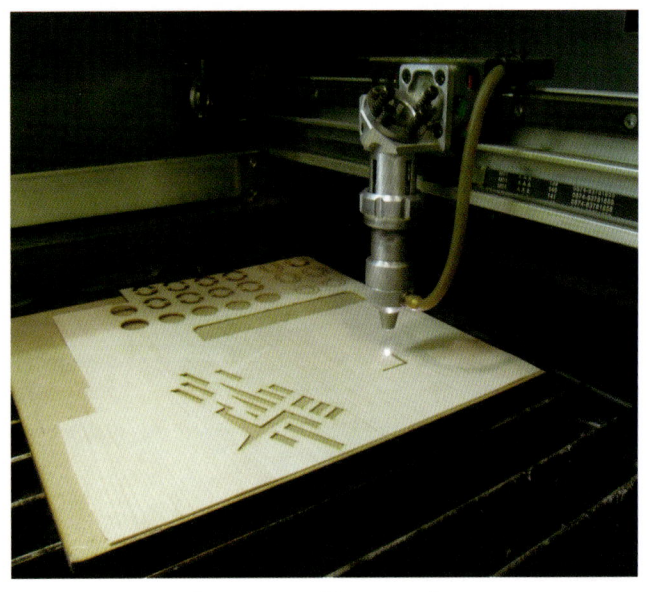

The process of laser cutting.

COMMISSIONING A MODEL

scale showing wall thicknesses, but a 1:20 detail will concern itself with the materials that will make up the wall thickness.

Paper scale drawings allow for dimensions to be read or measured, either using scale rules or by multiplying scale factors of these. Having a thorough understanding of this allows you not to be overawed when looking at drawings for a model, especially digitally when the drawings are 1:1 scale. In most cases the drawings will not have been prepared for a model maker so the range and quality of information, though variable, will in most cases exceed what is needed.

What to leave in and take out: finding the balance

Deciding on the level of information when making a scale model can be tricky, and careful reasoning needs to take place early on. It is very much scale-dependent; print out an elevation of your building once scaled, to view what will be seen when the model is made. In most cases the 'less is more' approach works to keep models from becoming too fussy or cluttered: on screen it is easy to become lost in the detail – for example, six fenestration detail lines when at scale will measure barely a millimetre across. Printing out drawings at scale for your model will give you a true sense of what you will and won't see in the model, as demonstrated in the drawings

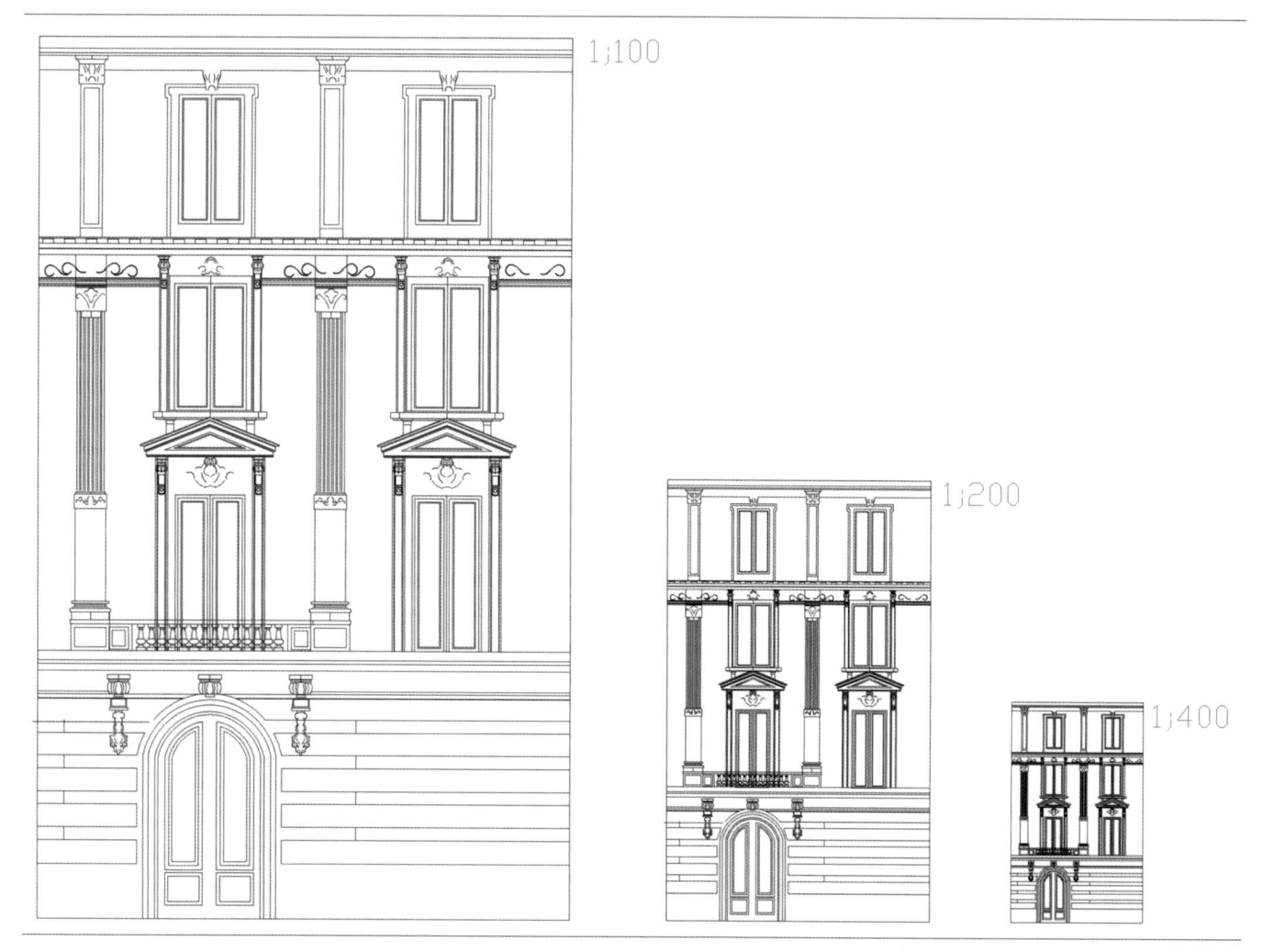

An elevation scaled to three different sizes: 1:100, 1:200, and 1:400.

125

above. The drawings show the same design at three different scales: 1:100, 1:500 and 1:750. As you can see, the difference in the workable information is pronounced.

The process of commissioning a model should be a rewarding part of any project. Imparting the excitement to the model makers of seeing a building in three-dimensional terms for the first time should make for the most engaging models.

Making your own model

If you are going to produce a model yourself, then beyond the practical techniques and processes that are laid out within this book are some general points of motivation and practicality that should be understood.

Be careful of 'model making' yourself into a corner: often, whether through tiredness or the threat of an imposing deadline, decisions can be made that jeopardize the completion or quality of what would otherwise be a fine model. For example, neglecting to get enough of the correct material such as a timber veneer at the start will mean that during the build you have to buy more, which may not match. Putting off making a decision on a component can leave you unable to construct a key elevation or element because you didn't want to think about it. Making the decisions and understanding the process that you are going to follow saves time and energy later on. Work out a plan and stick to it rather than making constant adjustments to your work as you go along; this could lead to an accumulative error throughout your work which will eventually need to be resolved.

Don't be intimidated. Most models at the beginning will appear overwhelming; the people around you will often have been working on the design for long periods of time and will complacently assume you have the same working knowledge of the project. Stop, take a deep breath, and question everything you need to know to build the model. You will often have too much build information and much can be disregarded – the drawings you have been given may be full detailed schematics that are intended as working drawings, produced to build the building not the model, so take only what you need.

As the job progresses the picture will become clearer: there is no way that you can understand every detail, building condition, pavement layout or ground level at first glance, so try to avoid making hasty decisions that may come back to haunt you later. The best bet is to take some time to gather an understanding of the basic principles of the model, come up with a general plan, then start working on something broad. I usually start with the floor plates to ask questions of the rest of the model: what are the ground-floor heights, how will the elevations work with the floors, how will the walls keep the floors up? This process allows you time to digest more slowly the important aspects of the model. Alternatively, building a flat base board may ease some of the pressure; the project suddenly becomes smaller and more achievable once the extents of the model are there in front of you.

Perfectionists have no place in the model-making industry: if you want to worry yourself with producing the perfect model then there isn't a company that exists that will be able to afford the models that you produce. Deadlines and budgets need to be met. Beyond this point there is no such thing as the perfect build, and attempting to achieve this will drive you, any employer and your client mad. There are always compromises that have to be made in the construction of a model; clearly a 'that will do' ethos is unacceptable, but if something has been built to a high standard then trying to alter it in pursuit of perfection will only undermine and often ruin all your hard work. Getting carried away with an element of embellishment in a model might satisfy your own pride but may either jeopardize the chance to meet a deadline or make for an uneven model: if some areas appear overworked, other parts of the model will appear light, leading to an uneven model and hinting at inconsistency or a poor concept of the finished article. When making any component of a model, have a finished view in your mind's eye. This will help in keeping to the straight and narrow and allow you to maintain a schedule of work that gets the job done with fantastic results.

An interview with Mark Luggie

How did the integration of laser-cutting technology into the model-making industry work?

Millennium Models was the first company in London to purchase a laser cutter for use in its workshop; this was new technology to model making. It took time to adjust to using it, as people were still learning the full potential of what could be achieved with this new technology. Architects at this time were still providing hard-copy or paper drawings and we were still using routers and other more traditional power tools to produce model components such as floor plates – this is the process where we made a master jig of one floor, then with material of either acrylic or MDF stacked together for the correct number of floors, we used the router to cut all of the floors from the master jig. The hand-held routers cut through the laminated sheets with the jig as a guide tool to follow the shape and accurate floors could be produced that were all the same. This method was very effective but time-consuming and there was a fair amount of finishing and sanding to do to get all of the floors ready to start the model build. Even though it takes time now to prepare drawings to be programmed for the laser-cutter, it is time well spent: an entire kit of parts – floors, elevations and any detailing – can be designed on screen, to levels of accuracy that would have been impossible in the past. Much more time is spent in front of the computer now compared to the number of man-hours that used to be spent routing and then finishing these floor plates with hand tools.

Can you describe the period before model makers used laser cutters?

In my first few years in the industry it was usual in an office of, say, fifteen people, for there to be only one computer which was most commonly used for office administration. This was pre-Internet and email, and correspondence was made in person, by mail or by fax, and digital photography was unheard of at this point. Virtually everything was produced by hand, so there were more model makers per job and larger time frames to build the models than today. This meant that there were more saws and hand tools. A lot of the skills and techniques like using ruling pens to paint window frames onto glazing layers have now disappeared, using saws to process timber or acrylic for an elevation, building layers with hundreds of rectangles of acrylic to represent window apertures. I remember when you could spend weeks producing eleva-

MODEL MAKER'S PROFILE: MARK LUGGIE

Mark studied Model Design and Model Effects BA (Hons) at the University of Hertfordshire, winning two student prizes for work of merit and graduating in 1998. Mark then became a freelance model maker for different companies across London. This developed into a full-time position with Millennium Models Ltd, building on his workshop expertise to become Studio Manager. In 2006 Mark moved from Millennium Models Ltd to be part of a new model-making company, Base Models Ltd. His work ethic, experience and industry contacts have helped build Base Models into a successful, thriving business, with a reputation for high-quality models.

Mark Luggie, Director of Base Models, at home in his studio. To make all different sizes of models a studio space doesn't have to be big: organisation and thinking ahead are essential aspects in planning a model.

tions that would now take a day to produce with modern approaches.

What were the changes in construction and technique?
In the period before computer-aided design, architects would supply a roll of drawings showing plans and elevations and you would use rules and veneer gauges to measure drawings to work out and understand the scale for the model. Drawings were supplied at scale and you would work out all the details you required from these. One big difference is that you would have one dedicated architect to follow the project from beginning to end; email means that you can easily have correspondence with many people at an architectural practice where you used to liaise with one representative from the architecture firm. This can lead to problems these days where the vision of the finished article can become blurred if there are lots of people involved in the production of the model. Because the technology allows lots of people to get involved and digital photography allows for progress shots to be taken and emailed, the number of people involved has grown. Some projects now may have five or six architects involved at three or four different companies; finding someone to supply the vision for the model then can become a skill in itself! The best models are produced when there is a clear voice behind the build.

When laser cutting was introduced did you require specific CAD training?
When I left school I did a Civil Engineering training qualification which focused especially on skills as a draftsman. I was trained to use CAD Version 8 which offers no images on screen (this was before Graphical User Interface, or GUI, where you see the image created in front of you on screen). You had to type in code using an X and Y axis to create co-ordinates that showed you, only when you printed the document, where your lines were. This system has kept me ahead of the curve in CAD and has stood me in good stead even today as it enables me to translate 2D into 3D and this training gives me a strong understanding of the ever-increasing intricacies of the AutoCAD systems.

How was laser cutting used when it was first introduced?
It takes time for all of the possibilities of a new technology and tool to be explored. With the laser cutter the uses of engraving and cutting made us see the potential very quickly; however, in the early days we used the technology primarily for signage and exterior detailing rather than using it to create core parts of the build. As its uses became evident, traditional machinery became much less integral than previously. The laser cutters allowed for new ways to represent buildings, such as floor slab stacks or laser-scribed detailing to elevations. The laser cutter completely changed the look, style and finish of architectural models, so completely changing the industry as a whole – people, skills sets and time frames have all changed.

Have the uses of CAD changed with the integration of laser cutters?
We didn't really use CAD before laser cutters, although the relationship was reasonably symbiotic. At the time that we started to invest in these new technologies, their integration was only made possible because of the other major change that was taking place during this same period. Many architects became more proficient using CAD and once architects began to supply plans digitally (without us needing to draw the plans in CAD which would be very time-consuming and not practical to redraw a whole scheme), then the true potential of the laser-cutting components became realized.

More recent changes in CAD are that architects can use a new type of CAD which will translate the 2D drawing into a virtual rendering of the scheme on your computer. This offers a way to gain an idea of a 3D format and could represent a gradual shift away from physical models; however, nothing can compare with the clarity of a traditionally produced model.

There is a potential pitfall for architects using CAD that in time you will have architecture students only being trained to design a building on-screen and as this gives a two-dimensional perception of a building, this may create a lack of understanding of how to fully understand the site and the building and how it works within its environment. It is important that a model can express a sense of style and 'feel' beyond what a computer can offer, how a building can be used, and how people can interact with it – I believe that a true sense of the building is essential in a design process and a 3D physical model is still the best way to show the true clarity of a design.

What do you look for from architects when you are briefed on a new job?
Appreciation of the story! Sometimes you are in a brief and you need the architects to say what they want from the model as a whole – this can help to decide what is important and to make the decisions about what to emphasize so that you can provide the best model to the brief. This way of 'selling' the

design needs no more than a pencil, sketchbook and a bit of trust at its core. Understanding floors, levels and elevations are job specific and vary, but the failure or success of how a model is received will ultimately come back to the model maker's grasp and understanding of the story of the design. This will always be the most important piece of information I need to give the project its best result.

In terms of more tangible information then the most common question I get from architects is usually about the format of drawings. The best format for a drawing to be sent to me is a 2004 DXF. This works on everything. In addition I often get asked what scale I want the information in; as a rule I prefer to receive all drawings at 1:1 scale. We then can scale the drawing, and this stops any confusion, especially these days where information often comes by email in dribs and drabs. Someone trying to do your job for you often results in it being wrong. The build process (where you're attempting to learn and understand a building, its levels and context often in a few short weeks) and the full picture – its back story and purpose and identifying the need it is trying to fulfil – are essential to make a model. This is what asserts its value – not in terms of just its monetary value but what the model can do. They can often produce a sense of theatre to the process: when someone walks into a room and reveals the model it is a physical, tangible vision of their design. This is what a good model should do; add a bit of excitement and theatre to the reveal, presenting what you want in the best possible light. Production of the object, building design, and a technically correct model to me are secondary to the overall purpose, which comes back to the model telling a story. Everyone relates to a model, which isn't necessarily the case of a computer-generated fly through, or a rotating CGI image. People will bend on one knee to peer through a model; they wouldn't do this with a computer image.

Do you think you are making 'better' models now with the new technology than fifteen years ago?
Model makers don't need steady hands any more. In a sense those craft and hand skills have been devalued by the new technologies in the model-making industry; conversely when you see a handmade crafted model it has an intrinsic charm and value. 'You build on cost and you borrow on value', as Paul Reichmann put it. The industry is probably producing more accurate and technically superior models now but because of the way the industry has changed, the increased pressure on deadlines and in many cases because of the devaluing of the skills sets, there is a falling value for the budgets for models. This has led to perhaps the story behind the model being lost. Many model makers have gravitated purely towards just high-quality production of models, which is obviously a prerequisite, but in many cases the exploration of a language and the story have become lost. You feel at some point there will be a backlash, and the need to communicate with the model will again become the focus.

What are your 'top ten' tools?
Hands, scalpel and blades (it has to be a Swann-Morton and the blades need to be 10A), Rabone Chesterman steel rule, veneer gauge, 123 or angle blocks, sable brushes, modelmaker's plane, laser cutter, cabinet scrape, and a sharp sanding block.

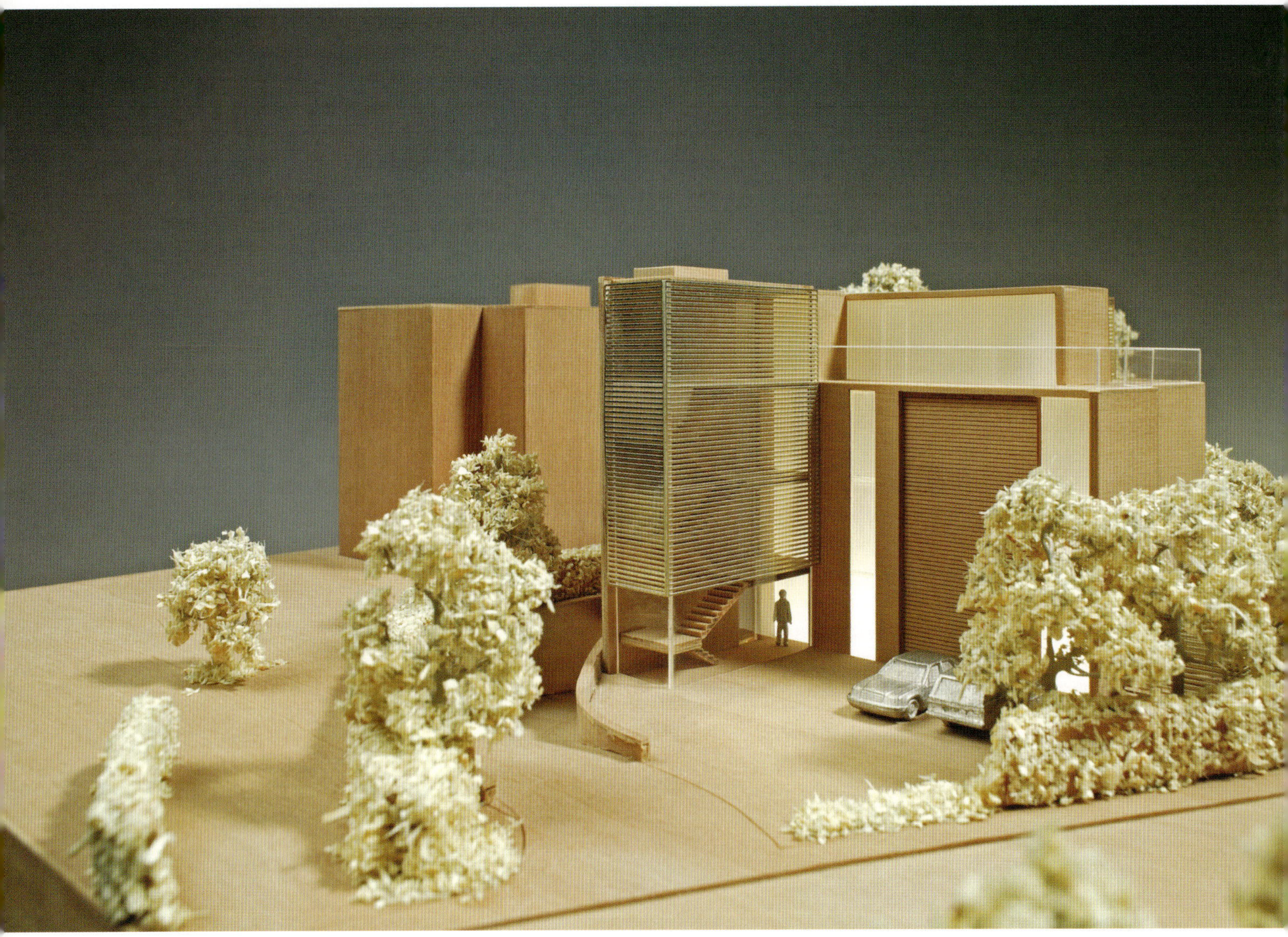

CHAPTER 8

THE FUTURE

In about 23BC, Vitruvius described the following problem:

> There are some things which, when enlarged in imitation of small models, are effective, others cannot have models, but are constructed independently of them, while there are some which appear feasible in models, but when they have begun to increase in size are impracticable .... So too, in some models it is seen how they appear practicable on the smallest scale and likewise on a larger.
>
> Vitruvius, The Ten Books on Architecture, translated by Morris Hicky Morgan

Architecture is a constantly changing discipline, with new technologies allowing for more design freedom. As the history of model making was explored at the beginning of this book it would seem appropriate to look to the future of an industry that started with the architects themselves before becoming a specialism of its own.

The model-making industry as we know it today has only been in existence for the last hundred years or so. Now model making is a career in its own right with its own qualifications and, like architecture itself, is a continuously developing world with an ever-changing skills set. In the past the models were either produced by the architects themselves or commissioned from other professionals – carpenters and masons being the best examples – and this approach still lies behind architectural model making today: they were craftspeople who had an inside view of the construction industry and benefited commercially from their involvement in the processes of the construction industry. There is no doubting the skill and dexterity of the people who are now professional model makers, but as the industry incorporates new technologies, many of the techniques that used to define the model maker as a skilled artisan have changed – and in many cases become redundant.

Future technology

Until now, the plans and elevations that make up an architect's drawings have provided the initial insight into the architect's imagining; these coupled with an architectural model have been the way that a design is best communicated to a client. Computer renderings have taken the place of drawn visuals to provide an image as an insight for the consumer to understand the design, but often only from one angle, and that angle chosen by the architect, often to best represent their design. Beyond this, the three-dimensional 'fly through' is built upon the rendering but still offers a controlled view of the design: there is no room for the viewer to deviate to areas of interest or concern. The ability to move around unrestricted, to touch and interact with an environment that still hasn't been built has largely been unthreatened as the preserve of the architectural model. The architectural model then, with the help of three-dimensional CAD and three-dimensional printing could (depending on one's viewpoint) either be ready for a new lease of life or the retirement home.

LEFT: **1:100 Swiss mountain pear and metal-etched traditional architectural model.**

■ THE FUTURE

Three-dimensional modelling

This is the process of developing a mathematical representation of any three-dimensional surface of an object via specialist software. The product is called a three-dimensional model, which can be displayed as a two-dimensional image or still through a process called three-dimensional rendering or using a computer simulation of physical phenomena. Three-dimensional models are represented as three-dimensional objects using a collection of points in space, connected by various geometric line-and-shape. It is worth realizing from a physical model maker's perspective that none of the above uses of the word three-dimensional actually relates to anything physical being produced, it is all on the screen. These programmes now produce three-dimension prints.

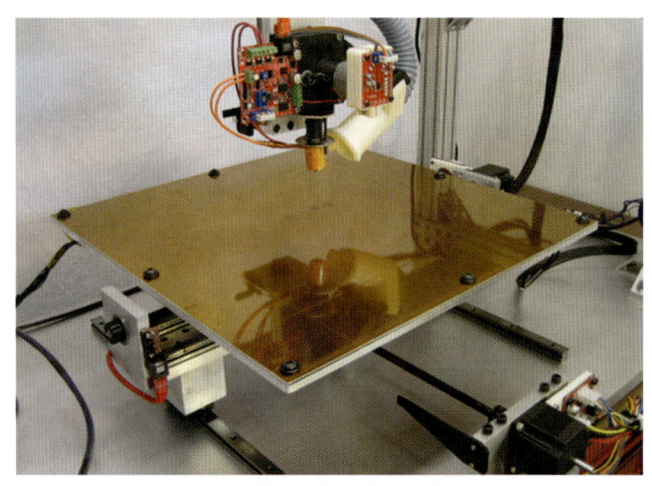

Three-dimensional printing.

Three-dimensional printing

Three-dimensional printing is exactly what it says: the creation of objects through the seemingly sci-fi technology of printing in three dimensions; the entire process from comport model through to finished print in a range of materials can be achieved in a matter of hours. What this could mean for the model-making industry is that accurate, scaled models could be automatically constructed without the crude tools of a scalpel or saw.

It works by printing layers one on top of another to create a three-dimensional object. (If you print a square onto a piece of paper and layer up enough squares you will eventually end up with a cube.) Instead of printing with ink, in most cases a fine white powder is used instead. This type of three-dimensional printing is known as Z Corp. There are now more sophisticated technologies at hand giving arguably cleaner, more accurate results. The main differences are found in how

Three-dimensional model of a family of tables, designed and computer-modelled by D*Haus.

THE FUTURE

thing, but the time invested in the production of the computer model is often disproportionate to the need for the product (or in this case the model). It can be an expensive and time-consuming process to produce a seamless, accurate computer model. It is often the case that models are needed to better understand what is on the screen, so a 'Catch 22' situation remains: to produce the drawings to make the model you almost need a model to produce the drawings. However, once the computer programmes that support the three-dimensional printers become further integrated with everyday practices then the idea of printing models will take hold further; a time will come (when the skills involved are all computer-based and the printers are small, relatively clean machines) when most architectural practices will have one of these, alongside the plotters and printers that make up today's print rooms. This will arguably lead to a greater emphasis on

Example of powder three-dimensional printing.

the layers are constructed: some methods use melting or softening materials to produce layers, such as selective laser sintering (SLS), while others lay liquid materials that are cured (SLA). Each method has its own advantages and disadvantages. Most companies producing three-dimensional printers offer the option of either powder or polymer printing. The quality of the prints often relies on the quality of the computer model. This is where the main downfall of this burgeoning industry currently lies: it is one thing to be able to print some-

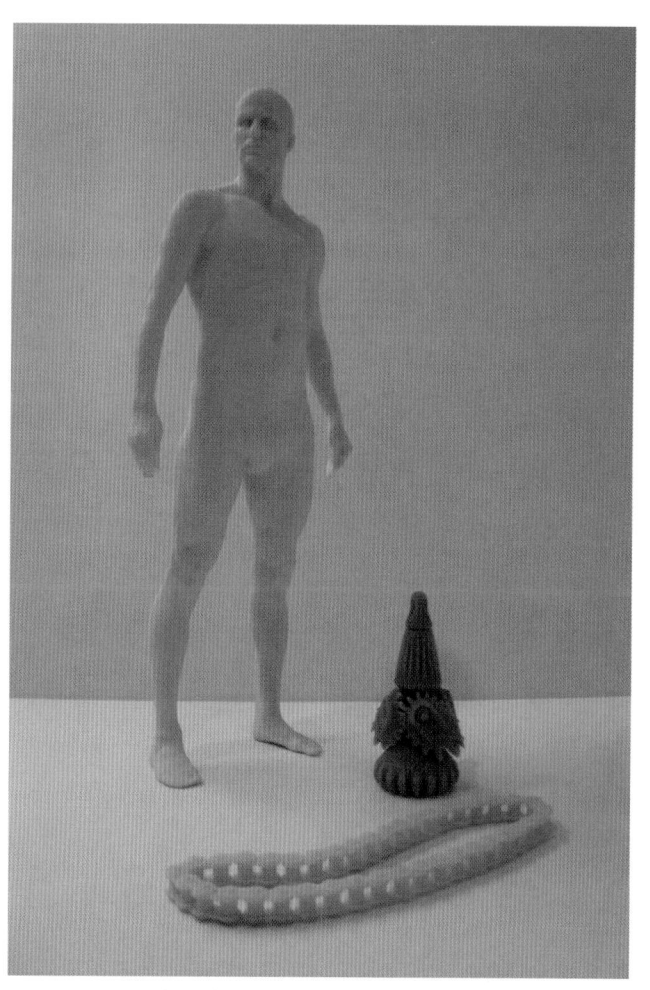

Examples of SLS three-dimensional printing.

133

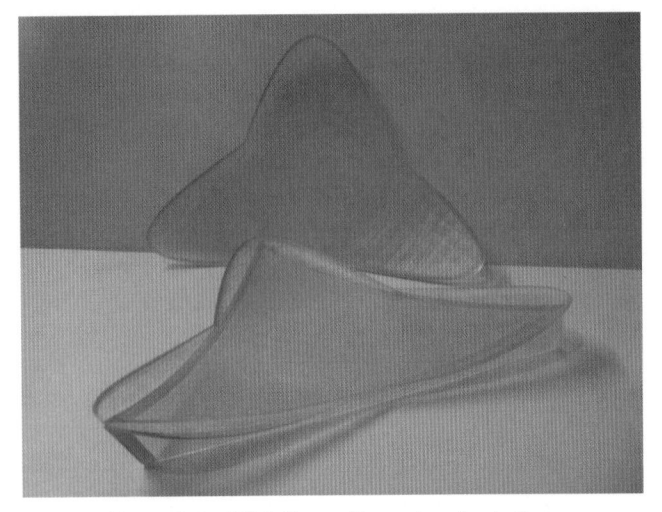

■ THE FUTURE

Examples of SLA three-dimensional printing.

models: just as desktop publishing programs have led to an increased output of print products such as flyers and brochures, three-dimensional printers will make models more readily attainable, and therefore there is potential for model making to have a more integrated role within the architectural practice, albeit in a different capacity.

This new technology might have you believe that the all-nighters and cutting foam board with a scalpel will become a thing of the past, but it is more likely that the future of three-dimensional printing will offer an integration with the model-making process, probably replacing many time-consuming operations and delivering a greater level of accuracy in the reproduction of countless models. There may therefore be less need for specialist architectural model makers, in the same way that laser cutting changed and sharpened the model-making industry upon its arrival. Ultimately this is perhaps not something to be lamented, but to embrace, allowing the architects themselves to interact with their designs and develop them with the use of models. The key to the mass use of the three-dimensional printer in the office environment will be the development and working practices of programs such as three-dimensional AutoCAD. It will become easier to make the transition from on-screen three-dimensional computer models to three-dimensional printed models in the hand, and this will help with the design process.

Architectural model makers have to follow new trends in technology, to allow for the ever-increasing sophistication of design concepts. What is achievable within architecture is increasing by the day; the engineering of complicated, organic shapes directly lends itself to the technologies involved in three-dimensional printing. This perhaps is the beginning of the integration of three-dimensional software, and model makers will need to have experience of the new technologies as they become available.

The rise of in-house model making

Over the past thirty years or so, architectural practices have started to hire individual model makers directly, setting up small model-making studios in-house. This has to a certain extent contributed to a reduction in the workload of the more established model-making companies.

To understand the reasons why this practice is becoming popular, we must look at the changing demands that the modern world of architecture is putting on architects and consequently on the model makers who work for them. The increasing limitations on time that have driven the design process (due to the growth of technologies such as the Internet and CAD) have resulted in architects themselves no longer having the time to produce maquettes, thus leading to the role of an in-house model maker. Over time the role might develop and grow, along with the architect's practice, producing more 'finished' architectural models: having a designated person on hand who understands the architect's thoughts, works to the same deadlines and is essentially in the same room to discuss, question and develop the design can mean all the difference when nurturing early stages of the design.

Although many of the skills are identical to those required by an external model-making company, an in-house model maker often works more closely with their clients, develops better people skills and has an active imagination to overcome the problems that a lack of machinery or sophisticated tools might present, giving this role a unique perspective on the process of designing a building. Some of the largest architecture companies in the United Kingdom, such as Foster + Partners, Raphael Viñoly architects, and Rogers Stirk Harbour and Partners, have already paved the way in creating in-house model shops.

It is beneficial for the design process to have a close working practice; in future years the model-making industry is likely to change further along these lines as the need for a quicker communication of the design increases, and cost of producing a presentation model becomes relatively more expensive.

If we combine this with the increasing accessibility of modern technology like laser cutters and now three-dimensional printing, the old idea of a model-maker's workshop with circular saws, sanders and spray shops is an expense an architectural practice need not concern itself with. As well as this, learning to use these new machines does not require the same level of trained specialism and safety implications as spray painting or operating saws, for example. After a short training course anyone can safely operate laser cutters and three-dimensional printers. The real skill will lie in the knowledge and understanding of the computer programs – an area in which many architects already have a key understanding.

Despite the variety of skills and the 'jack-of-all-trades' tag that seems to go with the model maker's job description, the new and diversifying technological avenues all seem to require the same overall criteria: they demand people who can! Partly because the model-making industry recruits from such a wide spectrum of disciplines, the role of model maker is perhaps becoming one of purely 'maker', transferring these skills through to architecture, furniture making, fine art, engineering, set design and product development, to name but a few walks of life. The abilities and skills that have taken model makers years to develop must surely have a place in the modern, technologically run, future.

Perhaps the best example of this consolidation of skills and talents can be seen at work within the Heatherwick studio, now famous for its commercial and residential buildings, infrastructure and high-profile works of public art. Its best-known works, which caught the public's imagination, include the new look London 'Routemaster' bus and the London 2012 Olympic cauldron. Thomas Heatherwick's aim: 'to bring architecture, design and sculpture together within a single practice'. Work is carried out from a combined workforce that includes architects, designers and engineers. As the Heatherwick studio website suggests, their 'studio has always been a workshop for making models, experimental pieces and prototype.' This approach to architecture, design and engineering, although appearing thoroughly modern, does perhaps take its lead from the architects of the past who were master makers of their own design. The fact that this process is proving so successful for the Heatherwick studio is only a starting point: re-unifying the skills of making with the talents of design will provide better thought-out architecture and design.

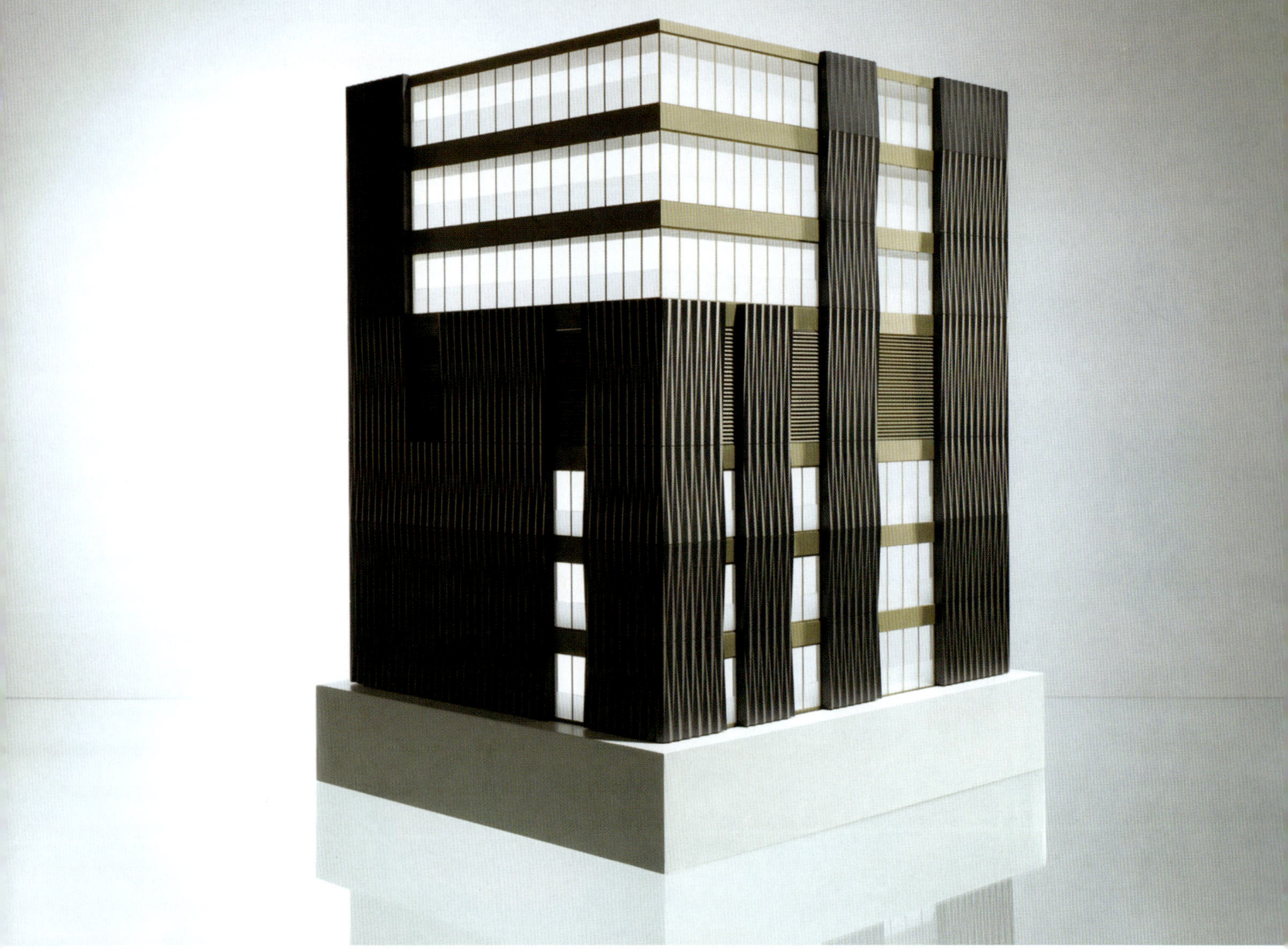

GLOSSARY

Acrylic
: The synthetic polymer of methyl methacrylate. This thermoplastic and transparent plastic is known under the trade names Plexiglas, Limacryl, R-Cast, Perspex, Plazcryl, Acrylex, Acrylite, Acrylplast, Altuglas, Polycast, Oroglass and Lucite and is commonly called acrylic glass or simply acrylic. Acrylic is used as an alternative to glass, and is the material of choice for fabrication of protective covers and display cases for models.

Articulation
: Any removable, interchangeable, or moving parts. A part of a model's functionality.

Atrium (pl. atria)
: A large, open space, often several storeys high and having a glazed roof and/or large windows. It is often situated within a larger multi-storey building and often located immediately beyond the main entrance doors. Atria are a popular design feature because they give their buildings a feeling of space and light.

Brise-soleil
: A structure used to protect a window from the sun, usually consisting of horizontal or vertical strips of wood, concrete, or metal.

CAD, computer-aided design
: (also known as CADD, computer-aided design and drafting) The use of computer technology for the process of design and design-documentation. Computer Aided Drafting describes the process of drafting with a computer. CAD software provides the user with input tools for the purpose of streamlining design, drafting, documentation, and manufacturing processes. CAD output is often in the form of electronic files for print or machining operations. CAD software generally uses vector-based graphics to depict the objects of traditional drafting.

CNC, computer numerical control
: A CNC controller reads and interprets inputted data and drives a carving tool, which creates the desired configuration out of a block of raw material by selective removal of it. CNC carving is one of the rapidly developing techniques widely used in model making for creating topographical models, prototypes and various parts. 'NC' refers to the automation of machine tools that are operated by abstractly programmed commands encoded on a storage medium, as opposed to controlled manually via hand wheels or levers, or mechanically automated via cams alone. The first NC machines were built in the 1940s and 1950s, based on existing tools that were

GLOSSARY

modified with motors that moved the controls to follow points fed into the system on punched tape. These early servo-mechanisms were rapidly augmented with analogue and digital computers, creating the modern CNC machine tools that have revolutionized the machining processes. In modern CNC systems, end-to-end component design is highly automated using computer-aided design (CAD) and computer-aided manufacturing (CAM) programs. The programs produce a computer file that is interpreted to extract the commands needed to operate a particular machine via a postprocessor, and then loaded into the CNC machines for production. Since a component might require the use of a number of different tools – drills, saws, etc. – modern machines often combine multiple tools into a single 'cell'. In other cases, a number of different machines are used with an external controller and human or robotic operators that move the component from machine to machine. In either case, the complex series of steps needed to produce any part is highly automated and produces a part that closely matches the original CAD design.

Composite Common term for the large family of engineered materials made of small fibres and particles, mixed with binding substance and formed into blocks and boards under high pressure and temperature. There are wood-based, plastic-based and mixed composites. All composites are widely used in modern model making due to their durability and, in some cases, light weight. Composites vary by density. The most popular composites in the model-making industry are MDF, Reshape and tooling boards.

Cross section Also simply called a 'section', this represents a vertical plane cut through the object, in the same way as a floor plan is a horizontal section viewed from the top. In the section view, everything cut by the section plane is shown as a bold line, often with a solid fill to show objects that are cut through, and anything seen beyond is generally shown in a thinner line. Sections are used to describe the relationship between different levels of a building's relationship that would be difficult to understand from plans alone. A sectional elevation is a combination of a cross section with elevations of other parts of the building seen beyond the section plane.

Curing A term in polymer chemistry and process engineering that refers to the toughening or hardening of a polymer material by cross-linking of polymer chains, brought about by chemical additives, ultraviolet radiation, electron beam or heat. In rubber, the curing process is also called vulcanization. Despite the wide variety of thermoset resin formulations (epoxy, vinylester, polyester, etc.), their cure behaviour is qualitatively identical. The resin viscosity drops initially upon the application of heat, passes through a region of maximum flow and begins to increase as the chemical reactions increase the average length and the degree of cross-linking between the constituent oligomers.

Eaves The eaves of a roof are its lower edges. They usually project beyond the walls of the building to carry rainwater away.

Elevation An elevation is a view of a building seen from one side, a flat representation of one façade. This is the most common view used to describe the external appearance of a building. Each elevation is labelled in relation to the compass direction it faces, e.g. the north elevation of a building is the side that most closely faces north. Buildings are rarely a simple rectangular shape in plan, so a typical elevation may show all the parts of the building that are seen from a particular direction. Geometrically, an elevation is a horizontal orthographic projection of a building on to a vertical

Epoxy	plane, the vertical plane normally being parallel to one side of the building. Architects also use the word elevation as a synonym for façade, so the north elevation is literally the north wall of the building. A material from the family of resins, epoxy (or Polyepoxide) is a polymer that cures when mixed with a catalyzing agent (hardener). Epoxy is used in the model-making industry mostly as glue.
Façade	Generally one exterior side of a building, usually (but not always) the front. The word comes from French ('frontage', 'face').
Fenestration	Refers to the design and/or disposition of openings in a building or wall envelope. Fenestration products typically include: windows, doors, louvres, vents, wall panels, skylights, store fronts, curtain walls, and slope-glazed systems.
Floor plan	A floor plan is the most fundamental architectural diagram, a view from above showing the arrangement of spaces in building in the same way as a map, but showing the arrangement at a particular level of a building. Technically it is a horizontal section cut through a building (conventionally at 1 metre above floor level), showing walls, windows and door openings and other features at that level. The plan view includes anything that could be seen below that level: the floor, stairs (but only up to the plan level), fittings and sometimes furniture. Objects above the plan level (e.g. beams overhead) can be indicated as dotted lines.
Foam	A large family of engineered materials formed by trapping a large quantity of air bubbles in liquid polymer that becomes hard as a result of chemical reaction or cooling. Foams vary in their chemical origin and density and are used widely in the model-making industry. The most useful ones are Styrofoam and high-density foams, which come as blocks and boards. High-density foams are a default material for CNC carving, prototype making and

	creating patterns for vacuum-forming.
Functionality	An important characteristic of the scale model, functionality includes articulation, effects and interactivity.
Interactivity	A complex of features allowing interaction with the model in order to provide optional or additional information about the subject(s). Interactivity is a part of model's functionality. In order to run and control such features the model is accompanied by a specially designed Interactive System (IS).
Juliet balcony	A glazed door (or doors) in an upper floor exterior wall with a railing to prevent occupiers from falling out (named after Shakespeare's *Romeo and Juliet*). The advantage is that the glazed door lets in more light than a simple window and is cheaper to create. Naturally a proper balcony would be preferable but in ancient towns was not always allowed.
Laser cutting	Popular in architectural model making. This technology is based on cutting parts out of a sheet of material using a high-power laser. The output of the laser is directed by computer software. Due to this technology the process of cutting walls, doors and windows for architectural models has become faster and much more efficient.
Laser engraving	The same process as laser cutting, being performed using the same equipment. The difference is that the laser beam does not go completely through the material, but halfway, engraving an ornament or pattern according to the software input. The technology is most useful in architectural model making and sign making/engraving.
Louvre	From the French (l'ouvert, 'the open one'), a window blind or shutter with horizontal slats that are angled to admit light and air, but to keep out rain, direct sunshine, and noise. The angle of the slats may be adjustable or fixed.
Mansard	A mansard or mansard roof is a four-sided hip roof characterized by two slopes on

GLOSSARY

	each of its sides with the lower slope, punctured by dormer windows, at a steeper angle than the upper. The roof creates an additional floor of habitable space. The upper slope of the roof may not be visible from street level when viewed from close proximity to the building.
Maquette	A French word for a scale model, usually defining a very general, low-detail model, built for quick study or to compose elements of a future high-detailed scale model, sculpture or collectible. It is incorrect to use the word 'maquette' to define a highly detailed scale model or replica.
Mezzanine	An intermediate floor between the main floors of a building, and therefore typically not counted among the overall floors of a building. Often, a mezzanine is low-ceilinged and projects in the form of a balcony.
Monochrome	Single-colour painting scheme.
Mould	In industrial replication, a negative of the master, a form in which castings are made by pouring in liquid material, which after curing becomes a hard copy (replica) of the master. Moulds differ in the material in which they are made and in their construction, depending on the type of technology for which a mould is created. The most useful moulds in the model-making industry are silicone rubber or RTV moulds, used for resin casting.
Mullion	A vertical structural element which divides adjacent window units. The primary purpose of the mullion is as a structural support to an arch or lintel above the window opening. Its secondary purpose may be as a rigid support to the glazing of the window. When used to support glazing, mullions are teamed with horizontal supporting elements called 'transoms'.
Multi-colour	Painting scheme of more than three colours.
Opalescent	Normally in model making this is a finish to acrylic, either achieved through paint finish or bought in sheet form. The effect resembles a milky iridescence like that of an opal.
Plan	See 'site plan'.
Product development	The process of a new consumer product's development, including both its technical development and marketing. The model-making industry provides a wide range of product development-related services including concept development, prototype and master making, and testing. Product development is a long and complex process: it requires professional expertise and proper funding.
Prototype	A representation of future product, its model in 1:1 scale. (The term 'prototype' derives from the Greek πρῶτος [protos], 'the first one', and τύπος [teepos], 'kind, type'.) Prototypes are fabricated of practically every consumer product in order to study, develop and present the future product. There are certain types of prototypes, depending on their purpose and target for representation. 'Appearance models' and 'Engineered models' (or 'Production Prototypes') are the most common types.
Rapid prototyping	A process of automatically manufacturing a physical object via interpretation of a virtual model and transferring this data into the physical space. Commonly, the process involves an input of a 3D virtual model of the desired object (via CAD or similar software); a computer then transforms it into thin, virtual, horizontal cross sections; finally each cross section is created in physical space, one after the next until the model is finished. It is described as a 'WYSIWYG' ('what you see is what you get') process, where the virtual model and the physical model correspond almost identically. Rapid prototyping techniques became amongst the most used for creating simpler prototypes, models and model parts. The most commonly used rapid prototyping techniques are SLS, SLA, CNC machining and FDM.

GLOSSARY

Requirements
(model requirements)
A description of the scale model, summarizing its features. It includes the type of the model, its purpose, scale and size, main elements, level of detailing, functionality and optional features. Accurate requirements allow the model maker to evaluate the project, its complexity, the time needed for its production and to quote the project accordingly.

Resin
A family of liquid multi-component plastics which are used for resin casting in RTV moulds, creating fibreglass and some other purposes. Resins include urethanes, epoxy and polyester.

Roofscape
A view of the rooftops of a town, city, etc.

Scale
The main characteristic of any scale model/replica, defining the relation of a model's size to the size of the original.

Scale model
A physical representation of a subject/scene that is smaller or, in some cases, larger than the original.

Scale replica
This phrase has almost the same meaning as 'scale model'; the difference between the two terms is that a scale model may be a representation of a pre-existing or imaginary subject; a scale replica represents only a pre-existing subject, however.

Scenery
Commonly in architectural model making, various elements such as people, vehicles, equipment etc. are added to the model so the observer can visually compare the model/project to the objects of familiar size and, therefore, have an accurate impression of the project's scale. Scenery elements also add some action and a sense of realism to a model. Adding high-quality, realistic-looking scenery elements to the presentation of sales and museum models is very important.

Section
See 'cross section'.

Site plan
A site plan is a specific type of plan, showing the whole context of a building or group of buildings. A site plan shows property boundaries and means of access to the site and nearby structures if they are relevant to the design. For a development on an urban site, the site plan may need to show adjoining streets to demonstrate how the design fits into the urban fabric. Within the site boundary, the site plan gives an overview of the entire scope of work. It shows the buildings that already exist and those that are proposed (usually as a building footprint), roads, parking lots, footpaths, hard landscaping, trees and planting. For a construction project, the site plan also needs to show all the service connections: drainage and sewer lines, water supply, electrical and communications cables, exterior lighting, etc. Site plans are commonly used to represent a building proposal prior to detailed design: drawing up a site plan is a tool for deciding both the site layout and the size and orientation of proposed new buildings. A site plan is used to verify that a proposal complies with local development codes, including restrictions on historical sites. In this context the site plan forms part of a legal agreement, and there may be a requirement for it to be drawn up by a licensed professional: architect, engineer, landscape architect or land surveyor.

SLA, stereolithography
Rapid prototyping technique.

SLS, selective laser sintering
Rapid prototyping technique.

Square
Not only an essential tool for making but also a term to describe the relationship of one surface to another; it means that a 90° angle has been achieved. An example of its use could be the square edge of a piece of material or the placement of a building in context to surrounding buildings ('the building is sat square').

Styrene
A second, frequently used name for polystyrene, the most useful plastic material in model making. Styrene is in fact not polystyrene itself: also known as vinyl benzene, it is an organic compound which, under normal conditions, is an oily liquid. Styrene is the precursor to polystyrene.

141

Transom	A transom is the term given to a transverse beam or bar in a frame, or to the crosspiece separating a door or the like from a window above it.
Vacuum-forming (also vacuform)	A simplified version of thermoforming, whereby a plastic sheet is heated to a forming temperature, stretched onto a single-surface pattern or into a single-surface hard mould, and held against the pattern or mould by applying a vacuum between the mould surface and the plastic sheet. The vacuum-forming process can be used in model making to make complex configured hollow parts for models and prototypes and product packaging. Normally, draft angles must be present in the design on the mould for easy release of the formed plastic. Vacuum-forming is usually restricted to forming plastic parts that are rather shallow in depth; otherwise a plastic sheet is formed into a structurally weak cavity. Suitable materials for use in vacuum-forming are usually thermoplastics, the most common and easiest being polystyrene. Vacuum-forming is also appropriate for transparent materials such as PETG and acrylic, which are widely used to produce clear domes and skylights for architectural models, canopies and windows for aerospace replicas, for example.

INDEX

123 block 100, 102, 104
20 fenchurch street 45
3D printing 91
acrylic 15, 18, 22, 23, 24, 27, 29, 30, 42, 44, 46, 88, 105, 137
activator 23, 24
actual size 40
adhesive 26
aerial photography 109
Alberti, Leon Battista 9, 10
angle blocks 23
aperture 85
arbour 28
architect drawings 131
architectural model making 7
articulation 137
atrium 137
balsa 30
band saw 28
base 93, 95, 97
base board 26, 100, 126, 127
base models 127
base print 96
Battersea Power Station 45
Bauhaus 10
belt sander 27
blade 29
blind reveal 36, 38, 84, 111, 113, 115
block of flats 11
block work model 16
bonding 26
brick coarse 38, 110
brick work model 10
brief 35
brise-soleil 137
Brunelleschi, Filippo 10
brushes 26
budget 15, 16, 35, 37, 39, 42, 44, 49, 123, 126
building 25, 26, 36, 38
CAD (computer aided design) 10, 21, 49, 50, 60, 72, 73, 81, 94, 99, 104, 124, 127, 128, 131, 134, 137
calculation 40
calculator 22, 46
calliper jaw 23
campanile 10
canopy 30
car body filler 25
cardboard 9, 49, 55, 107
carpenter 25
carpet tape 24
case study 36
cathedral 10
cedar 31, 32
CGI 129
chemiwood 16, 28, 32, 33
cherry 31, 32
Chinese dynasties 9
chloroform 26
circle cutter 54
circular saw 28, 30
cities 21
city planning 11
clients 16
CNC 137
colour palette 36, 47
colour-coding 25
commissioning 123, 124, 126, 131
communication 123
competition 8, 38
competition models 44
composite board 33, 138
computer 11, 29, 45
computer technology 10
concept 126
conceptual model 35, 38, 43
construction 14
construction industry 131
contact adhesives 26
context 41, 46, 70, 93, 115
contextual buildings 113
contour 16, 93, 95
contour stack 96
contour step model 97
cork 31, 33
craft 11
craftspeople 25
crosscut slide 28, 29
cross-grain 33
cross-sectional model 86, 138
cube 49, 54, 55
curing 138
curved edges 16
curving roof 30
cutting 28
cutting board 25
cutting-in 119
cyanoacrylate 23
cylinder 49, 50, 60
datum 94, 95
De Pictura 9
De Re Aedificatoria 9
deadline 126, 129
design development model 43
detail 37
developers 11
dichloromethane 26
Di-clo 26
disc sander 27
double-sided tape 24, 46
Dremel 30
dust extractor 29
Eagles, Justin 16
eaves 138
electronics 21
elevated model 38
elevation 15, 22, 23, 24, 39, 40, 46, 67, 86, 124, 125, 127, 128, 131, 138
elevation studies 80
Empire State Building 21
engineer's square 22, 23, 46
engineering 14
engrave 97
engraving 29
epoxy 139
equation 40
equipment 21, 49, 50, 74, 80
etch 15, 44
exhibition model 43
eye protection 29
fabrication 27
façade 139
fenestration 125, 139
film tape 24
floor counting 109
floor heights 126
floor level 15
floor plan 15, 139
floor plates 38, 46, 127
floor slab 15
floor stack 38, 71, 72
floor stack model 37, 80
foam 43, 46, 139
foam board 26, 27
Foster & Partners 72, 89
functionality 139
gherkin 72
Giotto 10
glazing lines 36, 38
glues 24, 26, 27, 33, 46, 119
ground levels 46
hand skills 21
hand-drawn sketch 11
health and safety 21, 28
Heatherwick Studio 135
highlighter 25, 46
hot wire cutter 27, 46
housing development 11
IBM 10
in-house model shop 89
industry scales 39, 40
in-house 123, 134
interactivity 139

143

INDEX

jelutong 31, 32
jig 30
juliet balcony 139
kits 11
lacquer 32
laminating 24, 27
landscape 14, 15, 25, 27, 39, 40, 44 113
landscape architects 21
landscaping design model 14
large-scale buildings 32
large-scale models 32
Lasdun, Denys 9
laser cut 99
laser cutter 45, 127, 128
laser scribe 16, 29, 139
laser-cutting 11, 15, 28, 44, 49, 60, 124, 134, 139
lighter fluid 24
lighting 14
lime 31, 32
liquid acrylic 26
lithographic tape 25
London Routemaster bus 135
louver 139
Luggie, Mark 127
machine tools 21
mansard 139
maple 31, 32
maquette 11, 43, 44, 134, 140
marketing model 11, 13
masking tape 22, 24, 25, 46
massing 27, 36, 38, 39, 42, 67, 69
massing model 37, 70
master plan 71
materiality 113
materials 98
MDF 25, 27, 33, 49, 74, 117, 127
measuring 22
metal square 61
methylene chloride 26
mezzanine 44, 140
micro drill 27
model animations 27
model definitions 43
model maker's plane 26
modelshop 26, 27, 45
modernist movement 10
monochrome 140
Morgan, Morris Hicky 131
Morgan, Sam 89
mould 140
moulding plane 30
mullion 140
multi-colour 140

museum model 14
nave 10
needle-nose pliers 24
nozzle 26
oak 31, 32
offsite 28, 32, 33, 36, 109, 110, 111, 116, 117, 119
opalescent 140
paper 9
paper grades 25
paper study 24
pavement 16
paving patterns 36
pear 31, 32
people 36, 39, 42, 86
pergola 14
perspex 27, 36, 49, 69
petg (plastic, glycol-modefied polyethylene terephthalate) 27
pipette bottle 23
planning 42
planning meetings 32
planning model 11, 43, 44
planning stage 36
planning submission 35
plans 10, 140
plastic weld 26
plexiglas 27
plod 25
plotter 133
plywood 22,33
polyester resin 25
polystyrene 27
powertool 28, 30
presentation model 11
printer 133
product development 140
prototype 140
push stick 28, 29
PVA (polyvinyl acetate) 26
pyramid 49, 50, 58
quote 124
rapid prototyping 140
reference material 93
reference points 110
renaissance 9
requirements (model requirements) 141
resin 141
road layouts 36
Roahacell 27
roofscape 25, 36, 42, 116, 141
router 30
sales model 43
sander 47

sanding block 25
sandpaper 25
saw 47
scale 11, 15, 16, 21, 22, 39, 70, 107, 115, 116, 126, 127, 128, 132, 141
scale drawing 124, 125
scale model 141
scalpel 22, 24, 46, 50, 52, 54, 61, 80, 107, 132, 133
scenery 39, 40, 141
schedule 124
schematics 126
scheme 49, 68, 69, 115
scheme model 111
scribe 22, 23, 24, 120
sea level 94
section 141
sectional model 38
sheet material 24
site plan 141
sketch model 11, 24, 26, 27, 45, 46, 96, 123
sketchbook 45
sketches 42
skill base 21
SLA, stereolithography 141
slabs 106
SLS, selective laser sintering 141
spindle moulding machine 30
spray adhesive 24, 46
spray paint 15, 27
spray-finished 16
square 141
square edge 22
stack 23, 98, 104
stacking model 27
stairs 36
Stanton Williams Architects 45
steel rule 22, 46
stone 9
street furniture 44
structural components 14
structural elements 14
studio 11
study model 8, 11
styrene 22, 27, 43, 141
styrene micro strip 46
styrofoam 27, 46
substrate 119
super glue 23, 24
survey 109
suspended ceiling 15
table saw 28, 29
tape residue 24

teaching model 14
techniques 37, 49, 65
technological 11
Tensol 12 26
thermoplastic 27, 30
three-dimensional modelling 131
three-dimensional 9, 21, 23
three-dimensional printing 21, 131, 132, 133, 134
tight-tolerance acrylic 27
timber 9, 28, 30
timescale 35
tool bag 11
tool lists 22-30, 46, 49-50, 74, 99, 119, 129
tooling board 33
top hatting 98
topographical 27
town planning 11
tracing paper 46
traffic flows 14
transom 142
trees 15, 27, 36, 44, 98, 107
tulipwood 31, 32, 33
tweezers 23
twentieth century 10
two-dimensional 11, 21
UHU 26
vacuum-form 21, 27, 29, 30, 33, 141
vegetation patterns 14
veneer 15, 22, 26, 33, 42, 44, 50, 60, 61, 64, 80
veneer gauge 23, 127
Vinoly, Rafael 44, 45
Vitruvius 131
walkway 14
walnut 31, 32
warp 29, 33
water level 100
weights 23
whittling 30
window apertures 38
window finishes 15
Wittgenstein, Ludwig 35
Wood, Philip 9
woodworking plane 26
workshop 28, 45, 47
Wykes, Phil 45